Laptops
FOR
DUMMIES®

by Dan Gookin

WILEY

Wiley Publishing, Inc.

Laptops For Dummies®

Published by
Wiley Publishing, Inc.
111 River Street
Hoboken, NJ 07030-5774

Copyright © 2005 by Wiley Publishing, Inc., Indianapolis, Indiana

Published by Wiley Publishing, Inc., Indianapolis, Indiana

Published simultaneously in Canada

WILEY

About the Author

This is Dan Gookin's 98th book on personal computers and technology. For over 20 years, Dan has been writing about technology, contributing articles to numerous high-tech magazines, and appearing on TV, radio, and other media.

Dan combines his love of writing with his interest in technology to create books that are informative, entertaining, and yet not boring. Having sold more than 14 million titles translated into over 30 languages, Dan can attest that his method of crafting computer tomes does seem to work.

Perhaps his most famous title is the original *DOS For Dummies,* published in 1991. It became the world's fastest-selling computer book, at one time moving more copies per week than the New York Times #1 bestseller (though as a reference, it could not be listed on the NYT Bestseller list). From that book spawned the entire line of *For Dummies* books, which remains a publishing phenomenon to this day.

Dan's most recent titles include *PCs For Dummies*, 9th Edition; *Buying a Computer For Dummies*, 2004 Edition; *Troubleshooting Your PC For Dummies*; *Dan Gookin's Naked Windows XP*; and *Power Office*. He publishes a free weekly computer newsletter, the "Weekly Wambooli Salad," full of tips, how-tos, and computer news. He also maintains the vast and helpful Web page, `www.wambooli.com`.

Dan holds a degree in Communications/Visual Arts from the University of California, San Diego. Presently he lives in the Pacific Northwest, where he enjoys spending time with his four boys in the gentle woods of Idaho.

Publisher's Acknowledgments

We're proud of this book; please send us your comments through our online registration form located at www.dummies.com/register/.

Some of the people who helped bring this book to market include the following:

Acquisitions, Editorial, and Media Development

Project Editor: Paul Levesque

Acquisitions Editor: Greg Croy

Copy Editor: Jean Rogers

Technical Editor: Mark Chambers

Editorial Manager: Kevin Kirschner

Media Development Manager: Laura VanWinkle

Media Development Supervisor: Richard Graves

Editorial Assistant: Amanda Foxworth

Cartoons: Rich Tennant (www.the5thwave.com)

Composition

Project Coordinator: Adrienne Martinez

Layout and Graphics: Andrea Dahl, Carl Byers, Lauren Goddard, Joyce Haughey, Stephanie D. Jumper, Jacque Roth, Heather Ryan, Julie Trippetti

Proofreaders: Rob Springer, Carl William Pierce, TECHBOOKS Production Services

Indexer: TECHBOOKS Production Services

Publishing and Editorial for Technology Dummies

　　Richard Swadley, Vice President and Executive Group Publisher

　　Andy Cummings, Vice President and Publisher

　　Mary Bednarek, Executive Acquisitions Director

　　Mary C. Corder, Editorial Director

Publishing for Consumer Dummies

　　Diane Graves Steele, Vice President and Publisher

　　Joyce Pepple, Acquisitions Director

Composition Services

　　Gerry Fahey, Vice President of Production Services

　　Debbie Stailey, Director of Composition Services

Contents at a Glance

Introduction *1*

Part 1: Choosing a Laptop Just for You *5*
Chapter 1: Sometimes You Can Take It with You 7
Chapter 2: Buying a Laptop Just for You 21

Part 11: 1 Have My Laptop, Now What? *33*
Chapter 3: Out of the Box and into Your Lap 35
Chapter 4: Laptop Goes On, Laptop Goes Off 43
Chapter 5: Basic Laptop Hardware Tour 65
Chapter 6: Windows and Your Laptop Software 87
Chapter 7: Expanding Your Laptop's Universe 113
Chapter 8: Power Management Madness 133

Part 111: Between Your Laptop and the World *147*
Chapter 9: All That Networking Nonsense 149
Chapter 10: Laptop to Internet, Hello? 169
Chapter 11: A Very Merry Modem 181
Chapter 12: Online Security 201
Chapter 13: Handy Web Browsing and E-Mail Tips 213
Chapter 14: The Desktop-Laptop Connection 225

Part 1V: On the Road Again *239*
Chapter 15: Before You Hit the Road 241
Chapter 16: The Road Warrior (Or Computing in the Strangest of Places) 251
Chapter 17: Laptop Security 257
Chapter 18: Giving a Presentation 269

Part V: Troubleshooting *275*
Chapter 19: Major Trouble and General Solutions 277
Chapter 20: Upgrading Your Laptop 289

Part V1: The Part of Tens *295*
Chapter 21: Ten Battery Tips and Tricks 297
Chapter 22: Ten Handy Laptop Accessories 305
Chapter 23: Ten Things to Throw in Your Laptop Case 311

Index *317*

Table of Contents

Introduction 1

  About This Book 1
  And Just Who Are You? 2
  Icons Used in This Book 3
  Where to Go from Here 3

Part 1: Choosing a Laptop Just for You 5

  Chapter 1: Sometimes You Can Take It with You 7

  The Power Cord Can Stretch Only So Far 7
        The Osborne 1 8
        The luggables 9
        The Model 100 11
        Hybrid beasts, or the "lunch buckets" 12
        Early PC laptops 13
        The search for weightlessness 15
        From laptop to notebook 16
        The modern notebook 16
        The future of the laptop 17
  Why You Need a Laptop 18
  Why You Don't Need a Laptop 19

  Chapter 2: Buying a Laptop Just for You 21

  Buy That Laptop! 22
        The five steps to buying any computer 22
        The hunt for software 22
        Figuring out how much basic laptop power you need 24
        Finding out what you don't need 25
        Special laptoppy issues 26
        Laptop expansion options 27
        Communications options 28
        Energy management hardware 29
        Docking stations and port replicators 29
  Hunting for Service and Support 29
  Where to Buy 31
  The Final Step: Buying Your Laptop 32

Part II: I Have My Laptop, Now What? 33

Chapter 3: Out of the Box and into Your Lap 35

Basic Box Unpacking 101 35
   Making piles for the various things in the box 36
   "How long should I keep the box?" 37
   When to send in the warranty 37
Setting Up Your Laptop 38
   Do you need to charge the battery? 38
   Is some assembly required? 39
   Finding a place for the laptop 39
   The last thing to do: Plug it in! 40
   "Should I plug the laptop into a UPS?" 41
What to Do Next? 42

Chapter 4: Laptop Goes On, Laptop Goes Off 43

Turning It On 43
   Before you turn on the power! 44
   Open the lid 44
   "Where is the power button?" 46
   "What is the moon button for?" 46
   Random power button symbols 47
   Power on! 48
A Brief Foray into Windows 48
   Windows for the first time 49
   Special deal software 51
   Windows every time 51
   Exploring the Start thing 52
Various Options for Turning Off (Or Not) the Laptop 54
   Properly shutting down your laptop 54
   "I need to restart Windows" 55
   Putting your laptop to sleep (Stand By) mode 56
   Waking up from sleep (Stand By) mode 57
   "What the heck is hibernation?" 57
   Turning on Hibernation mode 59
   Shutting down when the laptop doesn't want to 60
Changing the Whole On-Off Scheme of Things 60
   Setting the function of the power button 60
   Changing the sleep button's function 62
   What happens when you just close the lid? 62

Chapter 5: Basic Laptop Hardware Tour 65

Your 'Round the Laptop Tour 65
   A place for your CD/DVD 66
   Does Mr. Laptop have a floppy drive? 67

A home for Mr. PC Card 67
Mystery things called ports 68
A place for the old ball and chain 71
The thing's gotta breathe 71
Look at the Pretty Lights! 72
This Isn't Your Daddy's Keyboard 73
The general keyboard layout 73
Where did the numeric keypad go? 75
The Fn key is the Fun key! 76
Mind these specific keys 78
This Isn't Your Momma's Mouse 78
The mouse pad 78
Where is the wheel button? 80
IBM's "happy stick" keyboard mouse 80
Controlling the mouse 81
Get a real mouse! 82
Cleaning 83
Cleaning the case 83
Cleaning the keyboard 84
Cleaning the screen 84

Chapter 6: Windows and Your Laptop Software **87**
Places to Do, Things to Go 87
My Documents 88
My Computer 90
My Network Places 91
The Network Connections window 91
What's Important in the Control Panel 93
Setting the best Control Panel view 93
The optional Start menu approach 94
Display options 96
Network connections 97
Power options 97
System 98
Phone and modem options 99
Printers and faxes 99
Wireless link 101
Laptop-specific icons 101
Goodies in the System Tray 102
Where Your Programs Lurk 103
Installing new software 104
Removing old software 105
Software you want, software you don't want 107

Logging On to Windows 107
The User Accounts icon 107
Changing your password 108
Changing your image 109
Adding new accounts 109
Removing an account 110
Disabling the Guest account 110
Logging on as administrator 110
Do you really, really hate to log on? 111

Chapter 7: Expanding Your Laptop's Universe **113**
Beyond Your Lap 113
The miraculous expandability options of the USB port 114
Doing the USB thing 116
What are the A and B ends of a USB cable? 117
Connecting USB gizmos 118
USB-powered devices 119
Adding a hub 119
Adding external USB storage 120
Removing external storage 123
Using a PC Card 124
Inserting a PC Card 124
Using the PC Card 125
Removing the PC Card 125
Adding Some Big Boy Toys 126
Using an external keyboard 126
Connecting a second monitor or video projector 127
Using two monitors at once 128
Gotta getta mouse 128
Printing 129
Setting up the printer 129
Printing in Windows 131
Options for when you don't have a printer 132

Chapter 8: Power Management Madness **133**
The Battery Will Get a Charge Out of This! 134
Types of batteries 134
Finding your laptop's battery 136
Monitoring the battery 136
What happens when the power gets low 139
Charging the battery 141
The spare battery 142
Don't fall off the battery cycle! 143

Should you keep the battery in the laptop when
you use AC power all the time? 143
RIP battery 144
Managing Your Laptop's Power 144

Part III: Between Your Laptop and the World 147

Chapter 9: All That Networking Nonsense 149

Adding Your Laptop to an Existing Network 150
The hardware connection 150
Setting up the connection in Windows XP 151
Adding and removing your laptop to and from the network 153
Finding other computers on the network 154
Getting into another computer's disk drives 156
Accessing network printers 157
Sharing a folder on your laptop 157
Unsharing a folder 159
Networking with No Strings Attached (Wireless Networking) 159
The ABGs of 802.11 160
Wireless networking hardware 161
Connecting to a wireless network 161
Scanning for wireless networks 164
What if you don't know the SSID? 164
What is the computer's MAC Address? 166
Renewing your lease 166
Accessing a pay service wireless network 167
Disconnecting the wireless connection 167

Chapter 10: Laptop to Internet, Hello? 169

What You Need to Get on the Internet 170
Bonus Laptop Goodies Your ISP Can Offer 171
Getting ISP access from all over the country 171
Check for Web-based e-mail access 171
Connecting Your Laptop to the Internet the Ethernet Way 172
The Ethernet connection 172
Getting on the Internet 172
Connecting your laptop directly to a DSL or cable modem 173
Connecting to a router 173
Dial-Up Internet 176
Configuring a dial-up connection 176
Finding the connection 177
Making the dial-up connection 178

Dialing a specific connection 179
Don't forget to disconnect the dial-up connection! 179

Chapter 11: A Very Merry Modem 181

The Modem Hardware 181
Where the Modem Dwells in Windows 182
Setting the modem's volume 182
Adding special modem command settings 184
Options for disabling the modem 184
Adding an External Modem 185
Setting Up Dialing Rules 188
Location, location, location 188
Creating a new location 190
Area code madness! To dial or not to dial 191
Automatically using a calling card 193
Finding the Various Disconnect Timeouts 194
The general timeout 194
Timeouts for each session 194
Putting the Fax into Fax/Modem 195
Setting up the fax modem 195
To send a fax 196
Fax Central 199
Canceling a pending fax 199
Receiving a fax 200

Chapter 12: Online Security 201

Setting Up a Firewall 201
The Windows XP firewall 202
Monitoring the firewall 204
Setting Up Antivirus Software 205
Scanning for viruses 206
Shutting down your antivirus program 207
Good advice to help protect you from the viral scourge 208
Running Anti-Spyware Software 208
Protecting yourself from spyware 209
Anti-spyware software 210
How to tell if something is really spyware 211
Avoiding a Hijack 211

Chapter 13: Handy Web Browsing and E-Mail Tips 213

Web Browsing When You're Out and About 214
E-Mail Away from Home 215
Accessing e-mail on the road 215
Reading your e-mail on the Web 216

Getting a Web-based e-mail account 217
Accessing your e-mail from a friend's computer 217
Forwarding your e-mail 218
A forwarding mail rule for Outlook Express 219
E-Mail Options Worthy of Consideration 220
Omit your password 220
Disconnect after picking up e-mail 221
Disabling automatic checking 221
Sending everything in one batch 222
To pick up or leave on server 222
Skip messages over a given size 224

Chapter 14: The Desktop-Laptop Connection **225**

Connecting Desktop and Laptop 225
The easy way: Over the network 226
That ugly wire thing 226
Using the infrared port 228
Toiling with Windows Direct Connection 228
Synchronizing Files between the Desktop and the Laptop 231
Creating a Briefcase 231
Populating the Briefcase with stuff 232
Moving the Briefcase over to the laptop 233
Using Briefcase files on your laptop 233
Synchronizing the files 233
Accessing the Desktop from Elsewhere 234
Avoiding Windows XP Remote Desktop 234
Real Virtual Network Computing 235

Part IV: On the Road Again **239**

Chapter 15: Before You Hit the Road **241**

The Proper Laptop Case 241
Avoid the manufacturer's case 242
Things to look for in a case 243
Recommended brands 244
I'm Leaving, on a Jet Plane Check List 245
Things to do before you go 245
Things to pack in your laptop bag 246
Looming Questions at the Airport 247
Is your laptop case one carry-on bag or half a carry-on bag? 247
Laptop inspection 247
All aboard! 248

Up, up in the air 248
The secret 747 exit wall socket 249

**Chapter 16: The Road Warrior (Or Computing in
the Strangest of Places)** **251**

Café Computing 251
Where to sit? 252
Be a socket sleuth 252
Other tips 'n' stuff 253
Laptopping in Your Hotel Room 253
Dealing with the Low-Battery Warning 255
Mind the Laptop's Temperature 255

Chapter 17: Laptop Security **257**

Laptops Are Easy for the Bad Guys to Steal 257
What to Do before It's Stolen 258
Mark your laptop 258
Don't use an obvious laptop carrying case 259
Register the laptop and its software 259
Be mindful of your environment 260
The old ball and chain 260
Protecting Your Data 261
The BIOS password 261
Use the NTFS file system 262
Set a password on your account 263
Disable the Guest account 263
Lock Windows 263
Encrypt important files or folders 264
Disable the infrared port 266
Back up your data! 267
Having the Laptop Phone Home 268

Chapter 18: Giving a Presentation **269**

Setting Things Up 269
Creating the presentation 270
Hooking up to the video projector 271
PowerPoint Keyboard Shortcuts Worthy of Knowing 272

Part V: Troubleshooting **275**

Chapter 19: Major Trouble and General Solutions **277**

Soothing Words of Support for the Computer Weary 278
The Universal Quick Fix 278

The Miracle of System Restore 279
　　Enabling System Restore 279
　　When to run System Restore 281
　　Setting a restore point 281
　　Restoring your system 282
Safe Mode 283
　　Entering Safe Mode 284
　　Testing in Safe Mode 285
　　The laptop always starts in Safe Mode! 286
Common Problems and Solutions 286
　　The keyboard is wacky! 286
　　Making the mouse pointer more visible 287
　　The laptop won't wake up 287
　　Power management woes 287
　　The battery won't charge 288

Chapter 20: Upgrading Your Laptop **289**

How 'bout Some New Software? 289
　　Upgrading your software 289
　　Updating Windows 291
　　Upgrading Windows 292
Giving Your Laptop New Hardware 293

Part VI: The Part of Tens *295*

Chapter 21: Ten Battery Tips and Tricks **297**

Don't Drop the Battery, Get It Wet, Short It, Play Keep-Away with It,
　　Open It, Burn It, or Throw It Away 297
Every Few Months, Drain the Battery All the Way 298
Turn Down the Monitor's Brightness 298
Power Down the Hard Drives 299
Add More RAM to Prevent Virtual Memory Disk Swapping 299
Run as Few Programs as Possible/Close Unused Programs 301
Guard the Battery's Terminals 302
Avoid Extreme Temperatures 302
Store the Battery If You Don't Plan on Using It 302
Batteries Will Drain Over Time! 303

Chapter 22: Ten Handy Laptop Accessories **305**

Laptop Bag or Travel Case 305
Spare Battery 306
Docking Station or Port Replicator 306
Cooling Pad 306

Mini-Vac 307
USB Lamp 307
Full-Sized Keyboard 308
External Mouse 308
ID Card or Return Service Sticker 309
Theft Prevention System 309

Chapter 23: Ten Things to Throw in Your Laptop Case 311

Power Cord and Brick 312
Spare Battery 312
Mouse or Trackball 312
Screen Wipes and Cleaner 313
Laptop Lock 313
Removable Media 313
Headphones 314
Tools 314
Cables, Cables, Cables 314
Not the End of the List 315

Index *317*

Introduction

· ·

You've made a wise decision picking up this book, *Laptops For Dummies*. It's packed with tips, suggestions, examples, and just so full of laptop fun and frivolity that reading it will both inform and consume you. Consider your days of laptop bewilderment at an end.

All that aside, and given that relatively few people bother to read introductions, I've decided to fill the next several pages with scatological poetry banned by the Catholic Church.

Seriously, I'm glad you've decided to continue reading. I'm trusting that, like me, you find yourself suddenly blessed with or desiring to own a laptop PC. Yet you find that there is an utter dearth of good information on the topic. The laptop's box came with scant or no manuals. The Internet is vague on the subject. And quite a few other references are written from the utterly biased desktop PC viewpoint. I can assure you, gentle reader, that you'll find none of that hokum here.

This book takes you on a portable computer journey, from the dawn of the Let's-Bolt-A-Handle-On-It era to today's wireless mania. In the traditional *For Dummies* standard, this book is a reference. It assumes that you know nothing or find the subject daunting. If that's what you need to help you in your laptop life, then you've found your book.

About This Book

Everything between this book's card stock covers is unveiled here in a well-paced, informative, and often wit-laden tone. Information is laid out so that you need only read what you want to know and then quietly close this book, returning it to the shelf for when you need it later.

In writing this book, I assume that you may know a bit about computers, as most folks do today. But you may be utterly fresh on the idea of *portable* computing. Despite what they tell you, a laptop computer is not merely a portable version of the desktop computer. There is more to it, and this book is here to show you the ropes.

I divide the laptop experience into six handy parts:

Part I contains an overview of laptop computing, plus a handy how-to guide for buying a laptop to fill your portable computing needs.

Part II discusses using your laptop, its basic features, how Windows works with a laptop, plus important information on power management (a subject you won't find in a desktop computer book or reference).

Part III is about networking, the Internet, and getting your laptop to communicate with the rest of the world.

Part IV deals with taking your laptop on the road, and includes a special chapter on the hot topic of laptop security.

Part V covers laptop troubleshooting as well as various ways to upgrade your laptop's hardware and software.

Part VI is the traditional *For Dummies* "Part of Tens" — various lists for review or to help you get on your way.

And Just Who Are You?

Most of this book's readers are human beings who either own a laptop PC or want to buy one. You may already have a desktop computer, or perhaps you had a laptop a long, long time ago. Things have changed.

(You'll find that I use the word *laptop* here to describe the common portable computer. Others use the term *notebook*. You can read about why I prefer the term *laptop* in Chapter 1.)

This book assumes that you have a PC laptop, one that runs the Windows XP operating system. This book does not cover Apple's line of Macintosh laptop and notebook computers, nor does it address any PC laptops running the Linux operating system, or any other operating systems known or unknown, from this or any parallel universe or dimension.

Older versions of Windows are not covered here. When this book says "Windows" it refers to "Windows XP" specifically.

This book does not describe the basic operations of a computer, Windows, or your software. I've tried to keep the information specific to the portable aspects of the laptop computer. Beyond that, if you need more information about running your computer, then any standard PC or Windows reference will work fine.

Icons Used in This Book

This icon alerts you to something technical, an aside, or some trivial tidbit that I just cannot suppress. Feel free to skip over this information as you please.

The Tip icon notifies you to something cool, handy, nifty, or something that I highly recommend. For example, "Check your fly *before* you stand up to give your presentation."

When you see this icon, you can be sure it points out something that you shouldn't forget, or something I said earlier that I'm repeating because it's very important, and you'll likely forget it anyway.

Watch out and pay attention when you see this icon — it flags something bad or that could cause trouble. For example, "When it's dark, don't light a match to find a gas leak."

Where to Go from Here

As a reference, you can start reading this book anywhere. Open up the Table of Contents and pick a spot that amuses you, concerns you, or has piqued your curiosity. Everything is explained in the text, and stuff is carefully cross-referenced so that you won't waste your time reading repeated information.

As a supplement to this book, I offer a Web site and a free weekly newsletter. You can visit the Web site at

www.wambooli.com

Specific information for this book can be found at

www.wambooli.com/help/laptops/

For information on my free weekly newsletter, refer to

www.wambooli.com/newsletter/weekly/

Finally, I enjoy hearing feedback. If you want to send me e-mail, my personal address is dgookin@wambooli.com. I'm happy to answer questions about the book, but please be aware that I do not and cannot troubleshoot your computer. Still, I do promise to respond to all legitimate e-mail I get. So if you feel like saying, "Hi!" feel free to do so.

Enjoy your laptop computer. I'll see you on the road!

Part I
Choosing a Laptop Just for You

The 5th Wave   By Rich Tennant

"YOU KNOW, IF WE CAN ALL KEEP THE TITTERING DOWN, I, FOR ONE, WOULD LIKE TO HEAR MORE ABOUT KEN'S NEW POINTING DEVICE FOR NOTEBOOKS."

In this part . . .

*L*aptops aren't only for people who have laps; they're for everyone! That's because the laptop is the ideal portable computer, not only for use as your main computer but as a computer system that you can take with you whenever and wherever you go. It's the answer to that ancient riddle, "Where does your lap go when you stand up?" For the laptop at least, when you stand up, the laptop goes with you.

This part of the book introduces you to the laptop or portable computing concept. It includes a strategy for buying laptop computer, plus excuses for getting one — just in case you need to convince someone near or dear to you that your portable computing desires haven't been plucked from thin Ethernet!

Chapter 1

Sometimes You Can Take It with You

. . . .

In This Chapter

▶ Searching for a portable computer

▶ Looking back at the history of the laptop computer

▶ Deciding if you need a laptop

. . . .

*F*rom the time when the first computer was powered on in the early 1940s, users have craved mobility. I'm certain of it. Sitting in the lunch room, some guy with a crew cut, thick glasses, and a white lab coat popped up and said, "How 'bout we put wheels on the ENIAC? Then we could roll it out into the quad and work outside on a sunny day? Hey?" And so the dream was born.

This chapter provides an overview of the laptop computer concept. If you're uncertain as to what a laptop is, or how it can help you, then this is where you start reading.

The Power Cord Can Stretch Only So Far

Any computer can be mobile. The solution is simple: Just add a handle. I remember my first portable TV. It may have weighed over 40 pounds, but dangit, the thing had a handle, and therefore it was portable. Seeing that portability is often desired in a product, manufacturers were quick to add handles to everything, blessing products such as blenders, table saws, microwave ovens, and grand pianos with the gift of portability.

For computers, the desire to make it portable is a primeval one. It was a quest for the Holy Grail, but without a Holy Grail. That's because the true notion of what a portable computer is, and what it could offer, changed subtly over time.

The Osborne 1

The first successful portable computer was the Osborne 1, created by Adam Osborne in 1980. A computer book author and publisher, Adam believed that for personal computers to be successful, they would have to be portable.

Adam's design for the Osborne 1 portable computer was ambitious for the time: The thing would have to fit under an airline seat — and this was *years* before anyone would dream of actually using a computer on an airplane.

The Osborne 1 portable computer (see Figure 1-1) was a whopping success. It featured a full-sized keyboard, two full-sized floppy drives, but a teensy credit card-sized monitor. It wasn't battery powered, but it did have a handy carrying handle so you could lug the 24-pound beast around like an over-packed suitcase. Despite any shortcomings, they were selling 10,000 units a month (at $1,795 each, which included software — a first for the time). The cash was rolling in.

Figure 1-1:
A late-
model
Osborne.

By late 1983, sadly, Adam's company floundered, suffering from the onslaught of the new IBM PC and its legion of compatibles and clones. Yet the Osborne 1 proved that computers could be portable. In fact, it founded a new class of computer: the *luggable*.

The ancient portable computer

Long before people marveled over solar powered, credit card-sized calculators, there existed the world's first portable, human-powered calculator. Presenting the *abacus,* the device used for centuries by merchants and goat herders to rapidly perform calculations that would break human fingers.

Abacus comes from the Greek word meaning "to swindle you faster." Seriously, the abacus or *counting board* is simple to master, and in the deft hands of an expert, it can even out perform all operations on a calculator — including the square and cubic roots. In his short story "Into the Comet," science fiction author Arthur C. Clarke wrote of stranded astronauts using many abacuses to plot their voyage home when the spaceship's computer broke down.

The luggables

The Osborne was portable, but not conveniently so. Heck, it was a *suitcase!* Imagine hauling the 24-pound Osborne across Chicago's O'Hare airport? Worse: Imagine the joy of your fellow seatmates as you try to wedge the thing beneath the seat in front you.

Despite the inconvenience, the computer world recognized the value of portability. And despite the print ads showing carefree people toting the Osborne around — people with arms of equal length, no less — no hip marketing term could mask the ungainly nature of the Osborne: Portable? Transportable? Wispy? Like it or not, the computer industry itself devised the unglamorous term *luggable* to describe that type of computer.

Portability and communications

Long before the Internet came around, one item that was deemed standard on all portable computers was the ability to communicate. The laptop computer not only had to be able to talk with the desktop computer, to exchange and update files, but it also had to use a *modem* to communicate electronically over phone lines.

Nearly every portable PC from the Radio Shack Model 100 onward had to have a modem, or at least an option for installing one. This was in an era when modems were considered optional luxuries for a desktop computer. Portable computers required a modem to keep in touch with the desktop systems of the day while they were on the road. Special software was required, but once the connection was made, it was possible to keep files on the laptop updated even from the most remote of locations.

The luggables were an extremely popular class of computer. Never mind the weight. Never mind that most never ventured from the desktop that they were set up on, luggables were the best the computer industry could offer in the arena of portable computing.

The problem with the Osborne was not that it was a luggable. No, what killed the Osborne was that the world wanted IBM PC compatibility. The Osborne lacked that. Instead, an upstart Texas company called Compaq introduced luggability to the IBM world with the Compaq 1, shown in Figure 1-2.

Figure 1-2:
The luggable Compaq 1.

The Compaq 1, introduced in 1983 at $3,590, proved that you could have your IBM compatibility and eat it on the road — or anywhere there was a power socket handy.

But yet, the power cord can stretch only so far. It became painfully obvious that for a computer to be truly portable — as Adam Osborne intended — it was going to have to lose that power cord.

The Model 100

The very first computer that even remotely looks like a modern laptop, and was fully battery powered, was the Radio Shack Model 100, shown in Figure 1-3. It was an instant, insane success.

The Model 100 was not designed to be IBM PC compatible, which is surprising considering that PC compatibility was all the rage at the time. Instead, it offered users a full-sized, full-action keyboard, plus a tiny 8-row, 40-column display. It came with several built-in programs, including a text editor/word processor, communications, a scheduler/appointment book, plus the BASIC programming language, which allowed users to create their own programs or buy and use BASIC programs written by others.

Figure 1-3:
Radio
Shack's
Model 100.

The Radio Shack Model 100 was really all that was needed for portability at the time, which is why the device was a such a resounding success.

- ✔ The Model 100 provided the *form factor* for laptops of the future. It was about the size of a hardback novel. It ran for hours off of standard AA batteries. It weighed just 6 pounds.

- ✔ Despite its popularity and versatility, people wanted a version of the Model 100 that would run the same software as the IBM PC. Technology wasn't ready to shrink the PC's hardware down to Model 100 size, but the Model 100 set the goal for what users wanted in a laptop's dimensions.

Hybrid beasts, or the "lunch buckets"

Before the dawn of the first true laptop, some ugly mutations wandered in, along with a few rejects from various mad scientists around the globe. I call them the *lunch bucket* computers because they assumed the shape, size and weight of a typical hard hat's lunch box. The Compaq III, shown in Figure 1-4, was typical of this type of portable computer.

Figure 1-4:
The Compaq III.

- ✔ The lunch box beasts weighed anywhere from 12 to 20 or more pounds, and most were not battery powered.

- ✔ At this same time, color monitors were becoming the standard for desktop computers. For technological reasons, monochrome LCD screens were all that laptops could offer.

- ✔ Honestly, the lunch buckets did offer something over the old transportable or luggables: less weight! A late-model lunch bucket PC weighed in at about 12 pounds, or half the weight and about ⅙ the size of the suitcase-sized luggables.

Early PC laptops

The computer industry's dream was to have a portable computer that had all the power of a desktop computer, plus all the features, yet be about the same size and weight as the Model 100. One of the first computers to approach that mark was the Compaq SLT back in 1988, shown in Figure 1-5.

The Compaq SLT was the first portable computer that actually looks like one of today's laptops. It featured a full-sized keyboard, full-sized screen, floppy drive (this is before the era of CD-ROM), and a 286 microprocessor, which meant that the computer could run the DOS operating system of the day.

Figure 1-5:
The Compaq
SLT.

Weight? Alas, the SLT was a bowling ball at 14 pounds!

What the Compaq SLT did was prove to the world that portability was possible. A laptop computer was designed to feature everything a desktop computer could, plus run off batteries for an hour or so.

Calculating laptop weight: The missing piece(s)

When computer companies specify the weight of their laptops, I'm certain that they do it under ideal conditions, possibly at the North Pole or some other location where the earth's gravity field is at its weakest. The weight advertised is, like they say, "for comparison purposes only."

Commonly left out of the laptop's weight is what's known as the *power brick*. This is the AC adapter used to connect the laptop to a wall socket. When the laptop isn't running off of batteries, you need the power brick to supply the thing with juice. This means that the power

brick is a required accessory — something you have to tote with you if you plan on taking the laptop on an extended trip.

In the old days, what they didn't tell you in the advertisements was that the power brick often weighed half as much as the laptop itself! Either that, or the power brick was more bulky than the laptop, as seen nearby with the Dell 320LT's obnoxiously big power brick (and heavy 30-minute batteries). Lugging around such items is not very convenient. Things are better today.

The search for weightlessness

Just because the marketing department labeled the computer a "laptop" didn't mean that it was sleek and lightweight. For a while there, it seemed like anyone could get away with calling a portable PC a laptop, despite the computer weighing up to 20 pounds — which is enough to crush any lap, not to mention kneecaps.

In the fall of 1989, NEC showed that it could think outside of the laptop box when it introduced the UltraLite laptop, shown in Figure 1-6. It featured a full-sized screen and keyboard, but no disk drives or other moving parts! The UltraLite used battery-backed up memory to serve as a *silicon disk*. The silicon disk stored 1 or 2MB of data — which was plenty back in those days.

The UltraLite featured a modem, but it could also talk with a desktop computer via its serial port and a special cable. Included with the UltraLite was software that would let it easily exchange files and programs with any desktop PC.

The weight? Yes, the UltraLite lived up to its name and weighed in at just under 5 pounds — a feather compared to the obese laptops of the day. And the battery lasted a whopping two hours, thanks to the UltraLite's lack of moving parts.

Figure 1-6:
The NEC
UltraLite.

From laptop to notebook

The UltraLite marked the line between what was then called a *laptop* to what is today called a *notebook*. While manufacturers had perverted the term laptop to include heavy, bulky portables that were anything but lap-friendly (such as the bowling ball-heavy Compaq III), the UltraLite raised the bar and created the notebook category.

Any laptop that weighs under 6 pounds and is less than an inch thick is technically a notebook. Some even lighter units earned the moniker *sub-notebook*. But keep in mind that all these terms are for marketing purposes; today, all of these computers, regardless of weight, size, or what the brochure says, are called *laptops*.

The modern notebook

As technology careened headlong into the 1990s, it became apparent that users were desperate for three things from their laptop computers:

- Light weight
- Long battery life
- Full hardware compatibility with desktop systems

Over time, all of these were achieved — but at a price. Today, the Holy Grail of a lightweight, PC compatible laptop that boasts a long battery life isn't elusive, it's just expensive:

- **Weight.** Depending on how much you want to pay, your laptop can be anywhere from ½-inch thick to just under an inch thick and weigh in at between 2 to 6 pounds, such as the IBM Thinkpad shown in Figure 1-7. The weight and size also depend on the features you want in your laptop, with more features adding more weight.

- **Battery Life.** While the batteries themselves haven't improved much in the past several years, thanks to power management hardware and software, modern laptops can extend battery life from the once-standard two hours to about three or four hours.

- **Hardware compatibility.** Since the late 1990s, all laptops come with color screens just like desktop systems. They also sport CD-ROM or DVD drives, though floppy drives are seldom found in a modern laptop (and then usually as an external device). Laptops also feature modems, networking, and expansion options. Special laptop microprocessors and other hardware have been developed over the years, keeping the laptop hardware small and energy efficient.

Figure 1-7:
The author's IBM Thinkpad T-41 weighs in at 4 pounds.

The future of the laptop

Human laps aren't getting any smaller. Human eyes can only comfortably read text that's so big. But most importantly, human fingers have trouble with keyboards that are too tiny. Because of these limitations, the laptop of the future will probably remain the about same size as a laptop of today. (Even though scientists could make the keyboard and screen smaller, the human form wouldn't appreciate it.)

Technology will continue to make laptop hardware smaller, more energy efficient, and better able to handle the portable environment. But one area that needs vast improvement is battery technology.

The battery of the future will be the *fuel cell,* which is like a miniature power plant directly connected to your laptop PC. Fuel cell technology promises power that lasts for weeks instead of hours, which will prove a boon to portable gizmos of every kind — but only when it's perfected.

Presently, scientists are predicting that the first usable fuel cells will be available by the end of the decade, or around 2009. Until then, we'll have to slug it out with rechargeable batteries and power packs.

(Refer to Chapter 8 for more information on batteries as well as other power management issues.)

What about Tablet PCs?

This book doesn't cover the so-called Tablet PCs. These computers are essentially laptops, but without the keyboard; the tablet consists of only the monitor "half" of the laptop, on which you write information using a special pen or stylus. (Some Tablet PCs do have keyboards, though that kind of defeats the purpose.)

While the notion of the Tablet PC sounds intriguing (and I must admit that they are sexy), sales just aren't taking off. There's a reason for this: People prefer keyboards and want that method of input. Also the Tablet PC is really nothing new. Back in the early days of laptop computers, similar devices were introduced, and they too failed.

Unless someone dreams up some must-have reason for toting a keyboard-less laptop around, I predict that Tablet PCs will (again) drop off the computer radar screen.

Why You Need a Laptop

Obviously Adam Osborne was right: Computers need to be portable! The question should really be: Why buy a desktop computer that's stuck in one spot all the time?

Naturally, a desktop computer is more powerful, expandable, and cheaper than a laptop. *But you can't take it with you!* Well, you could, but by hauling all that desktop stuff around you'd really look like a dork.

On the other hand, it's impossible to look like a dork with a laptop. Imagine yourself sitting in that trendy coffee shop, sipping some overpriced caffeinated beverage while pouring over your e-mail and chatting on a cell phone — that's hip! That's so five-minutes-from-now!

Seriously, you want a laptop for one of the following reasons:

✔ **As your main computer**

Why dither over saving money with a desktop when you really want the portability of a laptop?

A desktop computer cannot pretend to be a laptop, but a laptop can certainly fake being a desktop: You can use a full-sized keyboard and monitor with your laptop. You can also connect any number of popular desktop peripherals such as a printer, scanner, external hard drive, and so on. But, unlike a desktop system, you're free to disconnect the laptop and take it with you whenever you want.

✔ **As a space-saving computer system**

Unlike desktops, you don't have to build a shrine to your laptop computer — that is, you don't need a computer desk. If space is tight in your house, apartment, or dorm room, keep the laptop on the shelf or in a drawer. Then set it up on the kitchen table or coffee table when you're ready to work. Forget about the constant mess and clutter that orbits the typical desktop computer station. Viva Adam Osborne!

✔ **As a second computer**

Why buy a second desktop computer when you can get a laptop and enjoy not only the presence of a second computer but the ability to make that computer system portable? Further, you can network the two computers together, allowing them to share the Internet connection, printers, as well as data and files. But you still have the luxury of having one system that's portable.

✔ **As your on-the-road computer**

Laptops let you take your work on the road. After a few moments of *synch* (transferring current files between your desktop and laptop, covered in Chapter 14), you're off and running to anywhere you like (though being in direct, bright sunlight can make it difficult to see the laptop screen).

When you return from your "road warrior" trip, you perform another synch, and both computers are all caught up for the day.

- Laptops let you escape the confines of your office and do work anywhere you like for a few hours. Or if there is power at your location, you can plug in and work all day.

- The laptop lets you take your work with you when you travel. It lets you experience the reality of using a computer on an airplane (which isn't as sexy as it sounds).

Why You Don't Need a Laptop

Laptops are not cheap. They're also expensive to fix. They can easily get stolen. The battery life never lives up to the printed specifications. It's tough to get work done on a jet or in a café because people either look over your shoulder or ask you questions about the laptop. Ack! But those are minor quibbles.

Thanks to their light weight, long battery life, and increasing computing power, laptops make an ideal computer for just about anyone. If you don't own a laptop today, you will someday.

Taking that laptop off to school

Once upon a time, your fellow students just knew that you were a computer geek when you hauled up your ancient "microcomputer" for installation in your dorm room. Today, they just know you're a geek if you don't have a laptop. (In fact, laptops are cool; desktop computers are very *five minutes ago* on college campuses.)

Laptops allow you to bring a full-powered computer with you anywhere on campus. You can get work done in your dorm just as easily as you can in the library or anywhere else your feet take you.

Most colleges and universities provide a laptop requirements sheet that tells you which type of hardware you should look for when purchasing a laptop for school. (But before you go, please refer to Chapter 17 on laptop security.)

Chapter 2

Buying a Laptop Just for You

In This Chapter

▶ Getting to know the five steps to buying a computer

▶ Understanding your software needs

▶ Getting the right laptop hardware

▶ Mulling over specific laptop options

▶ Expanding your laptop

▶ Networking and communications options

▶ Finding service and support

▶ Buying your laptop

*B*uying a laptop is like buying any big-ticket, pricey item: The more you know about what you're buying, the better chance you have of finding exactly what you need. An educated consumer is a wise and thrifty consumer. Plus, you don't want to feel like a clumsy doof when buying something technical like a computer.

Even if you're an old hand at buying desktop PCs, before you go shopping for a new laptop, you need to do a little research and investigation of the issues unique to laptops, such as weight, battery life, and wireless networking options. Therefore, to help you make the best decision possible, I present this chapter. Here you can read about the easiest way to buy a laptop, plus which special laptop features to consider. The idea is to get a laptop that perfectly suits your needs.

For more information on buying computers, including definitions and descriptions of various computer pieces parts, refer to *Buying a Computer For Dummies,* 2005 Edition, published by Wiley Publishing, Inc., and written by yours truly.

Buy That Laptop!

The best computer you can buy is the one that does what you need it to do. To find that computer, you have to ignore all the sales pressure out there, which is more oriented toward brand-name computer buying. That's really wrong, and someone should be severely slapped for pushing computers based on their brand names.

You don't buy a computer for the hardware alone. Low price isn't the reason, either. Instead, the reason you want a computer is to complete some task, to have the computer do work for you, or to help you get something done. When you approach the purchase with that in mind, you end up getting the best computer possible — not some brand name you have to upgrade in a few months.

The five steps to buying any computer

To get a computer that works perfectly for you, follow these five simple steps:

1. Figure out what you want the computer to do.
2. Find the software to get that job done.
3. Match hardware to the software.
4. Shop for service and support.
5. Buy the computer.

Two items here stand out more than the others. The first — often surprising to most folks — is to look for software before hardware (Step 2). That's because it's the software that gets the work done. Despite all the flash and glory that the hardware offers, software is more important. Nya!

The second item is found in Step 4: service and support. More important than finding a low price or deal is to find folks who will give you help when you need it and fix the silly thing in case it breaks. That makes sense, but it's crazy how people forget it.

The hunt for software

Allow me to distill this information for you: If you plan on getting a laptop as an extension of your desktop computer, then you'll most likely be running the same software on the laptop as on your desktop. In that case, your laptop's hardware requirements are identical to the desktop system. Bingo! You're done.

If your laptop adventure is new, then what you probably need is a basic laptop setup. You'll want to browse the Internet, plus you'll want a basic Office suite of applications. That's pretty much what a typical laptop user needs.

Beyond the previous two examples, you might be running specific software on your laptop. If so, find out what kind of hardware that software requires. For example, if the software needs 256MB of RAM, you'll have to be sure that your laptop comes with that much RAM. Ditto for hard drive storage, a CD-ROM, microprocessor power, and other hardware requirements. These are listed right on the side of the software box.

✔ The most important piece of software you'll need is the computer's operating system. For this book, I assume that you're using Windows XP. Generally speaking, any laptop powerful enough to run Windows XP can run just about any desktop software sold.

✔ You'll have to refer to the software license agreement to see whether or not you're allowed to install a single program on both your desktop and laptop computers. Most of the time, this is considered okay by the developer, in that it's not assumed that you will be using both computers at once. But some software developers, specifically Microsoft, do not allow multiple installations from the same set of software.

✔ Happily, most laptops come with all the software you need. You get an operating system, such as Windows XP Home or Professional. Plus you get Microsoft Office or a similar productivity suite of programs. Perhaps there is other software as well. Be sure to inquire about included or bundled software before you buy a laptop.

✔ Computer gamers prefer desktop systems over laptops, primarily because desktops can readily be modified and updated. With that in mind, if you plan on playing games with your laptop, be sure to get the latest, best video hardware, lots of video memory, and lots of RAM as well. But keep in mind that, unlike a desktop computer, you cannot update this stuff later. So plan ahead with your laptop configuration.

✔ Also note that the laptop's LCD monitor does not update as fast as a CRT, or traditional monitor. Gamers prefer CRTs.

✔ In the realm of graphics applications, die-hard graphic artists also prefer CRT, or traditional glass monitors, because they can more accurately reproduce a variety of colors. But note that it is possible to connect such a monitor to a laptop when the need arises. (Refer to Chapter 7.)

Figuring out how much basic laptop power you need

The three basic items you want to mull over in matching your laptop's hardware to the software you need are

- ✔ The microprocessor
- ✔ Memory or RAM
- ✔ Hard drive storage

The microprocessor is the laptop's main chip. It's not "the brain." No, your computer's software is the brain. It tells the microprocessor what to do. You want to ensure that you get a microprocessor that's plenty fast enough to deal with the applications you need *tomorrow.* It is worth the extra money to invest in a fast microprocessor now, which extends the useful life of your laptop by ensuring that you can run tomorrow's software before tomorrow comes. So find a laptop with the fastest microprocessor that you can afford, and then buy the next most expensive microprocessor. You'll be thankful later.

Memory is where the action happens in a computer, where the work gets done. If the software states that it wants more than 256MB of memory, then get a laptop with however much RAM the software requires. The more RAM your computer has, the happier it appears to be and the more your software will enjoy the computer.

Hard drive storage is the electronic closet where you'll store your stuff. This includes not only the computer's operating system, but all the software you get and later install, plus all the data files and junk you collect. Again, the software should tell you how much hard drive space it requires. The total space for each application should be totaled, then at least doubled to give you a general figure for how much hard drive storage you'll need.

- ✔ Laptop microprocessors are more expensive than their desktop counterparts. That's because the laptop microprocessors must be designed to use less power and generate less heat. That takes time, so their development cycle is longer, hence the added cost.
- ✔ When reading the hardware requirements on a software box, use the "recommended" values, not the minimum. For example, a program may request 256MB of RAM but really thirst for 384MB. If so, get 384MB — or more.

- ✔ RAM is where it's at! If you cannot afford a faster microprocessor, you can afford to buy more RAM. Pack your laptop with as much RAM as you can afford now.

- ✔ Buy the fattest hard drive you can afford. Especially if you plan on putting music on your laptop, you will need at least an 80GB hard drive for that, perhaps more.

- ✔ If possible, I recommend a laptop with at least 512MB of RAM in it. If you can afford 1024MB of RAM, get it. If you can afford 2048MB of RAM, get it, but don't e-mail me about it because it will make me terribly jealous.

- ✔ The things that consume huge amounts of hard drive space are graphics image files (such as digital photographs), music or audio files, and video files. If you plan on collecting any of these on your laptop, get a larger hard drive!

- ✔ By investing in the latest, fastest microprocessor, lots of RAM, and copious amounts of hard drive space now, you are extending the life of your laptop. That's a good thing. You want your laptop investment to last for years to come. So pay more now, and you'll earn it back down the road when you're still using your laptop while others are forced to buy a new one.

Finding out what you don't need

Laptops generally don't come with floppy drives. Ditto for Zip disks. If you want such a thing, it can always be added as a peripheral, but honestly you don't need it — and really don't want to be carrying around such a thing with you anyway.

Laptops also lack a desktop PC's internal expansion slots, though this is because most laptops come with all the options pre-installed (yet another reason for a laptop's high price tag). If you want to play expansion card poker with your computer, then you probably want a desktop PC and not a laptop.

Thanks to the laptop's expandability — primarily because of its USB ports — you can add most any desktop device as an external peripheral. But don't be fooled! You're buying a laptop for its *portability,* so you want extra options installed *when you buy* the laptop. Adding on extras is possible, but then you're tethering your laptop to other things, which reduces its portability.

More important than a floppy drive, consider getting a laptop with a memory card reader. A combination Secure Digital and CompactFlash card reader means your laptop can immediately read the same media used in digital cameras. You can even use that media as removable storage and as a way to swap information between two computers.

Special laptoppy issues

In addition to all the regular hardware, you'll need to consider the following five items when choosing a laptop:

- ✔ Weight
- ✔ Size
- ✔ Display size
- ✔ Battery life
- ✔ Battery type

Weight. Nearly all laptops sold today fall in the range of 4 to 7 pounds. The heavier laptops have more features. The lighter models may have fewer features or merely more advanced features, but they're generally more expensive. You pay more for light weight, but oddly enough you pay more for extra weight too, thanks to the added features.

Size. Most laptops are less than 1 inch thick and about as tall and wide as a small coffee table book. They could get smaller than that, but there is a limit based on the size of the keyboard and the size of the display. Speaking of which. . . .

Display. Recently, manufacturers have discovered that people love larger LCD displays on a laptop — despite the larger display adding to the laptop's size and weight. For a laptop being used at one location and only rarely going on the road, a huge display is wonderful. But if you want portability, and a longer battery life, consider a smaller display.

Battery life. Despite the claims on the brochure, most PC laptops last anywhere from two to three hours unplugged. They last even less if you do a lot with the laptop, which means lots of disk access and networking and stuff that requires copious amounts of electricity.

Battery type. There are many types of batteries, but what you want in your laptop is a Lithium-Ion battery. You do not want a Nickel-Cadmium or "NiCad" battery. The Lithium-Ion batteries can be recharged at any time and don't have the "memory" problem of NiCads. They also last longer and keep a more potent charge longer.

- ✔ There's nothing wrong with buying a 7-pound laptop that has all the features you need.
- ✔ Refer to Chapter 8 for more information on battery types and the memory problem.

- Stuff that's important to the overall weight of the laptop — the power brick and cord, extra batteries, disks, manuals, and so on — are not included with the basic tonnage calculation. Keep that in mind if weight is important to you.

- Larger LCDs are sweet, but they use up battery power more quickly and they add to the system's overall bulk and weight.

- The larger displays on a laptop are designed to be in the same presentation ratio as a DVD movie. Coincidence?

- A popular trick used to make the battery life seem longer is to specify the time used by two batteries. With some laptops, you can swap a drained battery with a fresh one, thereby extending your portable time. While there's nothing wrong with that trick, the extended battery time should not be used for comparison.

- Avoid any so-called laptop computer that does not run off of batteries. Shun it! Point, scream, and run away!

Laptop expansion options

Laptops use a special expansion card system no longer called PCMCIA. It was once called PCMCIA, and you may still hear that term bandied about. But because no one can remember PCMCIA, let alone what it stands for, PCMCIA was changed back in the 1990s, renamed first to *Fred* and then to *PC Card*. Despite this, I noticed in Office Max the other day that some guy called them PCMCIA cards. His name was Fred.

The PCMCIA, er, PC Card system uses special expansion slots and cards for adding options to your laptop. These cards are about the size of a credit card, though thicker (and without revolving debt). They slide into a special slot on the laptop's side, which is how you can add special options to your laptop. The options include a memory card reader, networking abilities, more storage, and so on.

Laptops may also use an exchangeable disk system. For example, the CD-ROM or DVD drive might be removable and could be replaced with a second hard drive or a floppy drive. This type of drive-swapping is usually specific to certain laptop models; you generally cannot swap drives between two laptops from different manufacturers, unless you're just incredibly lucky.

- Okay: PCMCIA stands for Personal Computer Memory Card International Association. Big deal!

- It's often said that PCMCIA stands for People Cannot Memorize Computer Industry Acronyms.

✔ Better than getting the swappable drive option is simply knowing exactly what you need in a laptop in the first place. Buying a laptop with non-swappable disk drives is cheaper.

 ✔ Other laptop expansion options are available through the same type of expansion *ports* available on desktop PCs. These include standard USB ports, as well as older serial and printer ports.

Communications options

Laptops thirst for communications! Therefore, they must come with an internal modem plus networking abilities, either wire-based Ethernet, or wireless networking, or often both.

Most laptops are adorned with infrared communications ports, which allow for communications with other infrared devices. Or I suppose the infrared ports exist so that you can use your laptop to change channels on the hotel room TV.

 ✔ Ethernet is provided on a laptop via internal circuitry and an RJ-45 port (or hole) on the laptop's case. If the laptop doesn't have this circuitry built in, then you can add it via a PC Card.

 ✔ Wireless networking is done via the 802.11 standard. The most popular version of this standard is 802.11g, though some older systems use 802.11b. (Some wireless laptops use both systems, 802.11g and 802.11b.)

 ✔ Yes, the 802.11h and 802.11i standard will most likely be available soon. Don't worry about them. A good gauge of which wireless standard to get is to look at what's available in the store. According to Fred at Office Max, it's 802.11g.

 ✔ Whoa! I just saw the 802.11n standard fly by!

 ✔ If the laptop doesn't come with wireless networking built in, it can be added via a PC Card. I recommend getting a card with an external, directional antenna.

 ✔ Avoid the temptation to fondle the external antenna.

 ✔ If the laptop lacks a modem, then you can also add a modem via a PC Card.

 ✔ For more on networking, see Chapter 9.

 ✔ No, sadly you cannot use your laptop to change channels on the hotel room TV. I have this information on authority from many who've tried.

Energy management hardware

While desktop computers come with some energy management features — the ability to suspend or sleep the computer, or the "hibernate" option — these features are far more necessary on a laptop. Primarily, energy management on the laptop is concerned with controlling the power drain on the battery.

Ensure that your future laptop has the ability to merely sip power when necessary. Chapter 8 has more information on various tricks to make this happen, but it helps to look for such abilities in your laptop before you buy.

When power is really important to you, consider getting one of the power-miser microprocessors as opposed to the high-speed, top-of-the-line models. This does save a tad on battery life, but keep in mind that a high-end microprocessor works better for extending the laptop's lifespan.

Docking stations and port replicators

One optional item you can purchase for your laptop is the docking station or port replicator. Despite these being optional, I highly recommend them.

The docking station or port replicator serves as a base for your laptop when it's not on the road. It can be used to recharge the laptop's battery, but more importantly, it has connectors that allow you to add desktop options to the laptop. In fact, you can keep the full-sized keyboard and monitor connected to the docking station or port replicator, and just pop off the laptop when you're ready to go on the road.

- A port replicator may be nothing more than an extra attachment that plugs into a special expansion jack (or hole) on a laptop. The port replicator then lets you plug in standard desktop peripherals to the laptop.

- Docking stations are generally more sophisticated than port replicators. They're also more expensive, and they smell better.

- There is no need for a port replicator when you buy a laptop that contains all the ports you need in the first place.

Hunting for Service and Support

Please don't make the mistake of shopping for the cheapest laptop in the world. You'll find it, of course! You'll see that the laptop direct from the manufacturer is one price, then there are higher prices, then there are lower prices, and prices even lower still. Be not tempted!

Extended warranties — Don't buy a laptop without one!

For the past 50 years or so that I've been writing about buying computers, I've had one consistent recommendation: Avoid the extended warranty! That's because computers are hardy, reliable devices. If a PC can live through the standard warranty period, then it will probably live forever. And repairing or replacing any item on a desktop PC is often cheaper than any extended warranty you can find. Laptops, however, are another beast.

Laptops lack the replaceable components of a desktop PC. Often when something breaks on a laptop, the entire unit must be repaired or replaced. That can be expensive. For example,

the monitor connector on a laptop may be only a 23-cent part. But if it breaks, the entire laptop motherboard must be replaced, which costs up to $1,000 — or more. That's also true for other items inside the laptop's case; fixing things just isn't cheap!

Because of the laptop's unique nature, I highly recommend getting a manufacturer's extended warranty. In fact, I *insist* that you get at least a four- or five-year warranty to cover everything on your laptop, full replacement and repair costs. That may set you back about $120 or so, but the price is worth it. It's an *investment*.

People who overlook service and support when they buy a laptop are doomed to despair. Unlike desktop computers, laptops contain specific, tiny, and expensive hardware. Those items aren't easily swappable components like similar items in a desktop system. Because of that, buying from an outfit that offers personal support is important.

Support is best offered as a free telephone call for help when you need it.

Service is the art of fixing your laptop. The best service happens when the fixit guy comes to your home or office. Otherwise, the laptop will have to be returned, either directly to the dealer or manufacturer.

✔ There is a difference between support for your laptop hardware and its software. The software is supported by the software developer, which is not the same company that makes the laptop hardware. Be aware of the differences before you make the call.

✔ A helpful tool in your support arsenal is my book, *Troubleshooting Your PC For Dummies* (Wiley Publishing, Inc.).

✔ There is nothing wrong with mail-in service. Just be aware that you'll be without your "baby" for a few days while it's being fixed.

✔ Some manufacturers only offer you a replacement laptop while yours is being fixed via mail-in service. That's a bonus.

✔ A lack of service and support is one reason some dealers (and large department stores and discount houses) offer laptops at such ridiculously cheap prices. Don't ever expect the employees in such a place to be able to help you, and the guy who cuts meat in the back isn't going to be able to fix your laptop, either.

Where to Buy

Obviously, you want to buy your computer at the location that's going to give you the best deal plus the service and support you need. Beyond that, I can't be specific (because no one has bought me off . . . yet). I can, however, highly recommend local dealers over buying from huge discount stores, office supply stores, chain stores, or even the Internet.

Local computer dealers have a reputation that only needs to be as big as the community they serve. While the prices may not be the lowest, the people you buy from and who offer you service and support are all local. They're people you meet face to face, maybe even your neighbors. As such, I believe you'll find the local dealers to be your best choice for buying any computer.

✔ Laptops are more of a commodity than desktop computer systems. Unlike the desktop system, you can just plug in a laptop, and it's ready to go; there is nothing to configure or set up.

✔ I highly recommend sticking with name brand laptops made by big companies you recognize.

✔ Beyond the local stores, buy your laptop from any place you feel comfortable doing business with. But don't forget your service and support options!

✔ Buying a laptop on the Internet is safe, though keep in mind where your support comes from!

✔ When considering non-local dealers, such as Internet or catalog dealers, ensure that they have a real street address so that you can verify their existence. Companies that list only an 800 number could be fly-by-night operations, and you may never see your laptop — or your money — again.

✔ Don't ever put money down on a laptop. Laptops come fully assembled from the factory, and there is no need to put money down to "hold" one.

⟵ If possible, pay for your laptop using a credit card. The law offers far more protection to credit card users than people who pay by check or (don't even think about it) cash.

⟵ When buying from the Internet or some other non-local dealer, verify that it does not charge your credit card until the order ships. This is standard practice, but apparently some dealers haven't got the word yet.

The Final Step: Buying Your Laptop

When you're ready to buy your laptop, buy it!

Don't sit and wait for a better deal or a lower price. That's because there will *always* be a better deal and a lower price. Hardware gets better and better. The price will always come down. Therefore, when you're ready to buy, take the plunge and buy! Waiting gets you nowhere.

Part II

I Have My Laptop, Now What?

The 5th Wave   By Rich Tennant

All right fellows - basketball today! Get changed and make sure everyone's wearing a mouse pad!

In this part . . .

Unlike personal robots of the future, your laptop isn't going to jump out of the box, introduce itself, and shake your hand. That would be a nice trick. The next best thing to that would be, of course, to steal one of those cute kids in lab coats that populate various television laptop computer commercials. You know the type: They're infinitely cheerful and eager to help. And I'll bet they don't eat much, either.

Even better than cheerful actors in television commercials is this book you have in your hands. This part of the book introduces you to your laptop computer. Here, you read about all its various features and important things to note — specifically things that differ between a laptop computer and its desktop counterpart. Consider this your *For Dummies* laptop primer on getting to know your new, best electronic friend.

Chapter 3

Out of the Box and into Your Lap

In This Chapter

▶ Unpacking the laptop

▶ Knowing what to keep and what to throw away

▶ Setting up the laptop

▶ Finding a place for your laptop

▶ Plugging it in

▶ Using a UPS (or not)

I find it puzzling that laptop computers come in such large boxes. It almost takes you back: "Whoa! I didn't order something *that* big!" A little faith and a few rips of the cardboard later reveal that the laptop is safely tucked inside, along with lots of foam peanuts or packing material. But there's a lot of other stuff in that box, too. Surprisingly, for many people, the instructions for setting everything up are not among all the packages, papers, and gizmos!

Breath easy, gentle laptop owner. This chapter was written to assuage your fears and dread about opening that box and setting up the laptop. As a laptop owner myself, I too have experienced the panic of not finding the friendly "Hello there! What to do next?" manual. Even a single sheet of setup instructions is better than the nothingness that accompanies most laptop computers. To make up for that lack, this chapter provides you with all you need to know on laptop unpacking and setup.

Basic Box Unpacking 101

No one tells a kid how to open presents on his birthday, and me telling you how to open the box your laptop came in is an equally futile exercise. Even so, after years and years of opening computer boxes, I do have a slew of tips and suggestions for you:

> ✔ If there are instructions on how to unpack the box, heed them! I refer specifically to labels like, "Open other side" or "Remove first."

✔ Be sure to open and free the packing slip (if any) attached to the outside of the box. That contains the shipping invoice, which you should look over to confirm that what was shipped is exactly what you ordered. (Often, the invoice may be inside the box instead.)

✔ Don't throw anything away! If the laptop is a dud, you'll want to return everything.

✔ Be sure to look for boxes within boxes. Also be on the look out for things stuck in the sides or ends of the foam packing material.

✔ Don't fill out any warranty or registration cards until you're certain that the laptop works.

✔ Always open computer equipment boxes with your hands. Never use a box cutter because you could slice into something important.

✔ Beware of those big, ugly staples often used to close cardboard boxes. They can go a-flyin' when you rip things open, poking out eyeballs or just lying in wait on the floor for a bare foot to stomp on by.

Making piles for the various things in the box

Laptops, as all computers, come with lots of junk. Some you'll want to keep, some you can toss. Right now, making the decision of what to keep and what to toss isn't the most important thing, so I suggest creating piles for the stuff that came with the laptops.

First, unpack the laptop. Remove it from any plastic bag or shrink-wrap. Don't worry about opening it (though the temptation may be great). Just set the thing on a table by itself.

Second, find all the various hardware pieces that came with the laptop. This includes the power adapter, power cord, extra batteries, phone cord, adapters, connectors, weird tiny gizmos that you'll probably lose eventually, and other things.

Third, make a pile for any discs (CD-ROM or DVD-ROM) that came with the laptop.

Fourth, make a pile for all the paperwork. There will be three categories of paperwork: manuals, warrantees, special offers, and weird pieces of paper, the importance of which cannot be determined.

Finally, place all the packing material back into the box, including the plastic bags, twist-ties from the cables, and those silica pouches they tell you not to eat (probably because the stuff inside tastes like candy).

- If the laptop came with a how-to manual, consider yourself lucky. Most laptops don't come with any how-to material whatsoever.

- Sometimes the only manuals that come with the laptop are directories listing the locations where you can get it fixed.

- Software discs are included even though the software may already be installed on the laptop. Don't toss away the discs! They were given to you so that you can reinstall the software in the future, should you need to.

After you get the laptop all set up, separate the piles into two stacks. The first is the laptop and anything you need to run the laptop. For most systems, this is basically the laptop itself and the power cord. (The battery will be installed inside the laptop.) The rest of the stuff should be kept elsewhere, either in a drawer or box.

I have a shelf in my office where I keep containers for each computer I own. The container holds all the stuff that came with the computer that I want to keep: the manuals, spare parts, and other documentation. I suggest you have a similar shelf or location for a container or special box for your laptop's extra stuff.

"How long should I keep the box?"

I recommend keeping the box and the packing material as long as you own the laptop. That way, should you need to ship the laptop to a repair center, or return it to the dealer, you'll have the original box.

When the laptop dies, you can then bury it in its original box, throwing them both out at the same time.

- Many dealers and repair centers won't accept a laptop unless it's packed in the original box.

- If you don't have the original box, you can order another one — but why pay for that when you can just save the original?

- No, you don't need to pack the laptop in a box when you take it on the road; slipping the laptop into a briefcase or any quality carrying case is fine for that. You'll only need the boxes if you plan on mailing or shipping the laptop.

When to send in the warranty

Wait a week to ensure that the laptop works and that you have everything you ordered. When you're satisfied, fill out and send in the warranty card.

Often times when you order a computer direct from the manufacturer, you do not need to fill in and return a warranty card.

In some cases filling out and returning the warranty card sets the start date for the warranty period. Otherwise, the warranty may start on the day the laptop was manufactured, which could have been three months ago! Read the card to be sure.

Setting Up Your Laptop

Features vary from laptop to laptop: Not every laptop has the same keyboard layout; the CD-ROM or DVD drive may eject forward, to the left, to the right, or might not even exist; connectors and holes may be on the sides, back or both; and the power button? Well, it could be *anywhere!*

Beyond the differences, if you squint your eyes tight enough, all laptop computers look basically the same. Setup for each is similar, so the sections that follow address issues that are the same for all laptop owners.

If you find any specific instructions regarding setup inside the laptop box or — should you be so lucky — if you find a manual, heed its instructions first. Then refer back here for a gentle review.

Do you need to charge the battery?

When setting up your laptop, the holiest piece of hardware is the battery. Om! It either came preinstalled (and perhaps even non-removable) inside the laptop, or it came separately and must be installed.

Install or set up the battery. Fortunately, this is one of those things where the instructions are actually included with the laptop. The instructions may tell you how to install the battery, or which doodah to remove to make the battery work, or other important battery preparations.

- ✔ You can use your laptop without the battery, but before doing that I recommend properly setting up the battery to ensure that it works.

- ✔ Some batteries come DOA and must be charged before use. This is normally done by installing the battery inside the laptop, then plugging the laptop's power brick both into the wall and into the laptop. Battery charging takes place automatically.

- ✔ It usually takes a few hours to charge a laptop's battery. The time depends on the type of battery, power management hardware, and whether or not you're using the laptop at the time.

✔ If the battery is already charged, then install it, and you're ready to go! Literally!

✔ The manufacturer may claim that the battery is fully charged, but don't be surprised if it isn't. No big deal; just install the battery and plug in the laptop. It will charge.

✔ I usually let my laptop's batteries charge overnight.

✔ Be sure to put any extra or spare batteries in storage when not in use. Chapter 8 discusses storing batteries.

✔ Also refer to Chapter 8 for more information on managing your laptop's battery and power management in general.

Is some assembly required?

Beyond that battery, you may be required to add some features to your laptop. Pray that such a thing doesn't happen to you! But I've known some laptops to arrive without memory, disk drives, and other options installed. When that's the case, it's up to you to properly install those items. I wish you the best of luck!

✔ Most laptops come fully assembled. In fact, installing extra features is not an option for many laptops.

✔ Fortunately, installing options such as memory or a network adapter are one-time affairs. Follow the directions closely. Read them over first before attempting the installation. In most cases, the operation proceeds smoothly. It also helps that most things are inserted in only one direction so that you cannot goof things up.

✔ Beware of Electrostatic Discharge (ESD). That tiny little spark you generate on a dry day could permanently damage your laptop. When installing options, always keep one hand touching the laptop's case. This helps lessen the potential of the dreaded ESD.

✔ If your laptop came with a docking station or port replicator, don't worry about setting it up or using it just yet. The laptop works fine without that optional feature, so I recommend using the laptop for a while before you need to mount the docking station or port replicator.

Finding a place for the laptop

Laptops can go anywhere. That means they can get up and go anywhere, anytime. With a fully charged battery, your laptop has a home wherever you go! Beyond that, you can place your laptop anywhere you like: the kitchen table, the coffee table, a real desk, a computer desk, in bed with you, and so on.

I do recommend keeping the laptop on a flat, steady surface. Try to keep it away or out of spilling range of any drinks or food you might be consuming.

When I use my laptop around the house, I like to keep it plugged in. For example, when I'm browsing the Internet while I'm watching a football game on TV, I'll put the laptop on the coffee table and plug it in just behind the couch. I keep the beer and Doritos well away from the laptop.

If your laptop doesn't have a permanent home, then do create a consistent storage place for it. I've seen laptops slid into bookcases between the Steinbeck and Grafton novels. You can keep the laptop in a drawer or cupboard, or in the box with the rest of the laptop stuff. But keeping it in the same place means you'll always be able to find it when you need it.

Avoid putting the laptop in a spot where it can overheat. Today's laptops get hot all by themselves. Anything you can do to help keep the laptop cool is good.

When the laptop has a docking station or port replicator, try to keep that part in the same place all the time. Set up a desk and put the docking station or port replicator in one spot. You might also keep various peripherals — such as a printer, big keyboard, mouse, full-sized monitor, scanner, and other toys — ready to go and plugged in. Call this location your *Laptop Shrine*.

One great way to set up a laptop is to place the laptop on an elevated platform above the desktop. Then use an external keyboard to type on, resting the keyboard on the desktop itself. That way the laptop's screen is at eye level, which will naturally make you sit with better posture and give you less neck strain than keeping the laptop down on the desktop itself.

- ✔ Although you can use the laptop anywhere, be aware of ergonomics! For example, when using the laptop on a coffee table, if you start to feel a pain in your back from hunching over, stop! Find a better, more comfortable place to work.

- ✔ Refer to Chapter 7 for more information on attaching devices to your laptop.

The last thing to do: Plug it in!

When you choose your laptop's final resting place — even if it's final only until you find a new resting place — plug it in, as illustrated in Figure 3-1.

Attach the power cord to the laptop's back or side. On newer laptops, the power cord connector may be color-coded yellow; the yellow hole is where the power cord plugs in. Otherwise, the power connector should be unique; it plugs in to no other hole on the laptop.

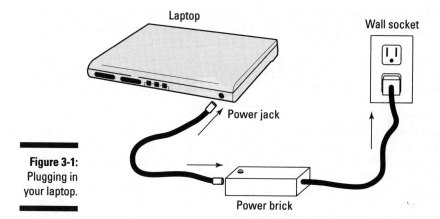

Figure 3-1:
Plugging in
your laptop.

Attach the power cord to the power brick, if necessary. Plug the power brick into the wall. Note that the power brick may also contain the plug that connects directly to the wall.

That's it. The laptop is now ready for use.

"Should I plug the laptop into a UPS?"

I advise my desktop computer readers in *PCs For Dummies* (Wiley Publishing, Inc.) to consider investing in a UPS, or Uninterruptible Power Supply, specifically one with both surge and spike protection. This device both serves to protect the computer from nasty things that can come through the power lines as well as to provide emergency power should the electricity go bye-bye.

A UPS for a laptop is unnecessary. The main reason is that your laptop already has a battery. Should you be running your laptop from an electrical outlet and the electricity goes off (or some doofus unplugs it), the laptop quickly and happily switches its power source over to the internal battery. Nothing is lost!

✔ Note that while you don't need a UPS for a laptop, I still highly recommend plugging your portable baby into a power strip with surge protection and line filtering. This helps keep the power your laptop uses clean and steady.

✔ It would be a wise idea to use a UPS for any external storage devices connected to the laptop. For example, plug an external disk drive into a UPS. You'll also do well to plug your DSL or cable modem into a UPS, as well as the router. But there is no need to plug a scanner or printer into a UPS.

> ✔ Generally speaking, if there is a lightning storm nearby, don't plug your laptop into the wall unless you're using a spike protection filter. If not, then just run the laptop from its battery until the storm passes.
>
> ✔ Refer to Chapter 8 for more battery information.

What to Do Next?

My guess is that after setting up your laptop, you'll want to turn it on and see how it works. That's covered in Chapter 4, which also contains details on using Windows XP on a laptop, plus it describes the many different ways to turn your laptop computer off — which can be confusing if you've never used a battery-powered computer before.

On the subject of batteries, I also recommend that you read Chapter 8 to bone up on how to treat your laptop's battery in a fair and just manner.

And before taking the laptop on the road, read Chapter 15, which covers a few nifty things you might want to consider before you venture out into the cold, harsh world with your new computer friend.

Chapter 4

Laptop Goes On, Laptop Goes Off

In This Chapter

▶ Turning on the laptop

▶ Finding the power button

▶ Starting Windows

▶ Locating basic Windows places

▶ Discovering options for turning off the laptop

▶ Putting the laptop into Stand By mode

▶ Hibernating the laptop

▶ Dealing with shutdown issues

▶ Changing the power button's function

Computers stopped coming equipped with on-off switches in the late 1990s. Laptops pioneered the trend. For some reason, computer scientists decided that consumers were just too satisfied with a reliable, obvious, trusty old on-off button. It gave users too much control to be able to turn off the computer at their whim. So an alternative was developed: the frustrating *power button.*

Unlike a plain, familiar on-off switch, the power button no longer turns the computer on and off. Well, it can be trusted to turn the thing on, but off? That's an entirely different matter, one that this chapter covers in depth.

Turning It On

Turning on your laptop is cinchy: Just press the power button. A blindfolded monkey on a sugar high could do that. But what the monkey — and many laptop users — cannot often do is *find* the bleeping power button.

It's a *power button,* not an on-off switch.

Before you turn on the power!

Ensure that your laptop is set up in the proper location and position for working. Yes, this even includes putting it on your lap. But more importantly, if there is a power source nearby, plug in the laptop! Always use that juice whenever you can. Save the battery for later.

- ✔ If the laptop has a docking station or port replicator, attach it per the instructions.
- ✔ Refer to Chapter 3 for more information on laptop setup.
- ✔ See Part IV of this book for information on taking your laptop on the road.

Open the lid

Believe it or not, the laptop must be in an open position for you to use it. It's difficult to see the screen and nearly impossible to use the keyboard with the lid closed. Many have tried. They all failed and, giving up in frustration, returned the laptop to the store and wrote the whole thing off as a high-tech folly.

Here's the catch: The lid has a catch, or possibly two! The catch is either a button that you push in or a little slider that you push sideways to release the lid. After you release the catch(es), the laptop's lid pops up slightly. You can then raise it up to an angle best suited for viewing, according to Figure 4-1.

- ✔ If your laptop has one catch that you must release to open the lid, it will probably be in the middle. If your laptop has two catch release buttons,they will be on the front corners of the laptop's lid. The catches will either be on the front or sides. Figure 4-2 offers some hints.

- ✔ The front side of the laptop is the side without all the connectors. (Though in the future, laptops may have connectors on the front.)

- ✔ It's possible to configure the laptop to be on without opening the lid, for example when using a docking station or an external monitor. Refer to Chapter 7 for the details.

- ✔ Do be aware that your laptop's cooling system is designed with the assumption that the lid will be open. Many laptop users who keep their systems on while closed have cooked their displays. Beware!

NOPE

NOPE

NOPE

YEP

Figure 4-1:
Adjust the
lid so you
view the
screen at an
angle that's
just right for
you.

DEFINITELY NOT

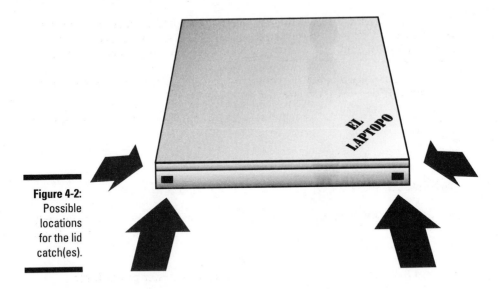

Figure 4-2:
Possible
locations
for the lid
catch(es).

"Where is the power button?"

Laptop designers have grown very adept at hiding or masking the power button. The most recent trend is to put the power button under the laptop's lid; you must open the laptop up to find and press the power button, turning the laptop on.

✔ Older laptops may have the power button anywhere, usually along one of the laptop's sides: front, left, right, or back.

✔ The power button may be a spring-slide switch that you must push in one direction and then release.

✔ Some power buttons are tiny push buttons, what I call "pray and press" buttons. There is no click or bump to the button's feel; you just press it in with your finger and pray that the laptop understands your intentions.

✔ You can put a red sticker dot by or near the power button's location in case it's easy to overlook. Even so, I find that a few times after opening the case and turning the system on, I remember where the button is. Of course, this won't help you use anyone else's laptop, because the power button is never in the same location twice.

"What is the moon button for?"

The moon icon labels a *sleep* button. This might be in addition to the power button, though on most modern laptops, the sleep button and power button are one and the same.

The moon icon is still used on many laptops to indicate when the computer is in sleep, or stand by, operation. So you may find that symbol on your laptop row-of-symbols thing, but not associated with any specific button.

✔ Sleep, or suspend, mode is covered later in this chapter, in the section, "Putting your laptop to sleep (Stand By) mode."

✔ See Chapter 5 for more information about the symbols you find on your laptop.

Random power button symbols

Blessed is the laptop owner whose laptop's power button has a symbol on it. And wise is he who recognizes the symbol as that of the power button. Let it be so. Amen.

Figure 4-3 displays a sordid sampling of laptop computer power button symbols.

Traditional power button symbol

Reset symbol (also used as power button)

Sleep symbol (also used as power button)

Figure 4-3:
Power
button
symbols
common
and
obscure.

Dot of Mystery (also used as power button)

Nerdy terms for starting a computer

Despite years of effort, the computer industry continues to use ancient and primitive jargon to mean "starting a computer." Among the lingo, you will find:

Boot. The oldest and most mysterious computer term, it basically means to turn the thing on or "pull it up by its bootstraps." In fact, *bootstrap* is an even older version of this term.

Cold boot. To turn the computer on when it has been off for a while. See *warm boot.*

Cycle power. To turn the computer off, wait a few seconds, then turn it on again. This is often required when you're trying to fix something.

Das Boot. Not a computer term at all, but the title of a German film about a U-boat in World War II.

Power up / power on. More human terms for turning the computer on.

Restart / reboot / reset. Often times, a computer needs to be shut down and then started up again. This can be done without turning off the power, and it's called a *restart, reboot,* or *reset.*

Start / turn on / switch on. Again, more human terms for turning the computer on.

Warm boot. Another term for a restart, reboot, or reset.

Power on!

To turn on your laptop, press the power button.

- Refer to the previous sections if you need help finding the button.
- If nothing happens, then the battery is most likely dead: Plug the laptop into a wall socket by using its AC adapter cord (or module or power brick thing).
- Be sure to check all the power cables! The power brick may wiggle loose from the wall socket cable.
- When everything is plugged in and nothing happens, then you have a problem. Contact your dealer or laptop manufacturer for assistance.

A Brief Foray into Windows

When your laptop starts you'll see some initial messages, perhaps a logo or graphic, then the computer's operating system — its main program — comes to life. For PC laptops, this program is Windows.

The laptop's Setup program

All modern PCs, laptops included, have a special Startup or Setup program. This program is not a part of your computer's operating system (Windows). Instead, it's built in to the computer's circuitry, or chipset, and it might also be referred to as the BIOS Setup program.

What the setup program does is to configure your laptop's hardware. It keeps track of such things as how much memory (RAM) is installed, the type of hard drive, whether or not you have a CD-ROM or DVD drive, plus other hardware options. The Setup program also keeps track of the time with the computer's internal clock, as well as other random things.

Be sure you know how to get into your laptop's Setup program. This is usually done by pressing one or more keys just after turning the computer on (and before Windows starts). On most laptops, the Del or F1 key is used to interrupt normal startup and get into the Setup program. (If your laptop uses a different key, be sure to make a note of it on this book's Cheat Sheet.)

One important item to know about in the Setup program is the security system, which usually includes a password. I don't recommend setting that password at this time (when you're just getting used to your laptop). Instead, see Chapter 17, which covers laptop security, for more information.

The version of Windows used on laptops is identical to the one used on desktop computers. There are some extra options included for laptops, specifically for power management and battery monitoring, plus there may be some other utilities and fun junk installed by the laptop manufacturer. Otherwise, it's the same Windows you know and despise.

The following sections cover a few of the places in Windows that laptop computer owners should be familiar with.

✔ For this book, the current version of Windows is Windows XP.

✔ For more information on Windows, refer to a bookstore near you and purchase a good Windows XP book. (The last time I looked, there were no books specific to Windows on laptops.)

Windows for the first time

When you first turn a brand-new laptop on, Windows goes through some gyrations and prompts designed to help you set up your computer. You'll be asked certain questions, such as which time zone you live in and your name and company name. This is designed to finish the installation of Windows, which was begun back at the factory before your laptop shipped.

Passwords

Windows lets you slap a password on your account, requiring you to type the password before you can use Windows. This is optional for an individual user, and completely unnecessary if you don't plan on using Windows in an environment where others can pick up your computer and snoop around. But for the office or school, I highly recommend creating an account with a password.

Because I'm the only one in my office, I use the same password on all my computers: none. That's considered an insecure password, but I use it because I'm the only one here, and it's easy to remember. If you're in a similar situation, consider a similarly simple password.

For situations where others could use your system, set a password that contains a combination of numbers and letters. For example, if you once lived at 4870 Elsa Road then `elsa4870` would be a suitable password. Another technique is to use two obnoxiously unrelated words and connected them with a number, such as `stinky7teeth`.

See Chapter 16 for more information on passwords and Windows XP security issues.

Whatever you do, make sure that you do not forget whatever password you've chosen! There is no way to recover Windows when you've lost or forgotten a password! I can't help you, Microsoft can't help you. Basically, you're screwed.

Heed the instructions on the screen! It's painless and it's over with quickly.

When you're asked to create user accounts, just create one for yourself. Don't bother creating one for each member of the whole fam-damily as well as your pets just yet. You can do that later, and then only if other people *really* need to use the computer.

- ✔ The name you enter as the administrator is used by Windows in various places.

- ✔ Do not forget the administrator's password! Refer to the sidebar, "Passwords," for more information.

- ✔ You don't have to use your own name for your account in Windows XP. For example, I type in the name I've given the computer instead of my own name. It really doesn't make any difference.

- ✔ Entering an Organization name is optional, though it's fun to specify fictitious organizations or something juvenile like "U.S. Department of Agriculture."

Special deal software

After setting up Windows for the first time, you may encounter some dealer or manufacturer-specific program or registration routine. For example, my IBM laptop came with some IBM help thingy I could sign up for. I opted not to and just cancelled out of the program.

You can always save registration for later. Generally, you find the registration program's icon either on the desktop or in the Start menu.

No, you don't have to sign up for AOL or EarthLink or MSN or NetZero or whatever other advertisements are included with the laptop. Feel free to skip over those programs or just delete the icons if you could care less.

Windows every time

After the initial setup, and every time you start your laptop after that, you'll be greeted with the graphical fun and folly of the Windows operating system. It may start right up, or you may have to log in first.

If you set your account up with a password, then you're prompted to enter the password before you enter Windows.

On laptops with multiple accounts, you have to choose your account name, and then enter the password before you can behold the glory that is Windows.

Whatever, eventually the Windows desktop appears on your laptop's screen, similar to what you see in Figure 4-4.

Note that many important things are pointed out in Figure 4-4:

- ✔ **The desktop.** This is your home plate, the starting point for all your adventures in Windows.

- ✔ **Wallpaper or background.** This is the image you see on the desktop. It's optional and it can be changed through the Display icon in the Control Panel. (More on that later in this chapter.)

- ✔ **Icons.** These are tiny pictures that represent files, folders, or programs inside Windows.

- ✔ **The mighty Start button.** This button pops up a menu that contains options for controlling the computer or starting programs.

> ✔ **The taskbar.** This doohickey displays a host of buttons used to switch between windows and programs opened on the desktop.
>
> ✔ **The System Tray or Notification Area.** This annoying little thing contains teensy icons that can help you do things on the computer, alert you to certain happenings, and it also shows the time and day.

Take a moment to find each of those items on your laptop screen right now. Don't touch the display to point them out! Just find them and point. (Maybe even say, "Oh, there it is!")

Exploring the Start thing

To get things done on the laptop, you need to run programs. These can be started from icons that appear on the desktop, or more likely, you'll use the Start button and its slab-o-stuff to choose which programs to run.

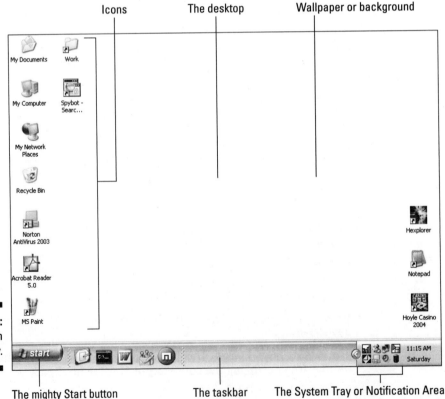

Figure 4-4: Windows in all its glory.

You can see the Start slab after clicking the Start button with the mouse. Figure 4-5 points out some of the common locations:

- ✔ **Your account image.** You can change this image by clicking it with the mouse.

- ✔ **The pin-on area.** These are programs permanently stuck to the Start menu.

- ✔ **Recently Used Programs menu.** These are programs you've used recently, except for that Hoyle game icon you see in Figure 4-5. I would never play games on my work laptop!

- ✔ **The All Programs menu.** Clicking this item displays a pop-up palette of program pickings. Any software that's been preinstalled on your laptop appears on that list.

- ✔ **Fun Windows places to visit.** These icons represent places to go in Windows where you can carry out interesting (or not) tasks and play or dawdle.

The pin-on area

Your account image

Fun Windows
places to visit

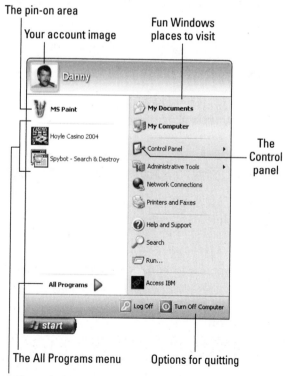

The
Control
panel

Figure 4-5:
The Start
button's
menu
thingy.

The All Programs menu   Options for quitting

Recently used programs menu

> ✔ **The Control Panel.** You'll visit here often as you mess with the computer and set various options. These are explored later in Chapter 6.
>
> ✔ **Choices for quitting.** Finally, the mysterious options for ending your session with Windows appear in the Start panel as well. Odd location; I would prefer a Stop button, but I don't work for Microsoft.

You'll discover more about using Windows and what all this stuff means in Chapter 6. For now, just knowing where things are is all you need to know.

Various Options for Turning Off (Or Not) the Laptop

Turning on a computer is easy. Once you find the switch, it's click (or press), and the thing fires up and is ever so happy to please you. But turning the computer off? That ain't so easy. That's because there are many options for turning a laptop off, leaving it on, putting it to sleep, or even sending it off to the electronic cave for some well-earned hibernation.

There is also the option of hurling the laptop discus-like out the window and the satisfaction of seeing it land and splinter into a zillion pieces. But that technique isn't really necessary to teach.

The following sections unravel the mysterious answer to the question, "How do I turn my laptop computer off?"

Properly shutting down your laptop

Here are the not-so-obvious steps you need to take to properly shut down Windows and turn off your laptop when you're done for the day:

1. **Save your work and close all your programs.**

   The generic Save command is Ctrl+S, though you'll be alerted whenever you close a program's window and the information has not been saved. Always save your stuff!

2. **Click the Start button.**

   Up pops the Start menu thing.

3. In the lower-right corner, click the Turn Off Computer button.

The Turn Off Computer box thing appears (see Figure 4-6). Don't be startled as the rest of the screen slowly fades to grayscale. (Yes, you're back in Kansas.)

Figure 4-6:
Things that
turn off your
laptop.

4. Click the Turn Off button.

The laptop turns itself off.

Yes, that's correct: The laptop turns itself off. When the screen goes dark, and the power lamp is dimmed, you can shut the laptop's lid and put it away.

But — honestly! — merely shutting down a laptop is so trite. There are far more interesting ways to end your laptop session, as covered in the sections that follow.

The "powerful" keyboard shortcuts for turning off the laptop are to press the Windows key (or Ctrl+Esc) to bring up the Start menu. Then press U for Turn Off Computer. Press U again to choose the Turn Off button.

If you change your mind, click the Cancel button, or press the Esc key, in Step 4. You'll be returned to Windows in its full, Technicolor, Oz-like glory.

"I need to restart Windows"

Occasionally, you'll be directed to reset the laptop, which is often referred to as "restarting Windows." To do so, heed these steps:

1. Save your work and close all your programs.

2. Click the Start button.

3. **Click the Turn Off Computer button.**

4. **Click the Restart button.**

   The laptop seems like it's turning itself off, but just before it does, it starts right back up again. Amazing.

Note that sometimes restarting Windows is automatic. You'll generally be given a choice: "Would you like to restart Windows now?" If so, click the Yes button, and things happen automatically. But if the process is stalled, such as you have an open and (gasp!) unsaved document, you'll have to interrupt things, take care of business, then manually restart Windows according to the preceding steps.

Putting your laptop to sleep (Stand By) mode

All laptops have a special low-power mode. In this mode, the computer is still on but power to certain areas is shut off. That way it's possible to keep the laptop ready for an extended period of time without wasting a lot of battery juice. This low-power mode is called Stand By mode, but many people refer to it as sleep mode.

To put your laptop to sleep, follow these steps:

1. **Click the Start button.**

2. **Click the Turn Off Computer button.**

3. **Click the Stand By button.**

   The computer quickly prepares to Stand By. You might hear a beep. Then it appears to be turned off, but — shhh! — it's merely sleeping.

The amount of time your computer survives in Stand By mode can be infinite. If it's plugged into the wall, then you can keep the laptop in Stand By mode as long as there is power. On batteries, Stand By mode lasts a long time, but how long is a guess. I'd say the laptop will be fine for anything up to an hour or so unless the battery is really low. In that case, you'd want to use Hibernation mode (covered later in this chapter).

- ✔ Yes, it's probably a good idea to save your stuff before entering Stand By mode. But it's forgivable not to when you need to suspend operations quickly.

- ✔ If you're going to quit all your programs before going into Stand By mode, then just shut down the laptop instead. Honestly, the laptop does mysteriously benefit from being turned off every once in a while.

- ✔ The moon light might be on when the laptop is in Stand By mode.

- ✔ I do recommend that you save your work before entering Stand By mode. The reason is just in case you don't get back to the laptop and eventually the battery does drain. If you save first, you'll be assured that your stuff is safe.

- ✔ Refer to Chapter 8 for information on checking how much charge is left in your laptop's battery.

- ✔ Sometimes Stand By mode gets "lost." When that happens, it's typically a software thing. Either you need to turn off the laptop and then turn it back on again, or your laptop's power management software needs updating. Refer to your laptop manufacturer's Web site for the latter.

Waking up from sleep (Stand By) mode

To revive a snoozing laptop, simply press a key on the keyboard or tap on the mouse pad. That wakes the sucker up, bringing it back to active duty.

- ✔ If you closed the lid to put the laptop into Stand By mode, then opening the lid usually wakes it up. See the section, "What happens when you just close the lid?" later in this chapter.

- ✔ I generally push the Ctrl key on the keyboard to wake up my sleeping laptop.

- ✔ The key you press to wake up the laptop is not passed along to whatever program is running. So if the screen says "Destroy all your data files? Y/N" and you press the Y key to wake up the laptop, nothing dastardly will happen.

- ✔ Sometimes it's necessary to press the power button to wake up a snoozing laptop.

- ✔ If the laptop doesn't perk up, then the battery is probably dead. Check the laptop's power-on lights. If they're off, then the battery is dead.

- ✔ If the laptop still won't wake up, then you may have a problem with the system's power management software. Try pressing (and holding) the power button until the unit either turns off or on again. Then try starting up the laptop as you normally would. Refer to your dealer or laptop manufacturer for updated power management software.

"What the heck is hibernation?"

Hibernation is a great feature that's often sadly ignored despite its great benefits. It's like Stand By mode, but instead of merely entering a low-power state, the computer is actually turned off. Everything in memory is saved, however, so that when the computer is turned on again, it's like you never left.

It just goes to sleep by itself!

Laptops are designed to go into Stand By mode when they're under battery power. They do this after a set period of inactivity (no typing or mouse movements). Again, the design here is to save power; if the computer thinks you're bored or off for a walk (or dead), it's going to slip off to sleep to conserve power.

The delay time after which the laptop automatically enters Stand By mode is set in the Power Options Properties dialog box, obtained through the Control Panel. Refer to Chapter 8 for the details.

Here's how to hibernate your laptop:

1. **Save your work.**

   Do this as a precaution; you should always save your stuff. Even so, there is no need to quit any applications now.

2. **Click the Start button.**

3. **Click the Turn Off Computer button.**

   The Turn Off Computer box thing appears. (Refer to Figure 4-6).

4. **Press the Shift key.**

   You'll notice that the caption beneath the Stand By button changes to read Hibernate. Keep that Shift key down!

   If the caption does not change, then your laptop lacks the Hibernation feature (or it hasn't been enabled).

5. **Click the Hibernate button.**

   The laptop hums for a few moments, then it hibernates and turns itself off.

That humming is the laptop saving everything in memory to disk. When the laptop turns itself off, it's really off. You can touch the keyboard or jiggle the mouse, and that won't wake it up again.

To rouse the laptop from its hibernated state, turn it on. Refer to section, "Power on!" earlier in this chapter. (Though that section merely says to press the power button on your laptop.) You may have to log back into Windows, but eventually you'll see the desktop and any open applications just as you left them before hibernating.

    ✔ The best way to tell the difference between a laptop in Hibernation mode or Stand By is that Stand By mode usually has that moon icon lit. In Hibernation mode, the laptop appears to be turned off. (Which it is.)

✔ I prefer to put my laptop into hibernation if I know I'm not going to be using it for longer than an hour or so.

✔ A big advantage of hibernation is that it's quicker to start the computer than a regular start up. I know hibernation fans who always hibernate their computers and never really turn them off.

✔ Unlike Stand By mode, you can leave your laptop in a hibernated state for as long as you wish. Even if the batteries eventually drain, the system will return to where you left it once the computer is plugged in and started again.

✔ On some laptops, I believe that Hibernation and Stand By modes are both the same thing, though I cannot prove it.

Turning on Hibernation mode

If your laptop seems to be unable to enter Hibernation mode, follow these steps:

1. **From the Start menu, choose the Control Panel.**

2. **Open the Power Options icon in the Control Panel.**

   Refer to Chapter 6 for more information if this Control Panel stuff has you perplexed.

3. **In the Power Options Properties dialog box, look for and click on the Hibernation tab.**

   If there is no Hibernation tab, then there's your answer: The laptop is not capable of hibernating. Oh well. (You might want to also check the laptop's Setup program to see if hibernation can be activated there. Refer to the sidebar, "The laptop's Setup program," earlier in this chapter.)

4. **Select the Enable Hibernation option by clicking the check box to place a check mark in it.**

5. **Review other options, if available.**

6. **Click OK to confirm the changes and close the Power Options Properties dialog box.**

7. **Optionally, close the Control Panel window as well.**

Some laptops may require you to restart Windows for this change to take effect. If so, refer to the section, "I need to restart Windows," earlier in this chapter.

Note that Hibernation mode requires hard drive space. When hard drive space runs low, it's possible that Hibernation mode won't work. Be aware of that.

Shutting down when the laptop doesn't want to

Unlike a desktop computer, you just can't yank that power cord from the wall on a laptop. The reason that doesn't work is that with the AC power gone, the laptop immediately starts using its battery. This can be very disconcerting when the system is locked up and you really, badly want to turn the sucker off.

If the computer just utterly seems to be ignoring you, press and hold the power button. Keep on holding it down, usually for five to ten seconds. Eventually the laptop will turn itself off.

Refer to Part V of this book for laptop troubleshooting information.

Changing the Whole On-Off Scheme of Things

As I've said throughout this chapter, your laptop doesn't have an on-off switch, it has a *power button*. While that may seem frustrating, it actually has one nice benefit: *You* control what happens when you press the power button.

While pressing the power button on a laptop that's off will turn it on, when the laptop is on, what happens when you press the power button is up to you. Now that's power!

Setting the function of the power button

To tell the computer what do to when you press the power button, abide by these steps:

1. **From the Start button's menu, choose the Control Panel.**

   Chapter 6 offers more help on getting to and using the Control Panel should you need it.

2. **Open the Power Options icon.**

3. **In the Power Options Properties dialog box, look for and click the Advanced tab.**

On the bottom part of the Advanced tab, you'll find a section roped off called Power Buttons, as shown in Figure 4-7. Note that you may not see all of the options as shown in that figure.

4. From the drop-down list under When I Press the Power Button on My Computer, choose an option.

There are five options:

A. Do nothing. The power button is disabled and not used for turning off the laptop. In that case, you have to use the Start button's Turn Off Computer command instead.

B. Ask me what to do. In this case, pressing the power button displays the Turn Off Computer message (refer to Figure 4-6). You choose what to do from that menu.

C. Stand by. The computer goes into Stand By mode.

D. Hibernate. The computer goes into Hibernation mode.

E. Shut down. The computer shuts down Windows and then turns itself off.

Figure 4-7:
Lording it over the power button.

Any of these items can be chosen and assigned to the power button.

For example, if you want the laptop to hibernate whenever you press the power button, assign that option to the power button's function.

5. **Click the OK button to set the option.**

   And the power button's function is changed.

6. **Close the Control Panel.**

This change does not affect the power button's duties for turning on or waking up the computer.

Note that not all of the options listed in this section may be available. It all depends on your laptop's design and whether certain functions have been enabled by the manufacturer. In other words, don't get all bent out of shape and yell at me just because I list an option that isn't on your laptop!

Changing the sleep button's function

If your laptop has a sleep button, you can use the Advanced tab of the Power Options Properties dialog box to set its function as well. Refer to the previous section, where the power button information also applies to the sleep button.

✔ Not every laptop has a separate sleep button; sometimes the Power button is the sleep button.

✔ The sleep button has the moon icon. Refer to Figure 4-3.

What happens when you just close the lid?

Ah, one of the great laptop mysteries, ranking up there with "Does the light in the refrigerator go off when I close the door?" is "What happens to my laptop when I close the lid?"

On my laptop, the sucker goes into sleep mode when I close the lid. That's handy for when the nasty manager comes over and tells me that I've spent too much time working in the restaurant, and he needs my table for an actual paying customer. It's close and run!

While it makes sense that the laptop goes into Stand By mode when the lid is closed, that's not always the case. Like the power button, you can determine what happens when you close the laptop's lid. Here's how:

1. **Choose Start⇨Control Panel and double-click the Power Options icon.**

2. **Click the Advanced tab.**

In the Power Buttons area, you'll find an option for what do to when the computer's lid is closed — just like for the power button. The options, however, are skinny:

    A. Do nothing. The laptop continues to stay on and happy when you close the lid.

    B. Stand by. The laptop blanks out into Stand By mode.

    C. Hibernate. The laptop becomes a bear and hibernates.

Obviously, the Ask Me What to Do option would be pointless with the lid closed, and the Turn the Computer Off option may be a bit drastic. But those three options make sense.

Yes, even the Do Nothing option makes sense. After all, if you want to keep your computer docked and use a larger screen and separate keyboard and mouse, it's handy to also keep the laptop's lid down.

3. Choose an option.

4. Click the OK button.

And the laptop's lid has newfound powers.

5. Close the Control Panel.

Again, I find the Stand By option to be the most logical choice. However, for situations where the laptop is plugged in all the time, perhaps the Hibernate option is the best choice.

Chapter 5

Basic Laptop Hardware Tour

In This Chapter

▶ Getting to know your laptop

▶ Finding various connectors and holes

▶ Understanding mystery symbols

▶ Using your keyboard

▶ Using the touch pad

▶ Cleaning your laptop

For being such a small thing, your laptop is lively with all sorts of goobers dotting its inside, outside, length, breadth, and width. There is so much to look at, that I've devoted this entire chapter to exploring the various features found on and about the typical PC laptop. So grab your laptop in one hand, this book in the other, and be prepared to take your basic laptop hardware tour.

> ✔ *Hardware* is the computer's physical part, the stuff you can touch. The *software* consists of instructions that makes the hardware do stuff.

> ✔ Not every laptop will have all the gizmos and pock marks mentioned in this chapter. Some laptops will have even more! Consider this a generic survey. For some items specific to your own laptop, the mysteries of what they do may never be solved!

Your 'Round the Laptop Tour

Rules? We don't need no stinkin' rules!

When it comes to designing a laptop, the rules are simple: There are no rules. Or it's just that the rules are so vaguely defined that they seem to make no sense to anyone.

For example, I've used laptops where the CD ejects on the right side and laptops where the CD ejects on the front. The only place I've not seen CDs eject from is the back of the laptop, which makes sense, or the left side, which is just another universal snub at all the left-handed people out there.

(There are some laptops with separate CD and DVD drives on either side. When both drives are open it makes the laptop look like a tiny airplane with retractable wings!)

The following sections mull over some of the many goobers you'll find clinging to or embedded into your laptop's sides (and perhaps even bottom).

A place for your CD/DVD

Please fetch your laptop and locate the spot where the CD or DVD is inserted.

Note that there are two types of CD/DVD drives. The first is the slot type; the disc is inserted into a slot. At some point the computer "grabs" the disc, pulling it all the way in. The second is the tray type; you push a button, and a disc tray pops out of the laptop's body, or the tray may pop out when you use an Eject command in Windows. You pull the tray out the rest of the way and pop the CD or DVD into the tray. Then you push the tray back inside the laptop.

CD drives may be labeled as CD, Compact Disc, or CD-RW or CD/R-RW or some combination of those. The word "disc" might also appear on the drive.

 DVD drives use the DVD logo (see margin).

Combination CD/DVD drives may use some combination of the logos.

And, of course, some drives may not use any labeling at all.

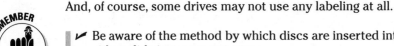

✔ Be aware of the method by which discs are inserted into the drive: either slide in or pop-out tray.

✔ For the pop-out tray, be sure you find and recognize the tiny button you press to eject the disc.

✔ It's a good idea to use the Eject command in Windows to properly remove a CD, specifically with the tray type of drive. In Windows, you open the My Computer folder and click the removable disc's icon. You then choose File➪Eject. Try it to get used to how it works. If you forget and just push the button to eject the disk, the computer may become frustrated and toss up an embarrassing error message.

Does Mr. Laptop have a floppy drive?

Most modern laptops don't come with floppy drives. Good riddance! If your laptop has one, then be sure that you can locate it on the laptop's case. It will be smaller than the CD/DVD drive opening, but essentially look about as big as a floppy disk on edge. A small eject button can be found near the opening.

If you're desperate to have a floppy drive on your laptop, then there are various external drives you can purchase. Try to get a USB-powered drive, which is more portable than the type of external floppy drive you have to plug in to the wall.

And that's all I want to say about floppy drives.

A home for Mr. PC Card

Locate on your laptop the spot where PC Cards are inserted. It may be an open hole on the side of the laptop, there may be a tiny "garage door" covering the hole, or the hole may be hidden behind a removable panel.

 I've often seen the PC Card garage labeled with the icon shown in the margin, though I'm not sure if this is a universal hieroglyph.

Note that some laptops sport a garage for two PC Cards, stacked one atop the other. Some laptops may have room for only one PC Card.

PC Cards are inserted into the slot "holy" end first. In fact, they fit in only one way. Push the card in all the way until it fully docks with the connectors deep down inside the laptop.

To remove the card, locate the eject button along side the slot, right next to the door. (See Figure 5-1.) Press the eject button all the way in, and the card pops out a little bit. You can then pinch the card between your thumb and forefinger, pulling it out the rest of the way.

An equal number of eject buttons appears along side the spot where the card slides in.

✔ Be sure to read the instructions before inserting a PC Card the first time. Some cards might require that the laptop be turned off before inserting the card.

✔ Note that some of the eject buttons pop out a ways from the laptop's case. Remember to push them back into the case when you're done with the PC Card. That way the knob won't snag on anything and possibly break off.

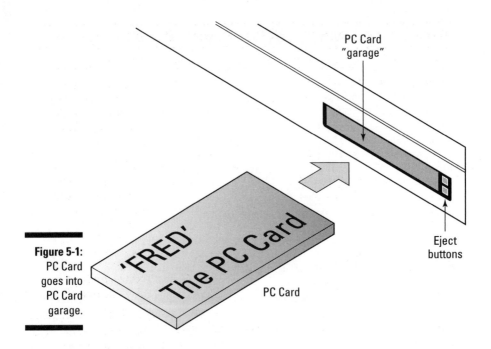

Figure 5-1:
PC Card
goes into
PC Card
garage.

Mystery things called ports

Despite their portability, laptop PCs come with just about all the expandability options found in desktop computers. These options are generally referred to as *ports.* They consist of connectors, holes, and plug-in-type things you use to add features and attach cables to your laptop, increasing its potential while at the same time limiting its mobility.

Each of these ports is configured in a certain pattern — a hole or a connector with a specific shape and whatnot. Each is also labeled with an appropriate hieroglyph, and they're often color coded. So if you're colorblind and cannot tell round pegs from square holes, just give up on all this nonsense right now.

Table 5-1 lists the pictures, symbols, colors, and duties of the various ports you may find lurking around your laptop. Try to find each one! Note that some may be hidden behind doors or sliding panels, and also that not every laptop manufacturer uses the color-coding scheme.

Table 5-1   Laptop Ports, Their Symbols, Designs, and Colors

Port Name	Configuration	Symbol	Color	Purpose
Custom	Non-specific	?	None	Most likely a connector for a docking station or external disk drive or some other form of expansion.
Digital video			White	Connecting a high-performance, external digital (LCD) monitor or TV.
Headphone			Forest green	For plugging in headphones, which automatically disables the laptop's speakers.
IEEE			None	Connecting high-speed peripherals. Also called the 1394 or FireWire port.
Infrared			None	For communicating with other infrared devices.
Keyboard			Purple	Add a full-sized, external keyboard.
Line in			Grey	Plugging in an external audio device.
Line out			Lime	Sending audio out/speakers.
Mic			Pink	Connecting a microphone.
Modem/phone			None	Attaching a modem for online communications or sending/receiving faxes.

(continued)

Table 5-1 *(continued)*

Port Name	Configuration	Symbol	Color	Purpose
Monitor			Blue	Connecting an external monitor or video display for presentations.
Mouse			Green	Attaching an external mouse.
Power			Yellow	For plugging the laptop into an AC power socket.
Printer			Violet	Attach a printer to your laptop.
RJ-45/Ethernet			None	Add your laptop to an Ethernet network or to connect to the Internet.
Serial			Cyan	An older port, though could still be used to add a mouse or for desktop-laptop communications.
S-video out			None	For attaching a desktop video projector or attaching the laptop to a TV or VCR.
USB			None	Allows a variety of components to be added to the laptop, including printers and disk drives.

If your laptop lacks most of these ports, then consider getting a port replicator or docking station.

A port replicator snaps on to a special expansion slot or connector on your laptop. It adds most or all of the features in Table 5-1, plus perhaps a few more. The port replicator may plug into the wall and supply the laptop with power, or it may just be a "cling-on" that snaps on to the laptop's rump for added expansion.

A docking station is a more sophisticated (and expensive) version of the port replicator. As with the port replicator, it allows you to add peripherals and expand the power of your laptop, but it's more of a base station or permanent location than a port replicator is. Some docking stations are even shaped like desktop PCs, but with an open maw into which you slide the laptop.

- ✔ Yes, the mouse hole and keyboard ports look alike. Use the pictograph next to the ports and the color codes to tell which is which.

- ✔ The RJ-45/Ethernet port may also have the icon shown in the margin labeling its trapezoidal crack.

- ✔ By the way, that Ethernet port and the modem port look awfully similar. Happily, one (the Ethernet port) is bigger than the other (the modem port).

- ✔ The power jack may appear differently from what's shown in Table 5-1. Be sure you don't plug the power cable into a microphone port!

- ✔ The IEEE symbol may be different on some laptops. Apparently the "Y" type of symbol isn't that universal.

- ✔ If your laptop has S-video out, note that the S-video connection is video only, not sound.

A place for the old ball and chain

To help prevent theft, your laptop has a special belt loop into which you can attach a security cable. That's the Universal Security Slot, or USS. The icon is shown in the margin.

- ✔ Note that the security cable must be attached to something solid and immovable to prevent the laptop from being stolen. Just threading a cable through the security hole doesn't do the trick.

- ✔ Refer to Chapter 17 for more information on laptop security.

The thing's gotta breathe

As you conclude your journey around the perimeter of your laptop, note where the breathing slots are. They may not be obvious, they may not even be there. If they are, note their location and try to keep the vents clear.

Look at the Pretty Lights!

Blinking lights have always been a part of computer history. They're a prime element of any computer in a science fiction TV show. That, and the fact that computers invariably blow up.

No, your laptop won't blow up. At least it won't shower you with sparks and moan about being unable to compute to the last digit the value of π. But beyond that, your laptop should sport a row of pretty lights. These are used to report the status of certain parts of the computer, as shown in Table 5-2.

Table 5-2	Pretty Laptop Lights
Symbol	*What It Could Possibly Mean*
☾	The laptop is in Stand By, or sleep, mode.
🔋	The laptop is running off battery power.
⏼	The laptop is on.
⛁	Shows hard drive access.
A	Illuminated to mean that the Caps Lock state is on. There may also be a light on the Caps Lock key.
1	Illuminated to mean that the Num Lock state is on. There may also be a light on the Num Lock key.
((•))	Indicates wireless networking activity.
✳	Indicates Bluetooth wireless activity.

Doubtless other pretty lights exist, some specific to your laptop's manufacturer. But thanks to that International Symbol Law, most of the symbols are pretty common. In fact, consider checking with Table 5-1 to see if any of those symbols appear on the laptop's pretty light strip as well.

Some lights may blink or change color. For example, the battery indicator may change from green to amber to red as the battery drains. The hard drive or wireless lights may flicker as access is being made.

When the laptop is off, none of the lights will be lit. This includes Hibernation mode as well. (See Chapter 4 for more hibernation information.)

This Isn't Your Daddy's Keyboard

The full-sized PC keyboard is an aircraft carrier! It's one huge boat! The thing was designed to be separate from the computer — a novelty back in 1981 — so that you could place the keyboard wherever you felt comfortable, even in your lap. But, golly! That keyboard is way too huge, even for the roomiest of laps.

The PC keyboard is big because it sports a lot of keys, 105 of them to be specific. Pretty much all the keys are used, too, which means they must also be found on a laptop's keyboard, and therein lies the rub. A laptop cannot have a huge, honking keyboard! So sacrifices and work-arounds were devised.

The following sections mull over the laptop's keyboard. Follow along with your own laptop as you read each section, noting how to use your laptop's keyboard and where the important keys dwell.

The general keyboard layout

Figure 5-2 illustrates a typical laptop keyboard layout, where all of the common keys found on the whopping desktop keyboard are scrunched down to laptop size. The design intends to let you type without the risk of breaking any fingers.

As with a desktop keyboard, you should be able to identify the following basic items on your laptop keyboard:

✔ **Alphanumeric, or "typewriter," keys.** These are the basic typing keys, each of which is labeled with a character (a letter, number, or punctuation symbol). When typing on the computer, pressing a key produces its character on the screen.

✔ **Shift keys.** The keyboard sports various shift keys used either alone or in combination with other keys. These include Shift, Alt, Ctrl, and the special Windows keys, Win and Context. The Win key appears in the bottom row between the Fn and Alt key in Figure 5-2; the Context key appears between Alt and Ctrl. Also note the Esc, or Escape, key found at the beginning of the top row of keys.

✔ **Function keys.** These keys are labeled F1 through F12 and are found on the top row of the keyboard, right above the number keys.

✔ **Cursor control keys.** These keys could be anywhere around the keyboard, though in Figure 5-2, they're on the top and bottom right. They include the four directional arrow keys, usually found in an inverted "T" pattern, as well as the Insert (or Ins), Delete (or Del), Home, End, PgUp (or Page Up), PgDn (or Page Down) keys.

✔ **Numeric keypad.** This is covered in the next section.

Figure 5-2:
Typical laptop keyboard layout.

Note that the alphanumeric keys are generally the largest, often the same size and with the same travel, or feel, that a desktop computer keyboard offers.

Some keys are small, Chiclet-sized keys. These are the less important and not often used keys, such as the function keys and the cursor control keys.

The text on some keys is color coded. That generally tells you which keys are used in conjunction with each other. For example, if the Alt key is green and the Num Lock key is green, that means that the Alt+Num Lock key combination is required to use Num Lock. (Also refer to the section, "The Fn key is the Fun key!" later in this chapter.)

At one point in the computer's history, the Function keys were programmable; you could tell the computer what to do when each key was pressed. In Windows, however, the function keys have taken on specific functions. For example, F1 is the Help key.

The cursor control keys are used to move the text cursor when editing text in Windows. They can also be used to help navigate through the Web. The keys may take on other functions in other programs as well.

Some keys are labeled with images or icons instead of text. For example, I've seen the Caps Lock key labeled with the letter "A" and a padlock symbol.

Your keyboard may have more or fewer keys than those shown in Figure 5-2, and the arrangement might be different.

Where did the numeric keypad go?

The first thing the laptop designers decided to sacrifice on their keyboards was the numeric keypad. But rather than just saw off that end of the keyboard, laptops since the Model 100 have used a combination numeric keypad/alpha keyboard.

This combination can be seen on your laptop by examining the 7, 8, and 9 keys. You'll note that these are also the top three keys found on the numeric keypad. Because of this, a shadow keypad is created using the right side of the alpha keyboard, illustrated in Figure 5-3. The trick, of course, is knowing how to turn the thing on and off.

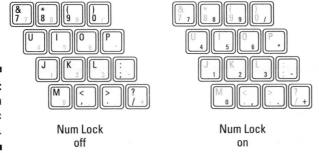

Figure 5-3:
The hidden numeric keypad.

Num Lock off

Num Lock on

Attempt these steps to turn the Num Lock on or off:

1. **Open a program you can type in, such as Notepad.**

   You can find Notepad by choosing Start⇨All Programs⇨Accessories⇨Notepad.

2. **Type** I just love Kimmy **into Notepad.**

   You'll find out why you adore Kimmy in a few steps.

3. **Find the Num Lock light on your laptop's strip of lights.**

   The light is your confirmation that you're in Num Lock mode and can use the embedded numeric keypad. (See Table 5-2.)

4. **Find the Num Lock key on your laptop's keyboard.**

   Somewhere on your keyboard is a Num Lock key. It might be called NumLock, or NumLk, or Num, or it might even be labeled with a symbol, as shown in the margin. Locate that key.

5. **Attempt to activate Num Lock.**

   Press the Num Lock key. If nothing happens, then try Shift+Num Lock.

   If the text Num Lock is listed in a different color, find the matching color key, such as Alt or Fn. Then press that key in combination with Num Lock.

   You're successful when the Num Lock light comes on. At that point, the keyboard has switched into numeric keypad mode.

6. **Try to type** I just love Kimmy **again.**

   It won't work. You'll get something like: 14st 36ve 500y. That's because most of the keys on the right side of the keyboard now have their numeric keypad abilities activated. It's great for entering numbers or working a spreadsheet, but rather frustrating at other times.

7. **Deactivate Num Lock.**

   Press whatever key combination you used to turn it on.

8. **Close Notepad.**

   There is no need to save the document.

Try to remember which key combination you used to activate the numeric keypad. Write it down in the book's Cheat Sheet just in case you forget.

The Fn key is the Fun key!

To make up for the lack of keys, early laptops came with a special function key, the Fn key. This was used in combination with other keys like a Shift key, giving those keys multiple purposes.

For example, in Figure 5-4, you see the keyboard from the old Compaq SLT. It's Fn (function) key is located in the lower-right corner, enclosed in a rectangle. Other keys with rectangles are activated when they're pressed with the Fn key. So the arrow keys also double as other cursor movement keys (lower right). But notice how the embedded numeric keypad also becomes an embedded cursor movement pad as well. (What a nightmare!)

Figure 5-4:
The Compaq
SLT
keyboard
(1987).

Most modern laptops retain the Fn key, but it's used primarily to activate *special* laptop functions. These functions share other keys on the keyboard, typically the Function keys. They're marked by special icons, and these are color coded to match the Fn key.

Sadly, there is no standard for these Fn keys and their functions. But among the many laptops out there, you'll find Fn key combinations that do the following:

✔ Turn the laptop's internal speaker volume up.

✔ Turn the laptop's internal speaker volume down.

✔ Mute the laptop's internal speaker.

✔ Increase or decrease the monitor's brightness or contrast.

✔ Activate an external monitor for giving a presentation.

✔ Activate Stand By mode.

✔ Hibernate the laptop.

✔ Lock the keyboard.

Take a moment to peruse your laptop and look over the Fn keys available.

Some of the Fn keys can be rather fun. For example, on my IBM laptop, Fn+PgUp is used to turn on a tiny keyboard light in the laptop's lid.

Mind these specific keys

In addition to the standard keyboard, or perhaps right along with it, your laptop may have some custom keys or buttons next to the keyboard. These are totally specific to the manufacturer, and you may never end up using them. But they're keys nonetheless.

The most common location for these keys is up above the keyboard, though I've seen them on the left and right sides as well. Some keys may be used to pick up e-mail, browse the Web, connect to a digital camera, or contact the vendor for tech support. I've also seen keys that control the display or speaker volume.

Use these keys if you will, but keep in mind that their functions are specific to your laptop. Don't expect to find similar keys on a desktop computer or even a laptop from another manufacturer.

 The special keys are controlled using specific software that must be loaded into Windows. If there is a problem with this software, or if you end up using an operating system other than Windows, don't be surprised when the special keys no longer function.

This Isn't Your Momma's Mouse

The marriage of mouse and laptop is an old idea. Even back before Windows, laptop users were aware of how handy a computer mouse could be. The problem was, unlike now, laptop users wouldn't accept a standard desktop mouse as a solution.

Figure 5-5 shows one funky solution to the laptop mouse problem. It's called a thumb-ball mouse. It plugged into the laptop's serial port and attached either to the lid or side of the keyboard, giving the laptop user a primitive pointing device. Yes, using it was as awkward as eating ice cream with a knife. But it was something.

The mouse pad

It took laptop developers years before they came up with the current solution: the mouse pad. Originally called a *touch pad,* the mouse pad allows you to control the mouse by gliding a thumb or finger along a flat surface. Buttons nearby emulate the left and right buttons found on your typical bar-of-soap mouse. (See Figure 5-6.)

Figure 5-5:
An early
model,
Microsoft
"thumb-
ball" mouse.

There is an art to using the mouse pad:

✔ You must be careful not to touch it in more than one spot. If you do, the pointer jumps about on the screen as if it were being electrocuted. Only touch the mouse pad in one spot with one finger.

✔ It helps to use your forefinger to move the mouse. Use your thumb to click the left-right buttons on the bottom of the mouse pad.

✔ A light touch is all that's required.

✔ The most difficult mouse operation is the *drag*. That's where you have to hold a button down while moving the pointer. With practice, this can be done — but you must practice! (Another excuse to play FreeCell.)

✔ Try to avoid accidentally hitting the right mouse button when you mean to hit the left one. This causes context menus to pop up in Windows. Very frustrating.

✔ Some mouse pads let you tap the pad to simulate a mouse click. You can check the Mouse icon in the Control Panel to enable or disable this feature; refer to the section "Controlling the mouse" later in this chapter for more information.

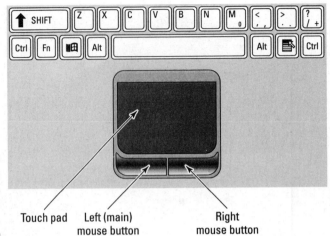

Figure 5-6:
The touch
pad mouse
thing.

Touch pad   Left (main)   Right
             mouse button   mouse button

Note that I like to refer to the mouse pad as such. Others may use the term *touch pad*. That's because a "mouse pad" can also mean a special mat on which you use a desktop computer's mouse. Whatever.

Where is the wheel button?

Most modern computer mice come with a *wheel button*. The button sits in the middle, between the mouse's left and right buttons, and is used to scroll, pan, or click for various effects. People love the wheel button, and obviously they want it on their laptops. Well, tough!

Sadly, there isn't a standard wheel button replacement on the common laptop mouse pad. Some manufacturers provide a button with similar features, but if you want a wheel button, you'll just have to end up using an external "wheel" mouse with your laptop. (And that's not a bad idea, anyway.)

IBM's "happy stick" keyboard mouse

Popular on some IBM models is a joystick-like mouse that looks like a pencil eraser jammed between the keyboard's G, H and B keys. IBM calls it the TrackPoint, though I prefer to call it a happy stick. Regardless, the gizmo is actually quite handy to use.

The idea behind the happy stick is that you can manipulate it by using the index finger of either hand. You can then use your thumb (either hand) to click the left or right "mouse" buttons, as shown in Figure 5-7.

Figure 5-7:
The
TrackPoint.

Note that a middle button exists in Figure 5-7. That's the "wheel" button, and it can be used with the happy stick to scroll information in a window. While it's not a full replacement for the wheel button on a mouse, it's a pretty neat trick.

- ✔ Like the mouse pad, using the happy stick takes some training and getting used to.
- ✔ Some IBM models come with both a happy stick and touch pad. You can use either one.

Controlling the mouse

Your laptop's mouse hardware is controlled by using the Mouse icon in the Windows Control Panel. By opening that icon, you'll find the controls for configuring and setting up your laptop's pointing device.

In addition to the standard mouse information, you may find a custom tab in the Mouse Properties dialog box, similar to what's shown in Figure 5-8. That's where you can configure the laptop's touch pad or custom pointing device. In Figure 5-8, the IBM's TrackPoint and touch pad mouse options are set.

✔ If you're a southpaw, use the Buttons tab in the Mouse Properties dialog box to switch the functions of the left and right mouse buttons. Do be aware, however, that most manuals refer to the main mouse button as being on the *left!*

✔ You can use the Pointers tab in the Mouse Properties dialog box to change the way the mouse pointer looks on the screen.

✔ Items in the Pointer Options tab can be used to help you locate a lost mouse pointer. Settings such as "pointer trials" and "show location" can also be used to help find hard-to-see mouse pointers on the laptop's display.

✔ Note that it's possible to disable your laptop's mouse pad. This is entirely acceptable if you plan on using an external mouse. (See the next section.)

✔ See Chapter 6 for more information on the Control Panel.

Figure 5-8:
Setting custom mouse options.

Get a real mouse!

The best solution for using a mouse on a laptop is to *get a real mouse.* No, not the furry rodent kind. Silly. A desktop computer mouse.

Consider getting a desktop computer mouse and using it on your laptop instead of the touch pad. Yes, it's one more thing to carry. But because desktop computer mice are so familiar, and people are used to them, it often makes sense for the laptop to have a "big computer" mouse.

✔ There are specialty computer mice available designed just for laptops. Some are smaller than regular mice, some come with retractable cords, some are even cordless!

✔ Buy your laptop a nice wheel mouse, and you'll never moan about your laptop missing a wheel button ever again.

✔ I've seen people on airplanes use real mice. Even in that cramped space, people will find a place to roll about the mouse. Pants legs work.

✔ Consider disabling the mouse pad if you attach an external mouse. Refer to the previous section.

✔ Be careful when you install the software for your external mouse. Sometimes doing so disables the software controlling the laptop's touch pad. My advice is to connect the external mouse and see whether it works. If it does, and you're happy, then just skip installing the software.

✔ Note that not all laptops come with a mouse port! If so, get a USB mouse and plug it into your laptop's USB port.

Cleaning

Now that you've been around your laptop a few times, you should do some cleanup. Look at all those tiny footprints! Look at those fingerprints! Yikes! If only your mother could see . . .!

Laptops are really robust beasts. They can go through a lot without cleaning. But when your mind does turn to it, heed the following sections.

✔ It's best to turn off the laptop before you start cleaning it.

✔ You will need a sponge or lint-free cloth as your cleaning tool.

✔ Isopropyl (rubbing) alcohol is also a good cleansing agent.

✔ If your laptop manufacturer has any specific cleaning instructions, directions, or warnings, please refer to them first over the instructions offered here.

Cleaning the case

The best way to give the case a bath is with a damp sponge. You can use standard dishwashing liquid, mixing it at about 1 part detergent to 5 parts water. Soak the sponge into the mixture, and then wring it clean. Use the sponge to gently wipe the laptop's case.

When you're done with the sponge, wipe off any excess moisture or dust using a lint-free cloth.

- ✔ Ensure that the sponge is dry enough that it doesn't drip liquid into the laptop.

- ✔ You might also want to use cotton swabs to clean some of the gunk from the cracks.

- ✔ Do not clean inside any disk openings or the PC Card slots. Never spray any liquids into those openings either.

- ✔ Avoid using detergent that contains strong chemicals (acid or alkaline). Don't use abrasive powders.

Cleaning the keyboard

Every so often, I vacuum my laptop keyboard. I use the little portable vacuums, either with the tiny (toothbrush-sized) brush or the upholstery cleaning attachment. This effectively sucks up all the crud in the keyboard. It's amazing to watch.

Some people prefer to clean the keyboard using a can of compressed air. I don't recommend this because the air could blow the crud in your keyboard further inside the laptop. Instead, use a vacuum.

Remember that it's best to have the computer turned *off* when you do this!

To clean the tops of the keys, use isopropyl alcohol. Soak it up into a soft, dust-free cloth, or use a cotton swab, and gently rub the key tops. Try not to drip any alcohol inside the keyboard.

Never use a spray cleaner directly on the keyboard.

Cleaning the screen

I've found the techniques used for cleaning an LCD screen, be it for a desktop or laptop computer, to be filled with controversy! Generally, no one recommends using any liquids because they could damage the LCD's delicate surface. Even so, you've gotta have something to rub with if you ever plan on getting that sneeze residue off the thing!

First, for general cleaning, get a soft, lint-free cloth. Use it to wipe the dust (pixel dust!) off the monitor.

Second, dampen a sponge or lint-free cloth with water. Be sure to wring out all the excess moisture. Rub the screen's surface gently. And don't get any excess liquid on or inside the monitor.

Let the monitor dry completely before closing the lid!

- ✔ Often times the keyboard will create "stains" on the screen. This is hard to avoid and even harder to clean off. To help prevent the stains, consider storing the soft lint-free cloth you use to clean the monitor inside the laptop, between the keyboard and screen.

- ✔ Office supply stores carry special LCD screen cleaners as well as the lint-free wipes that you can use to clean your screen and the rest of your laptop.

- ✔ One product I can recommend is Klear Screen from Meridrew Enterprises (www.klearscreen.com).

- ✔ Avoid using alcohol or ammonia-based cleaners on your laptop screen! This could damage the LCD screen.

- ✔ Never squirt any cleaner directly on a laptop's screen.

Chapter 6

Windows and Your
Laptop Software

In This Chapter

▶ Visiting common places in Windows

▶ Getting to the My Documents folder

▶ Finding networking things

▶ Using the Control Panel

▶ Setting up the display

▶ Finding important settings and options

▶ Abusing the System Tray

▶ Installing and removing software

▶ Changing log on options

▶ Logging in quickly

Computer hardware is pretty to look at, but without the proper software in charge, being pretty is all that hardware can muster. You need software to control your laptop. And unless your laptop has an Apple logo on it, that software will be Windows XP.

This chapter provides a stunning overview of Windows XP, with specific emphasis on those parts particular or particularly useful to your laptop. For more information on using Windows or using specific applications, refer to a cheerful bookstore employee near you.

Places to Do, Things to Go

Windows has some common places you often hear about, read about, and yearn to visit. The following sections summarize how to get there and what to do when you arrive. I might also point out some nice restaurants as well as places to buy souvenirs where the locals don't rip you off. (And where I get a modest kickback.)

You would think that the windows metaphor would carry itself throughout the Windows operating system. There should be a frame, a sill, a sash, a latch, a catch, and a pane. Yet of all these, there is only pain to be found in Windows.

My Documents

The most popular location in Windows is a folder called *My Documents*. As the name implies, it's where you store most of the stuff you create on your computer.

The easiest way to get to the My Documents folder is to open its icon on the desktop (see the margin). The folder's window pops open, revealing its marvelous contents — your stuff!

If the My Documents folder doesn't appear on the desktop, follow these steps to display it:

1. **Open the Display Properties icon in the Control Panel.**

   You can also right-click on any blank part of the desktop and choose Properties from the shortcut menu.

2. **In the Display Properties dialog box, click the Desktop tab.**

3. **Click the Customize Desktop button.**

4. **In the Desktop Items dialog box, General tab, put a check mark by the My Documents item.**

5. **Click OK to close each dialog box.**

   The My Documents icon now appears on the desktop.

You can also get to the My Documents folder from the Start menu. Clicking the Start button displays the Start menu, and one of the icons in the upper-right side is the My Documents folder.

If the My Documents folder does not appear on the Start menu, then heed these steps to display it:

1. **Right-click the Start button.**

2. **Choose Properties from the context menu.**

3. **In the Taskbar and Start Menu Properties dialog box, ensure that the Start Menu tab is up front.**

   Click on that tab if it's not.

4. **Click the Customize button.**

   This must be the Customize button by the Start Menu option, not the Classic Start Menu option.

5. **Click the Advanced tab in the Customize Start Menu dialog box.**

6. **Scroll through the list of Start menu items to find My Documents.**

7. **Select the Display as Link option.**

8. **Click OK to close each dialog box.**

   The My Documents icon now shows up in the Start menu.

Take a moment now to visit the My Documents folder. It contains your documents and the stuff you create, plus it contains other folders. Some of the other folders, such as My Pictures and My Music, are customized to hold specific types of files. (Pictures and music for the My Pictures and My Music folders, respectively.)

You can also create your own folders for specific types of files, or just to be organized. For example, I create a My Downloads folder inside the My Documents folder to keep all the silly files I download and save from the Internet.

✔ My Documents is really a folder, which is a storage container for files.

✔ The My Documents folder is located on your laptop's hard drive. So when you read about "saving this or that to the hard drive," the My Documents folder is the specific spot.

✔ You can quickly access the My Documents folder by using the Address drop-down list in any Save As, Open, or File dialog box. Press the F4 key to activate the Address drop-down list.

✔ Most of the Save As dialog boxes use the My Documents folder as the first choice for where to save your stuff.

✔ *Download* is the term for transferring a file from the Internet to your own computer.

✔ Folders are a very important concept for keeping your files organized. I would waggle my finger at you and explain all the benefits of using folders and on and on, but who has the time? So if you're serious, pick up my book *PCs For Dummies* (Wiley), and you can read more about organizing your files in greater detail.

✔ Your programs *do not* reside in the My Documents folder. No, they go in the Program Files folder. Refer to the section, "Where Your Programs Lurk" later in this chapter.

My Computer

The My Computer icon is home to all the goodies that dwell on your laptop. It should really be My Laptop, but your laptop is a computer, so I suppose you can let that oversight slide.

 You can find the My Computer icon on the desktop, or it can be accessed from the Start panel. Opening this icon reveals the My Computer window and its contents — various important places on your computer. Figure 6-1 shows a sample.

Figure 6-1 shows the fun My Computer things grouped by category: special folders, hard drive(s), and then removable storage. You might also find areas for a scanner or digital camera, plus perhaps other toys attached to your computer. The My Computer window gives you a central location from which you can access all of these devices.

✔ If the My Computer icon is not on the desktop or cannot be found in the Start menu, then refer to the previous section. The instructions for adding the My Documents icon are similar for My Computer; just substitute "My Computer" for "My Documents" and follow the steps listed.

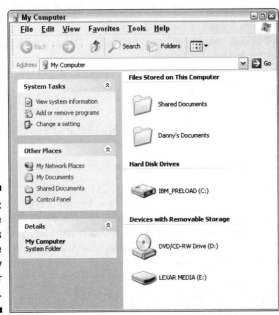

Figure 6-1: Some of the fun things you may see in the My Computer window.

✔ Note the panel on the left side of the window. It contains some common commands, plus other interesting places to visit on your computer. The commands, or System Tasks, vary depending on which item is selected in the My Computer window.

✔ You can eject a DVD or CD by choosing that drive's icon in the My Computer window, and then choosing File➪Eject from the menu.

 ✔ The icon for the CD or DVD drive may change, depending on whether you have a disc in the drive and what's on the disc. For example, music CDs have a special music icon, as shown in the margin.

My Network Places

Another place you might want to become familiar with is the My Network Places icon and its accompanying window.

 Find the My Network Places icon now. It might be on the desktop, or you may find it on the Start menu. It's also accessible via the My Computer window by clicking on the My Network Places link in the Other Places area (on the left).

Unless your laptop is connected to a network, and there are other computers on the network sharing resources (disk drives or printers), the My Network Places folder will be empty.

When your laptop is connected to a network, you can use the connection to send files between your laptop and the other computer(s).

If you cannot find the My Network Places icon on the desktop or Start menu, then refer to the section, "My Documents," earlier in this chapter. The instructions there also apply to the My Network Places icon; just substitute "My Network Places" for "My Documents" in the steps listed.

The Network Connections window

Another important place you should know how to visit is the Network Connections window, which sounds a lot like My Network Places, but it's not. The Network Connections window is where you manage the way your laptop connects to various networks, either wirelessly or wired.

 Getting to the Network Connections window is most easily accomplished by visiting the Control Panel and opening the Networking Connections icon. But there are other ways to get there as well:

✔ The Network Connections icon may appear in the Start panel. If so, click it with the mouse, and you're there.

✔ If you can see the little networking guys icon in the System Tray, you can right-click it and choose Open Network Connections from the context menu that appears, as shown in Figure 6-2.

✔ You can get to the Network Connections window from the My Network Places window by clicking the View Network Connections link in the Network Tasks panel (on the left).

Figure 6-2:
One way to access Network Connections.

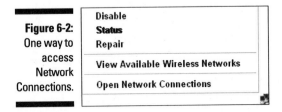

> Disable
> **Status**
> Repair
>
> View Available Wireless Networks
>
> Open Network Connections

The Network Connections window contains an icon for every network connection made by your laptop. You will see an icon for the wire-based Ethernet, wireless Ethernet, and any dial-up Internet services you may connect to.

In Figure 6-3, two network adapters are shown, one for wireless and another (that isn't connected) for the wire-based connection.

Sadly, Network Connections is one place you might end up spending many an unhappy hour trying to untangle some networking madness. I put that topic off until Chapter 9 of this book.

Figure 6-3:
The Network Connections window.

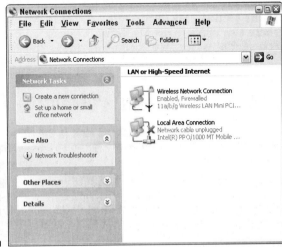

What's Important in the Control Panel

In Windows, you can work, you can play, or you can dink. *Dinking* is the art of adjusting and fine-tuning Windows, changing the appearance of this and the performance of that. It's playing with a purpose, and that play takes place in a land called the Control Panel.

To visit the Control Panel, you have several options:

⮑ Choose the Control Panel link from the Start menu thing.

⮑ From the My Computer window, choose either the Change a Setting link or the Control Panel link from the panel on the left.

⮑ Choose the Control Panel from any Address bar drop-down list.

⮑ Say, "Hey Control Panel!" really, really loud.

 Just about anywhere you see the Control Panel's icon (margin), you can click and get to the Control Panel. When you're there, you're free to dink.

Setting the best Control Panel view

You can choose how the Control Panel looks: the easy way or the best way.

The easy way, also known as the Category View, is shown in Figure 6-4. This way is all graphical and fun, but it takes far more steps to get things done there. On a laptop, time is battery power, so you'll probably want to switch to the Classic View.

Figure 6-5 shows the Control Panel's Classic View. In this mode, all the Control Panel's icons are visible at once, making each equally and quickly accessible.

To switch to the Classic View, click the Switch to Classic View link on the left side of the Control Panel window.

⮑ Note that some of the icons you see in your laptop's Control Panel contents will be different than what's shown in Figure 6-5.

⮑ Some laptop manufacturers include custom Control Panel icons, as do various hardware vendors. These icons are used to control hardware specific to your laptop, such as IBM's ThinkPad Configuration or the Iomega Active Disk icons shown in Figure 6-5.

⮑ Of all the icons in the Control Panel, only a handful play roles specific to a laptop computer. For information on icons not mentioned here, please refer to a good Windows reference.

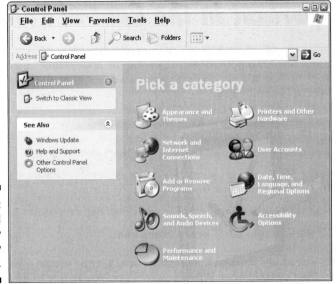

Figure 6-4:
The Control
Panel's silly
Category
View.

The optional Start menu approach

When finding the Control Panel takes too much time (and time is battery power on a laptop), you might consider another approach to accessing the Control Panel.

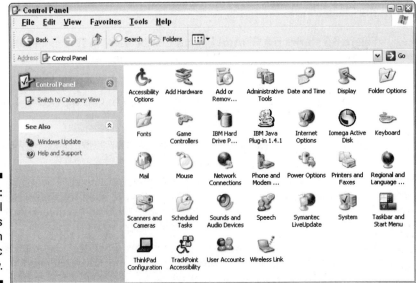

Figure 6-5:
The Control
Panel works
best in
Classic
View.

Figure 6-6 shows the options in the Control Panel as a fly-out menu on the Start menu. This is perhaps the best (certainly the fastest) way to access the individual Control Panel icons: Simply pop up the Start menu, and then use the mouse to choose Control Panel and then the individual icon for whatever your dinking needs.

The following steps configure the Control Panel as a fly-out menu on the Start menu:

1. **Right-click the Start button.**

2. **Choose Properties from the Start button's pop-up menu.**

    The Taskbar and Start Menu Properties dialog box appears.

3. **Click the Start Menu tab.**

4. **Click the Customize button by the Start Menu option.**

    You can only show the Control Panel as a menu when using the Windows XP Start menu, not the Classic Start menu.

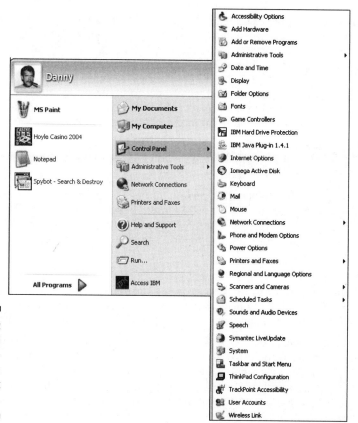

Figure 6-6:
The Control Panel's fly-out menu on the Start menu.

5. **In the Customize Start Menu dialog box, click the Advanced tab.**

6. **Locate the Control Panel item in the scrolling list of Start menu items.**

7. **Select the Display as Menu option beneath the Control Panel heading.**

8. **Click OK to close each dialog box.**

The Control Panel now lives as a sub-menu on the Start panel thing.

Prove that it worked by clicking on the Start button and finding the Control Panel item — it will now have a triangle indicating that it's a menu.

Display options

The Display icon is where you go to adjust your laptop's screen settings. You can set the individual colors, styles, and appearance of windows on the screen. You can set a screen saver. Or you can configure the screen's resolution and number of colors. These seem like items you might set only once, but of all the options in the Control Panel, this one is likely the most popular.

The Display Properties dialog box is shown in Figure 6-7. The ghost image of monitor number 2 is present because this particular laptop is equipped with an external video port for presentations. The Advanced button in Figure 6-7 is used to help determine which monitor the laptop uses.

✔ The quickest and handiest way to get to the Display Properties dialog box is to right-click on a blank part of the desktop and choose Properties from the pop-up menu.

✔ You need the Display Properties dialog box when you give a presentation with your laptop. It's where you configure the settings for the external monitor or video projection system.

✔ Your laptop's display has certain modes and resolutions that work best. For example, 800 x 600 or 1024 x 768. These and other resolutions are known as the *native* settings for the monitor. Although other resolutions might be possible, the results don't look good and could wreak havoc on the display.

✔ It may seem trivial, but by not setting a background image or wallpaper, Windows spends less time updating the screen. And time is battery life! To set a blank background image, click the Background tab in the Display Properties dialog box and choose "(None)" from the scrolling list.

✔ On the other hand, you can set the background image to anything you like, including pictures of the grandkids, your cat, or that exotic dancer at the Pink Pussycat who claims to adore you. To make this happen, click the Background tab and use the Browse button to locate the kids' picture on the hard drive. (It's most likely somewhere in the My Pictures folder.)

✔ You might also consider setting a lower resolution and number of colors for your monitor. The higher resolution/color settings require more video memory, which means more work for the computer, more power, and less battery life. If you can stand it, click the Settings tab in the Display Properties dialog box and choose a lower screen resolution for your laptop's display.

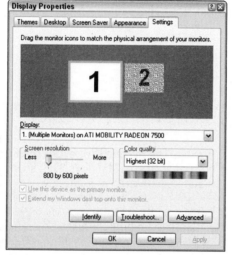

Figure 6-7:
The Settings tab of the Display Properties dialog box.

Network connections

The Network Connections icon is where you get access to your laptop's networking hardware. It's also where you may spend many mind-numbing hours configuring, correcting, and cursing the network settings.

For more information, refer to the section, "The Network Connections window," earlier in this chapter.

Power options

The Power Options icon is your main location for adjusting how your laptop uses the battery. The settings in the Power Options Properties dialog box enable you to control how the laptop goes to sleep and hibernates, control the power button's function, as well as control the settings for bossing the battery itself.

The Power Options Properties dialog box is shown in Figure 6-8. Note that some tabs are specific to the IBM ThinkPad laptop used to capture the image; the items without the black laptop icon are generic Windows tabs. You may find hardware-specific tabs in your Power Options Properties dialog box as well.

In addition to the Power Options icon, the Control Panel on your computer may have its own icon for your laptop's battery or power supply.

Chapter 8 has more information about your laptop's battery and power management issues.

System

The System icon is a central location for controlling your laptop's hardware and for minor troubleshooting.

Figure 6-9 shows the Hardware tab of the System Properties dialog box. One important button in that tab is labeled Device Manager. That's a prime hardware troubleshooting spot you may be directed to someday.

Clicking the Device Manager button displays the Device Manager window, which gives you access to the complete list of your laptop's hardware. A quick scan of the list determines whether or not everything is functioning properly; malfunctioning hardware is flagged with a yellow circle icon. Disabled hardware appears with an X by it.

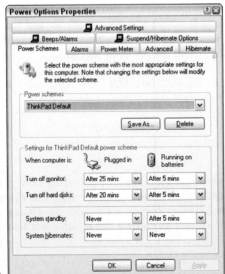

Figure 6-8:
The Power
Options
Properties
dialog box.

Figure 6-9:
The System
Properties
dialog box.

You can do other fun things in the System Properties dialog box, as covered throughout this book.

✔ You can also access the System Properties dialog box by right-clicking on the My Computer icon and choosing Properties from the context menu.

✔ You might consider disabling software you don't use to help save battery power. For example, on my laptop, I disabled the internal modem. Refer to Chapter 21 for details on this and on other tricks for saving battery life.

Phone and modem options

The Phone and Modem Options icon is used not only to set up the modem, but to configure phone dialing for when you're away from your home or office. This is a necessary thing to do on the road and is covered in Chapter 11.

Printers and faxes

Use this icon to help your laptop recognize a printer. Or when you're connected to a Windows network, you'll notice any shared printers automatically appear in the Printers and Faxes window.

Figure 6-10 shows a sample Printers and Faxes window. Three types of printers are shown in the figure: a fax, a network printer, and a local printer.

Fax printer   Network printer

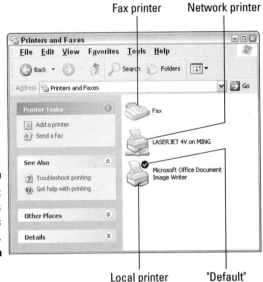

Figure 6-10:
The Printers
and Faxes
window.

Local printer   "Default"

Faxing works just like printing, except that the printer is a fax machine in another location. Also, the faxing is controlled by the laptop's internal modem, so you need to have an internal modem (and have it enabled) for faxing to work.

To add a printer to your laptop, click the Add a Printer link on the left side of the window. Then follow the instructions and steps in the wizard to add your printer. Also refer to your printer's documentation; note that some printers must be connected before their software is installed; for other printers, the software must be installed first.

Network printers are found and displayed automatically each time your laptop connects to a network. The network must have other Windows computers on it, and those computers must be sharing their printers for the printer to show up in the window. Note that network printers have "plumbing" beneath their icons.

 The dark circle with a check mark in it represents the *default* printer, or the printer that Windows uses whenever you haven't specifically chosen another printer. To set the default printer, right-click on a printer icon and choose Set as Default Printer from the context menu.

  ✔ The local printer shown in Figure 6-10, Microsoft Office Document Image Writer, is actually a *virtual* printer. I have no idea what that is.

✔ To share your laptop's printer with other computers on the network, right-click the printer's icon and choose Sharing from the context menu.

✔ If your fax machine doesn't appear in the Printers and Faxes window, click on the Set Up Faxing link on the left side of the window. After you run a setup wizard, click the Install a Local Fax Printer link.

✔ You can also use third-party faxing software, which often is better than the fax system presented by Windows.

✔ To send a fax, choose the fax from the list of printers in the Print dialog box. Then follow the instructions on the screen.

✔ Yeah, I dislike the word *default* as well. But it's common computer lingo meaning "the option chosen for you when you don't want to chose anything else."

Wireless link

 The Wireless Link icon is used to control your laptop's oddball infrared communications port (if your laptop has one).

You can use the infrared port to transfer files between two computers or to upload pictures from a digital camera to your computer. Note that both devices must have and support the same kind of infrared port — and use the same type of protocols — for this to happen.

✔ Also refer to Chapter 17 for some security issues regarding the infrared port.

✔ Okay, I may be a bit harsh with the term *oddball,* but this is my book. So there!

Laptop-specific icons

 Beyond the fun and exciting Control Panel icons I mention in previous sections, watch out for some icons specific to your laptop in the Control Panel. These may help you configure your laptop, set up special hardware, plus there might be better versions of the original icons that come with Windows. (For example, a better battery management tool.)

The function of those laptop-specific icons is too diverse for me to document here. My advice is just to open a few of the Control Panel icons and see what they do.

Goodies in the System Tray

The System Tray is that obnoxious little area to the far right of the taskbar. It's also known as the Notification Area, illustrated in Figure 6-11.

Figure 6-11:
The System
Tray lurks
on the right
end of the
taskbar.

People are of two minds about the System Tray. Some ignore it. The rest allow the System Tray to bug the living heck out of them. They obsess over it. But really, it's just a tiny place for storing programs that may, from time to time, need your attention.

 The icons in the System Tray also give you quick access to many common places in Windows. For example, if the twin networking buddies icon indicates that your network isn't working, you can double-click on the icon to get to a networking dialog box and address the issue.

 If any of the items in the System Tray annoy you, try right-clicking on them. Often this produces a context menu where you can choose an Exit or Quit command. If not, then try finding a Properties command, or access the window that controls the little icon. You'll usually find a turn-me-off item there.

✓ The day and date appear in the System Tray. This option is controlled from the Control Panel's Taskbar and Start Menu icon, Taskbar tab, the item titled Show the Clock.

✓ The speaker, or volume control, is made visible using the Control Panel's Sounds and Audio Devices icon, Volume tab, the item Place Volume Icon in the Taskbar.

✓ The networking buddies icon is controlled by the Control Panels Network Connection icon. Open that icon and then open the network connection icon in the Network Connections window. Inside the Network Connection Status dialog box, click the Properties button. In the next dialog box, you'll see an option titled, Show Icon in Notification Area When Connected.

How to disable those annoying balloon tips

One of the most irritating aspects of the Notification Area is that occasionally up pops a yellow balloon that says something just so dumb and obvious that it makes you want to stab your laptop screen with a knife. The notices are often useful — such as that you're properly connected to the wireless network, or your battery is getting low. But the annoying part is that they don't automatically go away. They linger. They annoy. They incite anger!

Disabling the balloon tips is possible, but it requires editing the Windows Registry, which is not a beginner's task. If you're up to it, heed these steps to eliminate the balloon tips for good:

1. **Choose Start⇨Run.**

   If Run isn't available on the Start button menu thing, press the Win+R key combination to summon the Run dialog box.

2. **Type** regedit **into the box.**

3. **Click the OK button.**

   The Registry Editor opens.

4. **Open the following folders, each contained inside the other:**

HKEY_CURRENT_USER
  Software
  Microsoft
  Windows
  CurrentVersion
  Explorer
  Advanced

5. **In the Advanced folder, right-click in the right side of the window.**

6. **Choose Edit⇨New⇨DWORD Value.**

   The new value is created and ready to be renamed.

7. **Type** EnableBalloonTips.

   This replaces the text "New Value #1" in the right side of the window.

8. **Double-click the EnableBalloonTips item you just created.**

9. **Ensure that zero is entered as the Value Data.**

10. **Click OK.**

11. **Close the Registry Editor window.**

12. **Restart Windows for the change to take effect.**

Where Your Programs Lurk

There is a place for everything, and for everything there is a place. My Documents is for your stuff. My Computer is for the computer's stuff. The Control Panel lets you control things. And for the software you install and use, there is the Program Files folder.

Yes, it should be called My Programs. But it's not. Apparently the folks in the Document and Programs departments in the Windows development group don't speak to each other.

The Program Files folder isn't any place you visit often. It's not high on the tourist list. It doesn't even have a flashy icon. You can go there if you like:

1. **Open the My Computer icon.**

2. **Open the hard drive C icon.**

   It might be labeled `Local Disk (C:)`, or it may have another first name. But the last name is always `(C:)`.

   At this point, you might see a screen telling you to go away and leave the contents of your computer alone. You can choose to ignore this warning.

3. **Open the Program Files folder.**

   You may get another warning here. That's kind of the idea: There is really nothing for you to do in the Program Files folder other than peek around.

4. **Close the Program Files window.**

   Bid adieu.

 Instead of manually adjusting your software directly in the Program Files folder, you use a special icon in the Control Panel. That's where you go to install or remove the software on your computer (mostly remove). Those topics are covered in the sections that follow.

Installing new software

The easiest way to install new software on your computer is to stick the software's CD into your laptop's CD-ROM or DVD drive, close the drive door, and then watch as the installation program runs. Follow the instructions on the screen, and then you're done.

✔ If the program doesn't automatically install after you insert the CD, then open the My Computer window. Double-click the CD drive's icon. Look for any SETUP or INSTALL program icon. Double-click that icon to open the installer program and set up the software.

✔ Some programs require that you restart Windows before installation is complete.

✔ The reason you occasionally have to quit all other running programs is that such programs may interfere with the installation process. Also, should the computer automatically restart when the installation is over, you could lose unsaved data in any running program.

What's the use of the Add or Remove Programs icon in the Control Panel? At this point, nothing. You could waste time with it and use it to help you install new software. But, honestly, sticking the CD into the drive will automatically install software for you. So why bother with the extra step?

Removing old software

The only time you really need to use the Add or Remove Programs icon is when you want to uninstall a program. Using the icon is the official and best way to uninstall software that you no longer need, want, or that you now detest.

Here is how you remove an unwanted program from your laptop's hard drive:

1. **Open the Control Panel Add or Remove Programs icon.**

   A list of installed programs appears, similar to the ones shown in Figure 6-12.

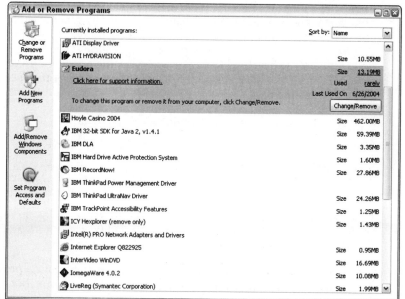

Figure 6-12: Hunting down a program to remove.

2. **Locate the program you want to remove in the list.**

3. **Click on the program.**

   You see some bonus information displayed, including the amount of space the program occupies (13.19MB in Figure 6-12) and how often the program has been used ("rarely" in Figure 6-12).

4. **Click the Change/Remove button to remove that program.**

   The *Change* part is weird, and I'm not comfortable with it. But apparently, some programs use this method to modify their installation. You can click the button, and nothing is uninstalled immediately, so it's hard to tell when a true change option is available.

At this point, what happens is that Windows turns control over to the uninstall program that came with whatever program you're trying to uninstall. You're prompted to go forward.

5. **Confirm that you want to remove the program.**

Or you may be presented with the illusive Change option. But if you elect to go forward, the program will be removed.

Removing a program erases its files from the laptop's hard drive. The uninstall program also resets certain options deep inside Windows, trying to change things back to how they were before the program was first installed.

Note that not every uninstall is successful. Sometimes pieces of the program, or its files, may remain behind.

Removing a program *does not* remove its associated data files. For example, removing a graphics program does not delete all the graphics images that you created with that program. After all, you created and own those files, and only you can remove them. Removing the files (should you want to) can be done in the My Documents folder, or wherever the application's data files are stored. Even so, my advice is not to delete them because other programs may be able to use the data.

- ✔ Remove programs that you don't use.

- ✔ Removing programs frees up space on your hard drive.

- ✔ Do not try to uninstall a program by just manually deleting a program's icon, folder, or related files. Always use the Add or Remove Programs icon to uninstall programs.

- ✔ Occasionally, you can find an Uninstall command on the All Programs menu (from the Start thing). Such a command sits in the same menu as the program itself. Very handy.

- ✔ When the Add or Remove Programs icon fails to remove a program, don't fret. You could manually try to delete the program, but odds are good you wouldn't fully remove everything or that you would damage other programs in the process. Today's hard drives are big and roomy, so just let the unwanted program be.

- ✔ If you're having trouble removing programs, I recommend Norton's Cleansweep utility. Not only can it free up hard drive space, but it often finds stubborn programs and removes them quite easily.

- ✔ The Add/Remove Windows Components item (on the left side of the Add or Remove Programs window) can be used to add or remove parts of Windows. You'll have to refer to a book on Windows XP for more specific information on that topic.

Software you want, software you don't want

Most laptops come with a host of software preinstalled. Don't feel compelled to use it. In fact, if you're annoyed by that software, simply refer to the previous section for the steps required to uninstall it.

You do not need to keep anything on your hard drive that you don't plan on using.

For example, if your laptop came with a wireless mapping tool and you don't ever plan on using it — or even don't know what the heck it is — freely delete it.

It's *your* laptop!

Logging On to Windows

The first time Windows slaps you in the face is when you need to log on. The following sections mull over your options for logging on, using a password, or just skipping the whole thing.

- *Log on* is the term used to identify yourself to the warden, er, to Windows. That way, multiple people can use the same computer and keep their stuff separate. It also helps the computer keep track of personal things, such as passwords, e-mail, and other junk.

- The term *log on* means to identify yourself. A *logon* is the name of your account or the word you use to log on.

- The terms *log in* and *login* can be used instead of *log on* and *logon*. They did that just to keep you confused.

- By the way, it's *log* as in *to write down*. It has nothing to do with timber.

The User Accounts icon

To modify the way you log on to Windows, you must first locate the User Accounts icon in the Control Panel. Opening that icon displays a list of the accounts for your laptop plus some tasks for modifying the way things are done, shown in Figure 6-13.

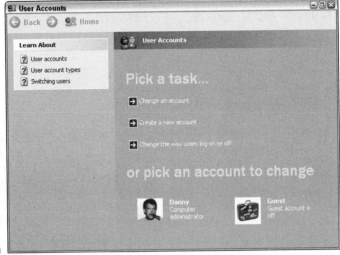

Changing your password

Computer security nabobs say you should change your password every few
months or so, more often in a high-security area. Whatever. If you're duty-
bound to change your password, go the User Accounts window (refer to
Figure 6-13) and click on your account's image. This opens a window similar
to the one shown in Figure 6-14.

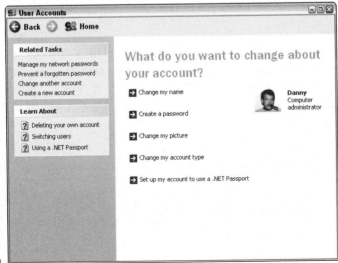

If your account lacks a password, click the Create a Password link.

To change a password, click the Change My Password link.

To get rid of your password, click the Remove My Password link.

No matter what you choose, follow the instructions on the screen for entering or deleting your password.

- ✔ The *strongest* passwords (that is, passwords that are the toughest to crack) use a combination of letters and numbers and are eight characters long or longer. Of course, such passwords are also easy to forget, so most people make the mistake of going with something short and simple.

- ✔ Never use the word *password* as your password. It's too easy to figure out.

- ✔ In situations where you're the only one using the laptop, and security around your home or office is not a concern, don't bother with a password.

- ✔ If you forget your password, then you're screwed. It's possible to recover Windows, but all your account information may be utterly lost and not retrievable. Keep that in mind when choosing a password.

Changing your image

To select a new picture for your account, click on the Change My Picture item (see Figure 6-14). This produces a window full of insipid stock photographs you can use for your account image. Or, if you're clever, you can click the Browse for More Pictures link and scour the hard drive for something more suitable.

Get a digital snapshot of yourself, your cat, your favorite car, or whatever and save that to your computer's hard drive. You can then select that image as your account's picture. You don't need to resize the image either; Windows does that for you.

Adding new accounts

To add another user to your laptop, click the Create a New Account link on the home User Accounts page (refer to Figure 6-13). Follow the instructions on the screen.

The *Administrator* level account is the best and allows the new user full access to all the laptop's features. Only create a *Limited* account if you don't really trust the person who will be using the account.

Don't be timid about creating a new account! If there are two or more people using the laptop, then each person should have his or her own account. This keeps your files separate and all your e-mail accounts, passwords, favorite Web sites, and so on all separate from each other.

Removing an account

To remove an account you no longer need, follow these steps:

1. **From the User Accounts home page, click the account you want to zap.**

   Refer to Figure 6-13.

2. **Click the Delete the account link.**

3. **Click the Delete Files button to clean up some disk space.**

   Click Keep Files only if you know how to dig in and retrieve any of that user's files that you want to keep.

4. **Click the Delete Account button.**

   And it's gone.

Disabling the Guest account

One account you might want to remove, or at least disable, is the Guest account. Honestly, it's a silly thing that was added to Windows. If you have guests, then honor them with the Guest account (if you really trust them). Otherwise, disable the Guest account:

From the User Accounts home, click the Guest Account icon. On the next screen, click the link that says Turn Off the Guest Account. That's it!

Logging on as administrator

For some reason, Windows users go bonkers when told that they need to "log in as the computer administrator." Honestly! You are already the computer administrator. There is no need to log in using a special account.

The secret Administrator's account

There is a secret Administrator account! You set it up when Windows was first installed and probably forgot about it. To access this account, you have to use a special logon screen where you manually type in usernames and passwords.

To set up the special logon screen, on the User Accounts home page, choose the link that says Change the Way Users Log On or Off. On the next screen, remove the check mark by Use the Welcome Screen. This reverts Windows back to a login prompt.

Next, choose Start⇨Log Off. Then click Log Off in the Log Off Windows dialog box.

When the login prompt appears, type **administrator**. For the password, use whatever was set when you first installed Windows. Yes, if you forgot this password, then you cannot use the administrator's account. Otherwise, you're into the system as an administrator and can make any modifications necessary.

You can confirm that your account has Administrator status from the User Accounts home page. If your account doesn't have Administrator status, then you'll have to ask someone who has Administrator access to update you.

To update a user to Administrator status, click the account on the home page. Then on the next page, click the Change the Account Type link. Follow the directions. La-di-da.

Do you really, really hate to log on?

If you're the only person using your laptop, and you dwell in an environment where it's unlikely that a bad guy, hooligan, or drooling three-year-old will pick the thing up with the intent to do damage, then you can live a login-free existence. Security experts would blanch at this, but it's possible.

First, remove the password from your account. Make it go away.

Second, ensure that yours is the only account on the computer. Disable the Guest account (if necessary).

That's it! The next time you start Windows, it should go right to the desktop and not display the login or Welcome-login screen.

Part II: I Have My Laptop, Now What? _____

Chapter 7

Expanding Your Laptop's Universe

In This Chapter

▶ Understanding the USB port

▶ Connecting a USB device

▶ Using a USB storage gizmo

▶ Working with PC Cards

▶ Adding an extra keyboard

▶ Connecting an external monitor

▶ Going beyond the laptop's mouse pad

▶ Printing from your laptop

▶ Printing when you don't have a printer

*L*aptops are all about portability. They help express the need for liberty, becoming unwired and untethered to the lines, anchors, and dependencies of the typical desktop computer system. Truly, freedom is walking around with a powerful computer system knowing that you can use it anytime, anywhere, especially in places where folks can look upon you with utter awe or seething red jealousy. That's really what it's all about.

Despite all that untethered, wireless malarkey, you gain a certain advantage by boosting your laptop system with a few of those wired, heavy, encumbering devices better known for their ease of use than their ability to let you prance carefree through O'Hare International Airport. This chapter is about expanding your laptop's power and potential by adding more devices. Sure, some of these gizmos are portable, but most are not. And each one is quite appealing in its own way. Regardless, welcome to the anti-portability chapter.

Beyond Your Lap

Your portable computer may lack the internal expansion options available to a desktop system, but externally, you can attach a whole slew of items to your laptop. Thanks to advancing technology, the list is nearly limitless. The only restrictions are how much you're willing to carry with you and, naturally, the size of your bank account.

(Then again, you don't have to carry all this stuff with you all the time.)

The miraculous expandability options of the USB port

The USB port is not the dock where boatloads of foreign students unload to attend the University of Santa Barbara. Nope, USB stands for Universal Serial Bus, and it's perhaps the best expansion option that lives on the outskirts of your laptop computer's case.

The idea behind the USB port was to replace many of the old standard ports on a computer with one, fast, versatile, and expandable system. The USB port has succeeded in meeting those needs, impressing everyone. The current USB 2.0 standard is perhaps the best type of expansion port available on any computer.

By using USB, you can add a variety of devices to your computer. I list the common ones in Table 7-1; many of those devices are covered in this chapter. In Table 7-2, I list many of the uncommon uses for a USB port — things that surprised even me! Check them out when you have time.

Table 7-1	Typical, Plain, Boring Uses for the USB Port
Device	*Typical Boring Usage*
External storage	Includes external hard drives, CD/R, DVD, and flash memory storage options, covered in the section, "Adding external USB storage," later in this chapter.
Printer	Lets you put things on paper. See the section, "Printing," later in this chapter.
Scanner	Sucks images from flat surfaces and reproduces them as graphics inside the computer. This topic isn't covered anywhere else in this book.
Network adapter	The USB port simply provides another way to add networking to your laptop, though note that a USB network device may be a bit more awkward than a PC Card network adapter, which better fits inside the laptop.
MP3 player	Lets you transfer your music files between the laptop and the player.

Device	Typical Boring Usage
Digital camera	Lets you grab photos from the camera's memory card and store them on the laptop. This can also be done directly by removing the camera's digital storage media, which is covered in the section, "Adding external USB storage," later in this chapter.

Table 7-2	More Unusual Ways to Use the USB Port
Device	**Unusual Thing It Does**
Legacy adapters	Allow you to connect ancient serial, parallel, joystick, and other devices to your laptop. This saves you from buying a port·replicator and allows you to continue to use legacy hardware with your newer laptop.
Mouse/Keyboard connector	Lets you connect an external mouse or keyboard (or both) to a laptop lacking a specific mouse or keyboard port. (And assuming that the mouse and keyboard don't have USB-specific connections.)
Sound hardware	Laptops lack the expansion options to add high-quality sound hardware, so the next best thing is to get external sound hardware provided by the USB port. For example, the Soundblaster Audigy can be added via the USB port to give your laptop full Dolby surround sound. (No word on how best to lug around the six speakers.)
Speakers	Going along with the USB sound expansion, you can get some mini-USB-powered speakers for your laptop. Everything you can't carry!
Video camera	For all your on-the-road video conferencing needs. (These may also be referred to as *Webcams,* though a Webcam is generally connected to the Internet full time.)
Little light	Imagine! A little light that plugs in and is powered by the USB port. Further, imagine it with a stiff-yet-twistable neck so that you can see the keyboard when you use your laptop in the dark.
Game controllers	Most of the hot new game controllers are USB-based.
Laptop coolers	These gizmos act like a fancy pad upon which to sit your laptop. They contain tiny, quiet fans that help keep your laptop cool, and they run from the power supplied by the USB port. (Also see Chapter 22.)

(continued)

Table 7-2 *(continued)*

Device	*Unusual Thing It Does*
Mobile phone recharger	This interesting USB gizmo lets you transfer some of the laptop's power to your mobile phone. Some may consider that robbing Peter to pay Paul, but I'm not really here to comment on the gizmos, just list 'em.
Security	Either the device uses the USB port to power an alarm on a cable lock, or a special security device that unlocks (or unscrambles) the laptop's data is plugged in to the USB port.
Bluetooth communications	If your laptop isn't equipped with Bluetooth wireless communications, then such a gizmo can be added via the USB port, allowing your computer system to chat with other Bluetooth-enabled devices.

Doing the USB thing

Your laptop may have one or two USB ports on its sides or rear. Refer to Chapter 5 for more information. Into those ports, you either plug a USB device directly, or you attach a USB device by using a cable.

For example, a memory card reader or flash memory disk drive may plug directly into your laptop, as shown in Figure 7-1.

Other devices use a USB cable to attach themselves to the laptop. For example, a USB printer or external hard drive connects to your laptop by using a USB cable.

Note that the same USB ports and the same cables are used for a variety of devices. As long as the devices are all USB standard, you can add them to any laptop with USB ports.

✔ If your laptop lacks USB ports, they can be added either by using a port replicator or (better) by using a PC Card with USB ports. See the section, "Using the PC Card," later in this chapter.

✔ USB cables come in a variety of lengths.

✔ Not every USB device needs a cable.

✔ Computer stores, as well as most office supply stores, keep a variety of USB cables in stock.

✔ USB cables cannot be longer than 12 feet. Any longer and the signal degrades. But note that for some devices, shorter cables are best.

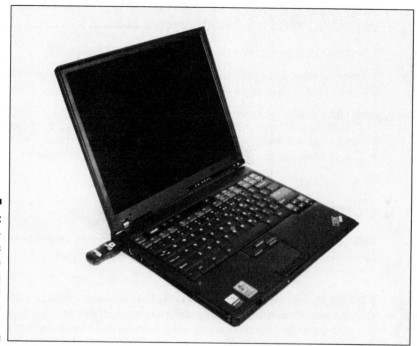

Figure 7-1:
A Jump-
Drive looks
more like
a diving
board when
attached to
this laptop.

✔ USB devices, even the cables, have the USB symbol on them.

✔ The current USB standard is version 2.0, often written as USB 2.0. This is a faster standard than the original USB, though it's still compatible with the older USB devices. USB 2.0 allows for high-speed devices such as external disk drives and CD/DVD players to be connected to a USB port. Ensure that your laptop has the USB 2.0 standard and that all USB devices support that standard. That way, you'll get the most from your equipment.

What are the A and B ends of a USB cable?

USB devices can use two types of connectors. They are known by the end of the cable that plugs in to the device. There is the A connector and the B connector.

 The A end is the rectangular end that plugs into the computer. It's often called the "upstream" end.

The B end of a cable has a D shape to it. This is the type of hole and cable connector fitted on USB devices. It's called the "downstream" end.

So, for example, to connect a USB printer, you plug the A end of the cable into your laptop and the B end into the printer. Ta-da!

✔ When you get a USB cable, you want a USB A-to-B cable.

✔ If you want a USB *extension* cable, then you want a USB A-to-A cable, or one that is labeled as an extension.

✔ There are other cable ends as well, though these are specific to the devices that they plug into. For example, your MP3 player may use a USB cable with an A connector on one end and perhaps a special connector on the other end that plugs only into the MP3 player.

Connecting USB gizmos

USB devices are a snap to connect — literally. You don't need to turn off the computer, run a special program, or wave a magic wand. Just plug in the USB device, and you're ready to roll.

✔ Keep your eye out for *pass-through* USB devices. These are USB thinga-mabobs that sport an extra USB port somewhere on their body. So you can plug the USB device into your laptop, and then another USB device into the first device. That way you don't run out of USB ports. (Also see the section, "Adding a hub.")

✔ Some devices are recognized the second that they're plugged in. A flash drive, for example, may be instantly *mounted* on your computer, its disk drive-like icon appearing in the My Computer window, ready for access. See the section, "Adding external USB storage," for more information.

✔ If the USB device has its own power switch, then you must switch the thing on before the computer will recognize it.

✔ It would be a Bad Thing to remove a USB storage device (disk drive or flash memory card) while your laptop is in Stand By (sleep mode), Hibernation mode, or turned off. Wait until the laptop is on again before removing the device. Otherwise, you could lose or scramble your files.

✔ Some devices, such as a scanner or printer, may involve extra setup. Be sure to read the manual that came with the device to determine whether you need to install special software before plugging in the device or turning it on.

✔ While you can just unplug a device, it's best to properly *unmount* it. Refer to the section, "Removing external storage," for more information.

✔ The ability to plug and unplug USB devices without having to turn the computer off or on is known as *hot swapping*. Sounds risqué, but it's not.

USB-powered devices

Quite a few USB doohickeys are self-powered. That is, they draw the electricity that they need from the laptop's USB port. The good news is that you don't need an extra cable, power supply, wall socket, or battery for that device. The bad news is that it sucks up even more of the laptop's precious juice even faster.

I tend to lean toward using USB-powered devices. They're more portable because you don't have to worry about taking along power cables or batteries. And anything that lightens the load is good.

✔ When looking for a USB peripheral for your laptop, get the USB-powered version.

✔ Most of the flash memory devices are USB-powered.

✔ Those cooling fan pads you can get for your laptop are also USB-powered.

✔ Not all USB ports provide proper power to run some USB-powered devices. Generally speaking, you must plug the USB-powered device into the laptop itself or into a powered hub for it to work.

Adding a hub

It may not seem practical, but your laptop can have up to 127 USB devices attached to it at any given time. Yes, all at once, too. That's one of the keys of the USB port's expandability. The way to add ports is by connecting a USB *hub* to the computer.

A USB hub is really nothing more than a gizmo with more USB ports on it. You plug the hub into your laptop's USB port. Then you can plug anywhere from two to four to eight USB devices into the hub.

✔ Some devices cannot be run from hubs, such as certain high-speed hard drives. In that case, the device must be plugged directly into the computer's USB port. Don't fret this: A warning message comes up and instructs you what to do when such a thing happens.

✔ There are two types of hubs, powered and unpowered. The powered hubs must be plugged in, but they also are necessary to supply more power to some USB devices.

✔ Obviously, a USB hub is probably not something you would want to pack in your laptop's case. The more cables the computer has, the less portable it becomes.

IEEE 1394 or FireWire gizmos

USB was one of two standards that emerged to replace the morass of expansion options and ports that plagued the PC for many years. The second standard is called IEEE 1394, or IEEE for short. Apple Computer refers to it as the *FireWire* standard, which is a cool but extremely scary-sounding name.

At one time, USB was considered the expansion option of choice for connecting items such as keyboards, mice, speakers, printers, and other low-speed devices. IEEE or FireWire was preferred for external storage or transferring video files because it was so much faster than USB. But that changed with the USB 2.0 standard, which is essentially as fast and as good as IEEE

(though not quite yet for digital video). That's why you won't find many IEEE ports on PC laptops.

Technically, IEEE works just like USB. There are cables, ports, hubs, and devices you can plug and unplug at your whim. Some devices — scanners and disk drives — may even support both USB and IEEE ports. (Though you can't use them both at the same time.)

If your laptop didn't come with an IEEE port and you need it, you can add one by using a PC Card. Especially if you plan on transferring movies from a digital video camera, IEEE is your best option.

- ✔ Note that there are smaller, more portable laptop-sized USB hubs available. Very quaint — and more portable than the desktop or full-sized USB hubs.

- ✔ One of the best ways to add more USB ports to your laptop is to get them on a PC Card.

- ✔ Each USB port on your laptop is considered a *root port*. The 127-device limitation is per root port, so if your laptop has two USB root ports, then it can access up to 254 USB devices.

Adding external USB storage

One of the most common thingies to add to a laptop is a USB storage device, such as a flash memory card reader or USB flash drive.

Both of these devices meld into your computer system just like any other disk drive. Or you can attach a real external hard drive or CD-ROM to your laptop's USB port, providing that those devices are USB-happy and properly powered. Here's how it works:

1. **Insert the USB mass storage device into your laptop's USB port.**

   And I am assuming that the computer is on and working at this point.

2. **You may hear an audible alert, a signal letting you know that Windows has found and detected the device.**

3. **Choose what you want to do with the device from the dialog box that appears.**

   Figure 7-2 illustrates this annoyance. Actually, it can be an advantage. If you just inserted a digital media card from your camera, you can choose one of the three options at the bottom of the list in Figure 7-2.

Figure 7-2: Annoying options after inserting a removable USB mass storage thing.

   I typically just click the Cancel button at the bottom of the window.

   You can disable the dialog box shown in Figure 7-2 if you like. Refer to the sidebar, "Getting rid of the annoying dialog box."

4. **Open the My Computer window.**

   Refer to Chapter 6 for how to get to this location. When you're there, you see the removable device *mounted* in the list of Devices with Removable Storage (if you have the window set up that way, as shown in Figure 7-3); otherwise, it just appears in the list with your laptop's other disk drives.

5. **Open the removable drive's icon to access the drive.**

   And there are its contents!

The USB storage device and its data can now be used like any other drive in your computer system.

You can leave the USB drive attached to your computer as long as you like. Refer to the next section for proper instructions on removing — or *unmounting* — the drive.

   ✔ *Mass storage* means some gadget that can store information just like a hard drive, CD, DVD, or silicon disk (flash memory, memory card, and that ilk).

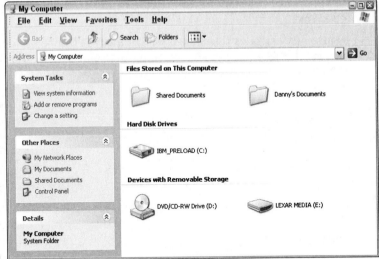

Figure 7-3:
The remov-
able drive
(Lexar
Media),
ready for file
and folder
action!

✔ A flash memory card reader can be used to read a Secure Digital or Compact Flash memory card. These are used in digital cameras to store images. So to transfer the images from your camera to the laptop, you just remove the memory card from the camera and insert it into the laptop's card reader.

✔ Your digital camera most likely stores its images on the memory card in the camera's folder inside the DCIM folder. That's odd, but it's how most digital cameras do things.

Getting rid of the annoying dialog box

If you don't like a dialog box appearing each time you insert a removable mass storage device (refer to Figure 7-2), you can direct Windows *not* to display it. Here are the secret instructions:

1. **Right-click on the removable drive's icon in the My Computer window (refer to Figure 7-3).**

2. **Choose Properties from the pop-up menu.**

3. **In the drive's Properties dialog box, click the AutoPlay tab.**

4. **Click the Select an Action to Perform option.**

5. **From the list of actions, choose "Take no action."**

6. **Click OK.**

These steps may not work for all removable devices, which is just plain annoying, but it's a fact.

Removing external storage

Yeah, you can just yank the USB drive out of the USB port. Unplug the thing! It works. But it's just not proper. Plus by doing so, you run the risk of losing some important data and seeing the fabled *Blue Screen of Death!* Better not risk it.

Just as there is a proper way to shut down your laptop, there is a proper way to remove any external storage you have plugged in. Here it is:

1. **Locate the Safely Remove Hardware icon in the System Tray.**

   The icon is pictured in the margin. It's not the easiest thing to see.

   If you cannot find the Safely Remove Hardware icon, then click on the Show More chevron just to the left of the System Tray.

2. **Click the Safely Remove Hardware icon.**

   A pop-up menu appears (after a brief pause), listing the removable storage devices attached to your computer, as shown in Figure 7-4.

Figure 7-4:
A list of removable devices attached to the laptop.

> Safely remove USB Mass Storage Device - Drive(E:)
> Safely remove TOSHIBA DVD-ROM SD-R9012 - Drive(D:)

3. **Click the device you want to remove.**

   For example, I clicked the item Safely Remove USB Mass Storage Device — Drive(E:), shown in Figure 7-4.

   If all goes well, you see an announcement that the device can be safely removed.

4. **Unplug or remove the device.**

The whole idea here is that you don't want to yank a storage device from your laptop before your software is done using it. Despite the fact that USB hardware can be hot swapped, unplugging something in use means that you may lose files. A bad thing.

✔ If you see a warning that the device cannot be removed, or "stopped," click the OK button. Locate whichever programs have open data files on the drive, save those files, and then close the programs. That should allow the drive to be removed.

✔ If you double-click the Safely Remove Hardware icon, the Safely Remove Hardware dialog box appears. It's basically a more detailed way to do the same thing described in the steps above.

✔ Refer to Chapter 6 for more information about the System Tray.

Using a PC Card

I must admit that the PC Card is rapidly becoming a thing of the past. Though it dominated laptop expansion for over ten years now, allowing users to add everything from mini-hard drives to network adapters to extra ports, the USB options are just far more numerous and flexible. In fact, if you go into a computer store today, you'll probably find only networking options available on the PC Card, which is kind of sad.

So while it may be on its last legs, the PC Card, or PCMCIA adapter, is still a part of the laptop landscape, and I give it due coverage in the sections that follow.

Inserting a PC Card

This is cinchy: Just stick the PC Card into the slot. It slides in only one way; the narrow edge with the holes goes in first. If the computer is on, then Windows recognizes the card instantly, as shown in Figure 7-5. At that point, you can start using the card, or whatever features with which it's just blessed your laptop.

Figure 7-5:
You just can't hide the instal- lation of new hardware from Windows.

Found New Hardware
VIA OHCI Compliant IEEE 1394 Host Controller

✔ Some cards may require extra software to make them go. It will state so in the card's manual. Other cards, like many USB devices, can just be plugged in, and they're off and running.

✔ The most common type of PC Card available today is a wireless networking card. Installing the card is only half the battle. The rest is properly configuring your laptop to connect to a wireless network. Refer to Chapter 9 for the gory details.

✔ The device installed in Figure 7-5 is an IEEE 1394 (or FireWire) port expansion card.

Using the PC Card

After the PC Card is inserted and properly set up, you can use its features. In fact, you can keep the card inside your PC for as long as you need those features.

Note that some cards hang out of the PC Card slot a bit. Some may have pop-out connectors. Be careful of those! They can get caught on things, so you might consider removing such the PC Card before you pack up and tote the laptop away.

✔ If you're adding USB or IEEE 1394 expansion with a PC Card, then you can start using those ports right away. Refer to the sections on using USB devices earlier in this chapter for more information.

✔ Adding a network device allows you to use that device — providing that networking options have been properly configured (as covered in Chapter 9). But after you've set up networking, you can remove and reinsert the networking PC Card as often as you like.

✔ Removable storage devices can be used after they've been inserted and recognized by Windows. But be sure to properly remove the device, as covered in the following section.

Removing the PC Card

Though all PC Cards can easily be pinched and yanked out of their cozy sockets, that's not the best way to treat your PC's hardware. Instead, follow these steps:

1. **Click the Safely Remove Hardware icon in the System Tray.**

   Refer to the section, "Removing external storage," earlier in this chapter for the details.

2. **Choose the device you want to remove.**

   A message appears telling you that the device can be safely removed.

3. **Pull the PC Card out from its slot.**

   Some cards need a bit of help here. You'll have to find a small button to the right of the card. Pushing the button in a ways makes it pop out about a half inch or so. Then press the button back into the laptop to help push out the PC Card.

Store the PC Card in a proper place, such as in your laptop bag or in a drawer or cubby with the rest of your laptop gear. The idea here is to keep the PC Card from being stepped on or crushed by a Big Gulp cup.

Adding Some Big Boy Toys

If you plan to land your laptop in one place all the time, then you'll probably want to upgrade its teensy portable features with some more robust desktop counterparts. Specifically, I speak of the keyboard, monitor, and mouse. Any of these desktop-sized items can be added to and used with a laptop instead of their feeble laptop counterparts. Use one. Use them all. It's up to you.

- ✔ Yeah, if you're really picky, you can even take a spare keyboard and mouse with you when you travel.
- ✔ Note that keyboards and mice do not need separate power supplies to work, but monitors do!
- ✔ If you really want a larger monitor with your laptop, and you want to take it with you, then consider upgrading to one of the many large-format or widescreen laptops with those sexy, humongous screens. They might not be as portable as smaller laptops, but *yowza!*

Using an external keyboard

If you miss the full size and action of a real PC keyboard, then get one! Just plug it into your laptop, either into the keyboard port or a USB port, whichever is available. You can start using the keyboard the second that it's plugged in.

Note that adding an external keyboard often does not disable the laptop's internal keyboard. You can use both! But you're probably not crazy enough to do that.

When you're done using the full-sized keyboard, simply unplug it.

✔ If all you're yearning for is to have a separate numeric keypad, then considering getting only that. You can pick up a USB numeric keypad, which is just the keypad and not the entire keyboard, at most computer stores and office supply stores.

✔ Sometimes, the only way you can add a non-USB keyboard to your laptop is by getting a port replicator or docking station.

✔ The standard color for a PC's keyboard connector — the hole somewhere on your laptop for plugging in the keyboard — is purple.

Connecting a second monitor or video projector

Most modern laptops are automatically equipped to handle two monitors, the laptop's own LCD and an external monitor. This is because many laptops are often used for storing and showing presentations, and it just makes sense to have the laptop all ready to go in that respect.

To add the external monitor, locate the monitor connector on your PC's rump. Plug in the monitor, and you're ready to go. You can use that monitor in conjunction with your laptop's LCD or as your laptop's only display.

✔ On some laptops, the same image appears on both the LCD and the external monitor.

✔ If you want to use the external monitor exclusively, then just close your laptop's lid. Most laptops are smart enough to see the external monitor and let you start using it, keeping the laptop's power on while the lid is closed. When you open the laptop's lid, control returns back to the laptop's LCD.

✔ Note that if you close the lid, it helps to have an external mouse or keyboard connected to the laptop so that you can still use your software.

✔ The monitor connector can also be an S-video connector. This allows you to connect your laptop not only to an external monitor, but also to many TV sets, VCRs, and DVD players. Refer to Chapter 5, Table 5-1 for more information.

Using two monitors at once

If you want to use two monitors at once, you need to direct Windows to do so. After connecting the second monitor, follow these steps:

1. **Open the Display Properties dialog box.**

   Refer to Chapter 6 for more details.

2. **Click the Settings tab.**

   You see both monitors displayed in the top of the dialog box.

3. **Click the second monitor.**

4. **Choose the Extend My Windows Desktop onto This Monitor option.**

5. **Click the Apply button.**

6. **Adjust the monitors' positions in the area near the top of the dialog box.**

   You can drag the number 1 or number 2 monitor around to help align the two desktops. Use the mouse to grab and drag each monitor into a proper position relative to each other.

7. **Click the OK button when you're done.**

Note that the laptop's LCD is always the first display. It will be the only display that contains the taskbar and Start button. And though you can drag windows and icons to the second display, they'll all hop back to the first display the next time you restart Windows.

Gotta getta mouse

A computer mouse is perhaps the best companion you can buy for your laptop. Not that flat, odd, mouse pad thing! I'm talking about a real computer mouse. Just grab your favorite desktop mouse and plug it into your laptop. It makes for a much more enjoyable laptop experience — even if you often have to use your thigh to roll the mouse around.

Mice makers are aware of laptop owners' fondness for "real" computer mice. So they have a whole line of options available to you. You don't have to get a full-sized desktop computer mouse. No, you can opt for one of those new mini-mice for laptops. They work just like desktop mice, but they're about half the size. Some are even wireless. And they're all better than using that silly touch pad.

Adding an external mouse may or may not disable your laptop's touch pad. If you do want the touch pad disabled, then use the Mouse icon in the Control Panel to disable it (providing that it's a hardware option for your laptop).

Printing

When Adam Osborne originally proposed the portable computer, portable printing was not part of the big picture. Instead, printing is something that can be done later. You can transfer your on-the-road files to your desktop system, or wait until your laptop is docked, before printing. But portable printing?

True, there are portable printers. I've used the Cannon Bubble Jet portable printer with my laptop. It's not that heavy, has full color, is fairly fast, and it runs off flashlight batteries. So there are on-the-road printing options if you want them.

Whether you're printing on the road or at home, the following sections describe how to set up and use a printer — or even a printer alternative — with your laptop computer.

Setting up the printer

Though the laptop comes with a connector mysteriously called the *printer port,* you probably want to use a USB printer with your laptop. Only if you already have a printer and it's a traditional (non-USB) model should you consider connecting it. USB is the wave of the future, man!

To connect the printer, follow these steps:

1. **Plug in the printer, but ensure that it's turned off.**

   Also, set up the printer with ink and paper and all that other good stuff according to the directions that came with the printer.

2. **Connect a USB cable to the printer and to your laptop.**

   Or if you just cannot stand my advice, plug a standard printer cable into the printer's rump or into your laptop's very expensive port replicator or docking station.

3. Turn on the printer.

Windows should instantly recognize the printer, as shown in Figure 7-6. Then, because you're using a USB printer, it will know the printer's name and brand and it will even completely install software for you, setting everything up just so.

When you're using the older printer-port type of printer, you'll probably have to use some kind of software installation disk that will just drive you nuts. Good luck!

Figure 7-6: Amazingly, Windows recognizes a USB printer. Wow.

After the printer has been set up and recognized by Windows, you can either print or you can save some energy and turn the printer off. You can even disconnect it when you don't need it. Reconnecting the printer simply reactivates its support in Windows.

- ✔ The printer port might not be available on your laptop. You may need a port replicator or docking station to access the old-fashioned, silly printer port.

- ✔ Leave your printer turned off when you're not using it.

- ✔ You can unplug the printer's USB cable without having to use the Safely Remove Hardware icon in the System Tray. Just unplug the cable and Windows bids adieu to your printer.

- ✔ Yes, it's not a good idea to unplug or turn off your printer while it's printing.

- ✔ If you're having trouble adding your printer, open the Control Panel and double-click the Printers and Faxes icon to display the Printers and Faxes window. Click the Add Printer task in that window to run the Add Printer Wizard, which should help you complete the printer setup task.

- ✔ Printers work by using a *driver,* which is a software program that controls the printer. Windows knows about many printers and comes with their driver software. For other printers, you need to find a CD with the driver software that came with the printer, or you have to visit the printer manufacturer's Web site to download the latest driver.

Printing in Windows

To print a document, e-mail, or anything in Windows, you use the File⇨Print command. This displays the Print dialog box, which can also be summoned by using the Ctrl+P keyboard shortcut. A sample of this dialog box is shown in Figure 7-7.

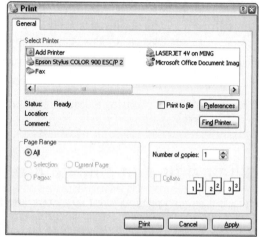

Figure 7-7:
A sample
of the Print
dialog box.

Here are the quick steps you can take to work through this dialog box:

1. Choose your printer from the list of printers.

This is also where you select the Microsoft Fax, or your computer's fax software, to send a fax.

Note that some printers visible in the window are network printers, available only when your computer is plugged into the network. Printing to them is fine; the document waits until you reconnect to the network before it prints.

2. Select the range of pages to print.

3. Select the number of copies.

4. Click the Properties or Preferences button to set individual printer settings.

For example, if you want to print in black ink only on a color printer, you would set that option by clicking the Properties or Preferences button, and then setting the printer's color in the dialog box that appears.

5. Click the Print button to print your document.

What about printing to disk?

Once upon a time, you could save printer information to disk like a file. Then you printed that file by sending it directly to the printer, either via a DOS command or by dragging that file onto your printer's icon. This worked well in earlier versions of Windows but does not work at all in Windows XP — despite the Print to Disk option still being available in the Print dialog box.

A great alternative for the old Print to Disk option is to create an Adobe Acrobat, or PDF, document instead. For this, you need to buy the Adobe Acrobat Writer software or an equivalent. The Acrobat Writer software appears in your laptop's list of printers. Select it for printing, and the result is a PDF document that's readable on just about any computer.

Also refer to Chapter 6 for information on setting a default printer, as well as where to find the Printers and Faxes window.

Options for when you don't have a printer

Only the truly clever can print when a printer is not available. And for the rest of us, I offer these suggestions:

- Most hotels have business centers where you can temporarily connect to a printer and get your stuff on paper.

- Some office supply stores offer printing services. Print shops and places such as Kinko's also have printers available for rent by the hour or by the sheet.

- Fax machines are printers. If you know of a fax machine nearby, just send your document as a fax. Note that plain paper faxes are preferred for this; avoid wax-paper faxes if possible. And note that faxes do not print in color.

As a last, desperate move, you might just try printing to the printer you use at home or the office, even though it's not connected. While this won't get you a copy right away, the item to be printed sits and waits on your computer until you're once again connected to the printer. At that time, it will *spool* out of storage and print as you intended.

Chapter 8

Power Management Madness

In This Chapter

▶ Knowing various types of batteries

▶ Locating your laptop's battery

▶ Monitoring battery usage

▶ Charging the battery

▶ Using a spare battery

▶ Conditioning the battery

▶ Disposing of dead laptop batteries

▶ Managing power usage in Windows XP

*T*he first efforts made by the engineering team to make things portable were done primarily to satisfy management and its quest for low-cost/high-return solutions. Stuffing a desktop computer's components into a single case and bolting a handle on top definitely makes that computer portable and satisfies management's desire for cheap solutions. Yet at some point, the engineers had to wonder whether they could do better.

Indeed, to make something truly portable, it must also be free of the power cord. The inspiration here just had to be the portable radio. It came with a handle but no power cord. Instead, the power was supplied via common flashlight batteries. Batteries. *Yes!* That must be the solution. For a computer to be truly portable, it must get its power from batteries instead of a wall socket. (And it still must have a handsome leatherette carrying handle.)

This chapter is specifically about the battery inside your laptop computer. The general topic, of course, is *power management.* That's the goal of using any battery; use it as you need it, but always with a mind to stretch that power as far as you can.

The Battery Will Get a Charge Out of This!

The thing that makes your laptop go on the road, or I should say the thing that *powers* your laptop on the road, is a battery. If your laptop "goes" on the road, be sure to clean up after it.

Having a battery in your laptop is not news. Even so, you may have some questions about the battery, and you probably want to know how best to use it and get better performance from it. Yes, indeed, you probably have a *battery* of questions! Ha! So before this paragraph degenerates further, the following sections touch upon battery issues, important and trivial.

Types of batteries

A battery by any other name would still sting like heck when your big brother fooled you into putting it into your mouth.

Just as a good gardener knows that there is more than one type of rose, so is there more than one type of battery. They all provide electricity. But yet between each battery type, there are plusses and minuses.

Alkaline. This is the most common type of battery, normally used in flashlights, portable radios, remote controls, smoke alarms, and kids' toys. The advantage here is that you can find these standard-sized batteries anywhere. A few portable computing devices (printers, handhelds) use them. But few laptops do. The reason is that they're not rechargeable. You use them, you throw them out (properly, according to the environmentally safe battery disposal rules of your jurisdiction).

Lead acid. The most common place to find the scary-sounding lead-acid battery is in your automobile. These batteries are durable, long-lasting, rechargeable, but they're also heavy and, well, *they're full of lead-acid!* Yikes!

More commonly, in a laptop computer, you'll find one of the following types of batteries:

Lithium-Ion. This is the type of battery you want to have in your laptop. It's lightweight and better performing than the other types of batteries. Unlike NiCads or NiMH batteries, Lithium-Ion batteries don't have The Dreaded Memory Effect. There is usually a rapid charging option with Lithium-Ion batteries, which is good when you're in a crunch. Finally, this type of battery is more environmentally friendly than the other types. And it has a cool-sounding name.

Fuel cells

Laptops of the future, as well as other portable devices, won't be using batteries any more. Instead, they'll be equipped with something called a *fuel cell.*

Fuel cells use a magical combination of chemistry and physics to provide power for a much longer period of time than a typical battery. When the fuel cell gets low, you simply add more fuel to it — similar to filling a gas tank. Then the fuel cell is ready to go, powering your portable electronics until it needs refilling again.

Certain types of fuel cells are available today, but they're still too large and bulky to be used with a laptop computer. The present time schedule states that by the year 2010, fuel cells will be small, light, and compact enough for use in laptop computers. When that time comes, power management on your laptop will become a different creature, and battery-saving tips and techniques will become a thing of the past.

Nickel Cadmium (NiCad). Of all the rechargeable types of consumer electronics batteries, the NiCad is the oldest. It's frowned upon now, mostly because this type of battery suffered terribly from The Dreaded Memory Effect. Even so, NiCads offer great performance and until the better battery technologies came along, they dominated the portable power storage market.

Nickel-Metal Hydride (NiMH). This type of battery was one of the first successful alternatives to NiCads. A NiMH battery is longer lasting than a NiCad, but sadly it suffers from The Dreaded Memory Effect just as badly as the NiCad.

✔ Of all these batteries, odds are very good that your laptop has a Lithium-Ion type. That's pretty much state of the art.

✔ Lithium-Ion is often abbreviated as LION. Because that's also the word for a big, ferocious kitty cat, I use "Lithium-Ion" in this book.

✔ You can confirm which type of battery your laptop has by looking at its label. Refer to the next section.

✔ If you haven't yet purchased a laptop, ensure that you get one that has a Lithium-Ion battery.

✔ A few laptops out there are still using NiMH batteries. This is fine, of course. But you might want to check to see if there is a battery upgrade option to the Lithium-Ion type.

✔ Your laptop might actually have a secondary, alkaline battery inside. It's used to power the laptop's internal clock, which keeps track of the time even when the laptop is unplugged or the battery has drained.

✔ There might even be a second (or third) battery in the laptop that keeps things powered for the minute or so that it takes you to swap a spent main battery out with a fresh one. See the section, "The spare battery," later in this chapter.

✔ Refer to the sidebar, "The Dreaded Memory Effect," for information on, well, The Dreaded Memory Effect.

✔ Using unapproved batteries in your laptop may lead to bad things, such as, oh, the laptop exploding.

✔ Another thing to look for is a *smart* battery. This type of battery contains circuitry that communicates with the laptop, letting it know the battery's condition so that you get better power control. Such batteries last longer due to better power management.

Finding your laptop's battery

Take a moment to locate your laptop's battery. Odds are good that it loads in on the bottom of the laptop, though many laptops have their batteries inserted through a hole or door in the side.

The battery may be labeled, describing what type of battery it is (see the previous section), as well as other information about the charge it holds, serial number, replacement information, and so on. Note that often this information may be printed on the laptop case instead of or in addition to being on the battery.

✔ Be aware of where your battery is stored in your laptop. You may need to remove or replace it in the future.

✔ Most laptops use a few sliding locks or clips to help keep the battery in place. Do not force a battery into or out of your laptop.

✔ Batteries get warm as they're being used. That's simply their nature. However:

✔ Watch out if the battery gets too hot! For example, the battery is too hot to touch or hold for more than a few seconds. That could be a sign of a malfunctioning battery, and such a thing *is* dangerous. Phone your dealer or laptop manufacturer immediately if you suspect that the battery is running hot.

Monitoring the battery

The laptop's battery drains as you use it, which is to be expected. In modern laptops, you should plan for at least two or three hours of active computer use under battery power. The rate of drain does vary, however, depending on what you're doing with the laptop. And, naturally, depending on what you're doing, that time may pass by rather quickly.

In Windows XP, you can monitor the battery by viewing the tiny battery icon in the Notification Area (or System Tray). The icon graphically shows how much power is left; the icon's color "drains" out as you use the laptop. But often that display is too tiny, so what you can do is point the mouse at the icon to see a pop-up bubble explain how much juice you have left, as shown in Figure 8-1.

Figure 8-1:
A good hour
is left on the
battery.

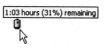

In Figure 8-1, Windows shows that one hour, three minutes are left for battery life, and the battery has about 31 percent of its power remaining.

You can also monitor the battery usage from the Control Panel's Power Options icon. The Power Meter tab offers up lots of juicy information on the battery's status, as shown in Figure 8-2.

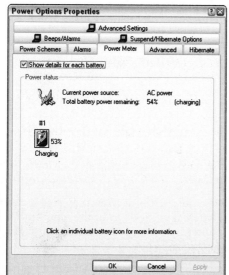

Figure 8-2:
The battery
is charging.
Fill 'er up!

The Dreaded Memory Effect

In the old days of the NiCad and even NiMH batteries, the mantra went that you had to fully discharge the battery, all the way down to zero, before you even considered recharging the thing. This was true and necessary: If you didn't fully drain the battery, then it began to lose its potency over time.

What happened, especially with NiCad batteries, was that the battery would "remember" how long it was used. So if the battery held one hour of power when fully charged, but you recharged it after only 30 minutes of use, then the former one-hour battery would become a 30-minute battery. That's The Dreaded Memory Effect.

To avoid The Dreaded Memory Effect and to prolong the life of their batteries, NiCad users would insist on fully draining the batteries each and every time they were used. Laptop owners would have to wait until their machines completely shut down before recharging. (Remember, NiCads are not "smart" batteries either.) Even so, some users would give up, and eventually their rechargeable NiCads would be down to only ten minutes of power — not enough.

Today's Lithium-Ion batteries do not have The Dreaded Memory Effect at all. You can use them for a minute, then recharge, and the battery will still be as good as it was when you bought it. So boldly use your battery without fear. And next time someone mentions The Dreaded Memory Effect, giggle with a smug laugh of confidence, secure in the knowledge that you're safe from the power problems of the past.

Your laptop manufacturer may have also included other battery tools, such as a battery monitor window, a special keyboard shortcut to display battery status, specific battery icons in the Control Panel, and so on. Be sure to review what you have, as often these tools can be better or more useful than what Windows XP offers.

- ✔ The battery icon may not appear in the Notification Area when your laptop is being AC powered.

- ✔ To ensure that the icon shows up, even when the laptop is plugged in, open the Control Panel's Power Options icon, click on the Advanced tab, and put a check mark by the Always Show Icon on the Taskbar option. Click OK.

- ✔ On some laptops, a different icon may appear in the Notification Area when the laptop is AC powered.

- ✔ The battery icon on your laptop's row-o-lights may also indicate how much charge is left by changing color or even the amount of light showing through. Refer to Chapter 5 for more information on finding the battery light or icon on your laptop.

- ✔ *AC powered* means being powered by electricity from a wall socket.

- ✔ *DC powered* means being powered by the battery.

✔ Smart battery technology is responsible for the ability of Windows to
determine how much power is left in the battery. But still be aware that
such a thing is an *estimate*. Different things can affect battery life. So
don't bet real money on how much longer your laptop can survive off
the battery.

✔ Refer to Chapter 6 for more information about the Control Panel in
Windows.

What happens when the power gets low

You know that terrible feeling you get immediately after a power outage?
You know, everything in the room goes dark or turns off. It's startling! Well,
the idea behind using your laptop is to avoid that feeling when the battery's
power starts to go.

Thanks to smart battery technology, your laptop computer gives you a good
deal of warning before the battery poops out. It's enough time to finish what
you're working on, save, close programs, and shut down the computer
properly.

Figure 8-3 shows the low battery bubble warning that Windows pops up.
That's the initial warning. A second warning appears just before the battery
dies. It should say, "I told you so," but actually, it just warns that a power-off
situation is imminent. At that point, the laptop ignores you and either shuts
down or goes into hibernation.

Figure 8-3:
Oops!
Quitting
time!

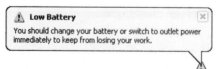

What the laptop does when the battery dies, or when the two warnings (
initial and imminent) appear, is set in the Power Options dialog box, Alarms
tab, shown in Figure 8-4.

The first warning is known as the Low Battery Alarm. You activate it by
putting a check mark by the Activate Low Battery Alarm When Power Level
Reaches option, as shown in Figure 8-4. Use the mouse to adjust the slider,
setting the percentage of battery life left when the Low Battery Alarm kicks
in. You can further use the Alarm Action button to tell Windows what to do:
to pop-up a warning, beep, or shutdown. (More on that in a moment.)

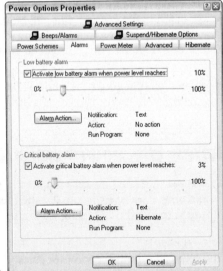

Figure 8-4:
Setting the
power-low/
power-gone
warnings
and alarms.

The second warning (refer to Figure 8-4) is the Critical Battery Alarm. I highly recommend activating this option and setting the slider to something low, such as the 3 percent shown in Figure 8-4. Click the Alarm Action button to see which options to take when the power does get low.

In Figure 8-5, you see the options available for when the power gets critically low. These things take place automatically, controlled by Windows. The computer can sound an alarm or display a message. But more importantly, you can direct the computer to hibernate, stand by, or shut down completely, as shown in the Alarm Action area of the dialog box.

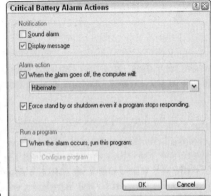

Figure 8-5:
Options for
when the
battery gets
critically
low.

Also notice the Run a Program area. If necessary, you can configure a certain program to run when the power gets low, such as a utility to immediately back up your work files to a flash memory card, send remaining e-mail, or a number of other options.

After the critical warning appears, the laptop does as its directed, shutting down or suspending or hibernating. It remains in this state until you either replace or recharge the battery, or you plug the laptop back into the wall for power.

✔ That critical battery notice is *serious*. Computer time is over! If you ignore the warning, your laptop will stop working. And so will you.

✔ When the low battery notice sounds or appears, and you are blessed with a second battery for your laptop, pop it in and keep working! Refer to the section, "The spare battery," later in this chapter.

✔ The best thing to do when power gets low: Plug in! This is why I always take my power cable with my laptop wherever I go.

Charging the battery

This is easy to do: Charging a laptop battery is done by simply plugging the laptop into a wall socket. Immediately, the laptop switches from battery (DC) power to AC power, and the power management hardware inside the laptop begins to recharge the battery.

You can recharge your laptop's battery whether the battery is fully drained or not. Especially if your laptop is using a Lithium-Ion battery, this makes no difference. Refer to the sidebar, "The Dreaded Memory Effect," for more information.

Note that Lithium-Ion batteries do have a rapid-charging option. This option is either available in a custom tab inside the Power Options dialog box, or it may be available through special battery software that came with your laptop. In a pinch, a rapid charge can save time. But normally, you want a nice, full, slow charge for your laptop's battery.

✔ I generally leave my laptop plugged into the wall whenever I can.

✔ There is no need to fully drain your laptop's Lithium-Ion battery every time you use it.

✔ It does benefit NiCad and NiMH batteries to be fully drained before they're recharged. That type of battery lasts longer and retains most of its potency if you fully drain it.

- ✔ Your laptop may come with — or there may be available — an external charging unit. You can use that to charge extra laptop batteries, should you have them.

- ✔ The battery continues to charge, even when the laptop is turned off.

- ✔ It's been said that if you're using a laptop while you're charging the battery, it will take longer to recharge the batteries than when the laptop is turned off. This might have been true once, but it is no longer true today; feel free to use your laptop while the battery is charging.

- ✔ Never short a battery to fully drain it. By *short,* I mean connecting the two terminals (positive and negative) directly so that the battery simply drains. This is very bad and can cause a fire. Don't do it.

The spare battery

One option you probably ignored when you bought your laptop was getting a second or spare battery. This is must for people who are seriously on the road or in a remote location where a long time is spent away from the power socket.

Before you use a spare battery, ensure that it's fully charged. Either charge it in the laptop, or use an external charger (if available). Put the fully charged, spare battery in your laptop case or in any non-conducting (metallic) container. Then head out on the road.

If your laptop has some type of quick-swapping ability, then when the power gets low, you can just eject your laptop's original, spent battery and quickly insert the spare battery. But be sure that your laptop can survive such a heart transplant before you attempt it!

If your laptop doesn't have the ability to hot-swap batteries, then just turn off (or hibernate) the laptop when the original battery is nearly spent. Remove the old battery, insert the fresh one, and then turn the laptop on again.

- ✔ Yeah, it's a good idea to get a laptop that supports hot-swapping batteries in the first place, if this is a trick you plan on pulling often.

- ✔ I recommend labeling the batteries with a Sharpie so that you don't get the two (or more) confused and accidentally insert a dead battery.

- ✔ You can buy a spare battery from your dealer, or also from stores that sell extra batteries, such as iGo (www.1800batteries.com) or Batteries.com (www.batteries.com).

- ✔ Be wary of generic batteries! Always try to get manufacturer or manufacturer-approved batteries for your laptop. Anything less and you can run the risk of setting your laptop ablaze! It's happened!

Don't fall off the battery cycle!

The act of draining and recharging a battery is known as a *cycling*. If you drain and then recharge a battery three times, you've just *cycled* the battery three times, or *thrice* as my eighth-grade English teacher would have said.

Cycling the battery plays an important role in keeping the battery conditioned. For example, when you first get a Lithium-Ion battery-powered laptop, I recommend conditioning the battery: Cycle it three or four times. That means use it, drain it, and then recharge it over and over again for three or four cycles.

To prolong the life of a NiMH battery, I recommend fully discharging it every three to five cycles. So after you use, drain, and recharge the NiMH battery about four times (or so), do a complete drain, and then recharge it again. That should help the battery last a bit longer.

Should you keep the battery in the laptop when you use AC power all the time?

Quite a few folks use laptops as their primary computer. If that's the case with you, and you keep the laptop plugged in all the time, then there is no need for the battery to be in the laptop.

In situations where you'll never use the laptop's battery, such as when it's more-or-less permanently docked, remove the battery. The laptop runs just fine without the battery, and by removing the battery, you'll keep it in good condition for when you do need it.

To store the battery when it's not in use, place it in a non-metallic (or non-conducting) container. Keep it in a cool, dry place. Over time, the battery will drain. That's just the way nature works. So if the battery has been in storage a while, don't be surprised if it's dead when you retrieve it. You can recharge the battery by inserting it into your laptop and charging it as described earlier in this chapter. It should work just fine.

If you do occasionally take your wall-bound laptop out on the road, then I recommend not removing the battery. Instead, every week or so, unplug the laptop and let the battery cycle. That keeps the battery healthy and reliable over the long haul.

✔ Yeah, there may be some laptops that refuse to run from AC power when the battery is missing. I've not heard of any, but they may exist. If so, keep the battery in the laptop and understand that if you don't cycle it every so often, it will eventually go bad.

✔ If you remove the battery, do consider plugging the laptop into a UPS (Uninterruptible Power Supply). The laptop's battery acts as a UPS, keeping the computer powered during brief outages and blackouts. So if you remove the battery, consider a UPS as an alternative — just as you would for a desktop computer. Refer to my book *PCs For Dummies* (Wiley), for more information on using a UPS.

RIP battery

Eventually, your laptop's battery will die. It's inevitable. Just as humans are subject to death and taxes, batteries are subject to death. (Fortunately, the government hasn't figured out how to extort tax money from a battery. Yet.)

You can tell when your battery is about to die by one unique trait: It suddenly becomes useless. It no longer holds a charge, and what charge it does hold is very low and unreliable.

Don't mourn a dead battery! Toss it out!

Note that batteries are considered to be toxic waste in most communities. You must properly dispose of or recycle dead computer batteries according to the rules of your community or jurisdiction. Never just chuck an old computer battery in the trash.

And don't get all Viking on me and try to burn your battery either. That's just a bad thing.

Managing Your Laptop's Power

You can do certain things to help your laptop's battery last a bit longer. On the short list there are things that consume a lot of power:

✔ The hard drive

✔ The CD/DVD drive

✔ The floppy drive (if you have one)

✔ The modem

✔ The network interface

✔ The display

Each of the above devices consumes power when it's in use. Obviously, by not using those devices or by rationing their use, you can save a modicum of power.

For example, by setting a lower resolution and fewer colors on the display, you cause the computer to use less video resources, though the overall savings there is minor. For more savings, consider not using the CD/DVD drive, which requires real power to keep it spinning (such as when you're watching a DVD movie).

But the real control happens by setting various timeouts in the Power Options Properties dialog box, Power Schemes tab, as shown in Figure 8-6. That's where you can disable or timeout certain laptop features and help extend battery life in a dramatic way.

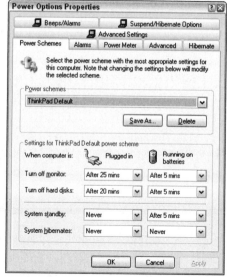

Figure 8-6: Scheming with Windows to conserve power.

Note the two major items in Figure 8-6: Turn Off Monitor and Turn Off Hard Disks. You can direct Windows to turn off those power-sucking hardware leeches after a given period of inactivity, greatly saving battery life.

In Figure 8-6, both the monitor and hard drive are disabled after five minutes of inactivity. This works just like Stand By, or sleep, mode: Power to those devices is quietly turned off. The hard drive stops spinning. The monitor goes blank. The devices wake up if needed, so if hard drive access is necessary, power is restored to the hard drive. And if you press a key or touch the mouse pad, the display comes back to life as well.

You can also use the Power Schemes tab of the Power Options Properties dialog box to set when your laptop automatically suspends or hibernates when under battery power.

When you find device custom settings that work for you, then save them permanently. Click the Save As button and type something like **My Scheme**. That way Windows remembers your settings, and you can choose "My Scheme" from the list, should Windows forget.

✔ Note that there are separate settings for when the laptop is plugged in and when it's running off battery power.

✔ Yes, you won't be seeing the screen saver if the monitor is suspended before the screen saver kicks in.

✔ It's a good idea to snooze the hard drive, especially if you don't plan on doing much hard drive access while using your laptop.

✔ Note that any disk access at all does wake up the hard drive, which requires an extra squirt of energy. If you set the hard drive to sleep after one minute, but it's constantly being revived, then you're actually *wasting* power. Try another setting.

✔ You can tell when the hard drive has been sleeping because it takes a wee bit longer for disk access to complete. (File saving, opening programs, browsing folders, and so on.)

✔ When a computer is plugged in, there is no reason to suspend hard drive operation. That will just annoy you.

✔ Another power-saving option is to run the laptop's microprocessor at a slower rate. This option is automatically controlled in modern laptops, though older laptops may have some manual control over the CPU or bus speeds.

✔ Refer to Chapter 4 for more information about Stand By and Hibernation modes.

✔ Refer to Chapter 6 for more information on the Power Options dialog box and the Control Panel in Windows.

Part III

Between Your Laptop and the World

In this part . . .

A portable computer need not be lonely. Sure, it can go out on the road and be far away from civilization, boldly taking technology where only geologists, the extremely adventuresome, or the utterly lost tread. Even at such great distances, your laptop can still be connected back to the real word. It happens with or without cables.

Despite its unencumbered nature, your laptop has the ability to connect itself with the rest of the electronic world quite well. This part of the book covers those connections, be they wire-based, wireless, or some combination of string and tin cans. Soon, you'll discover that, for being portable, you're laptop can be rather well-connected.

Chapter 9

All That Networking Nonsense

In This Chapter

▶ Understanding networking hardware

▶ Configuring your laptop for networking

▶ Connecting to the network

▶ Searching for computers on the network

▶ Sharing resources

▶ Un-sharing resources

▶ Understanding wireless networking standards

▶ Connecting to a wireless network

▶ Finding hidden wireless networks

▶ Disconnecting from the wireless network

*T*he idea of the personal computer was just that: personal. One computer for one person. That was the essence of the computer revolution back in the late 1970s and early 1980s. Before then, computers were all tangled and tethered together. The official term for that is *networked*.

In today's age of prolific PCs, once again there is the desire to network them together. While some may view this networking as a throwback to the era of domination and control, others look upon computer networking as merely a way to *share* things. And isn't sharing good?

This chapter covers some of the networking issues you may encounter as you take your PC on the road or keep it at home. Honestly, networking is the best way to keep your computer in touch. Whether it's just your laptop and the Internet, your laptop and one other desktop, or your laptop and the jillions of computers at your office, networking is necessary to know.

✔ You can also use a network to connect to the Internet. This subject is covered in Chapter 10.

✔ In an office setting, please make sure that you have your networking administrator, or one of his minions, assist in setting up your laptop for networking.

✔ This book does not cover setting up a wireless network or managing a wireless hub, switch, or router. I assume that such a device is already up and running for your wireless laptop to use.

Adding Your Laptop to an Existing Network

When it comes to computer networking, the most delightful words to enter your ear are *existing network*. That means that someone else has gone through the trouble and labored pain to bring the network into existence. You must further assume that the network is up and running and waits in eager anticipation to the addition of your laptop to its host of nodes.

The hardware connection

Networking is a combination of software and hardware, both working against each other to ensure that the experience is one of the most horrible of your life.

No, wait.

It's true that networking involves hardware and software. I'll admit to that. The software side is more difficult, so I put that off until the next section. The hardware side is rather simple: You need a NIC, or Network Interface Card, inside your laptop to make networking happen.

Most laptops sold today come with a NIC standard. You can tell it's there by looking for the RJ-45 hole or thing on the sides or back of your laptop's case. (Refer to Chapter 5.) If you see that hole, then your laptop is ready for networking. You just need to take a network cable and use it to connect your laptop to the network jack in the wall, to another PC, or directly to a network hub, switch, or router. That's it for the hardware side.

✔ Your laptop may also be ready for wireless networking. Refer to the section, "Wireless networking hardware," later in this chapter, for the grimy details.

✔ The cable you use to plug your laptop into the network is commonly called *Ethernet* cable. It's also known as *CAT-5*. You can buy it in assorted lengths, available at any computer or office supply store.

✔ *Ethernet* is the name of the computer networking hardware standard.

✔ RJ-45 holes look like phone jack holes, but they're slightly larger. Do not confuse them! If the Ethernet cable does not fit into the hole, then that particular hole is a phone or modem jack, not an RJ-45.

✔ A hub, switch, or router is a hardware device designed as a central locus for all computers on the network. Everything plugs in to the hub, switch, or router.

✔ A *hub* is simply a place where Ethernet cables from various computers (or printers or modems) plug into.

✔ A *switch* is a faster version of a hub.

✔ A *router* is a faster, smarter version of a switch.

✔ No, you don't really need a hub/switch/router thing. If you're just connecting two computers together, plug an Ethernet cable into each computer's NIC, and you can do what's called peer-to-peer networking. This is the fastest, most efficient way to connect two computers for exchanging information.

✔ If your laptop lacks a NIC or the RJ-45 hole, you can add one easily, either through a PC Card or by using a USB-Ethernet adapter.

Setting up the connection in Windows XP

I admit that Windows XP is brilliant when it comes to managing the network. All you really have to do is plug the Ethernet cable from an existing network into your laptop, and you're done. Any further fiddling isn't necessary. Or is it?

First, you can visit the Network Connections window. There you see any and all network adapters attached to your laptop. Figure 9-1 shows two network connections. The one labeled Local Area Connection is the standard Ethernet; the other is a wireless NIC.

Second, right-click on the icon for one of your network adapters in the Network Connections window, and then choose Properties from the pop-up menu. You then see the adapter's Properties dialog box, similar to Figure 9-2, which gives you access to both hardware and software settings for the network.

The settings listed in the networking hardware Properties dialog box don't normally need to be messed with. But yet there's a third place you should visit, one that may help clear up some connection issues.

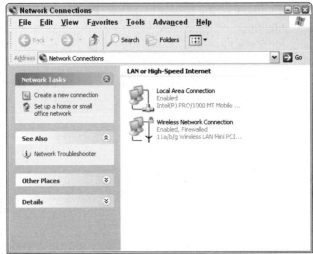

Figure 9-1:
The
Network
Connections
window.

Go to the Control Panel and open the System icon. Click on the Computer Name tab.

Figure 9-2:
Networking
hardware
and
software
settings are
controlled
here.

Each computer in the network must have two names to help identify it. The first is the computer's name. The second is the name of the workgroup to which the computer is assigned. In Figure 9-3, the computer's name is Chugger. The Workgroup name is CAT.

Note that all computers on the same peer-to-peer network should share the same workgroup name. If you're having trouble networking your laptop with your desktop at home, open the System Properties dialog box, Computer Name tab. Ensure that the computer's names are different but that the Workgroup name is *identical*. To change either name, click the Change button right there in the dialog box.

Fourth, and finally, you should check the My Network Places window to confirm that your computer is connected to the network and ready for action. This is covered in the next section.

✔ Note the task titled Set Up a Home or Small Office Network, shown in the Network Tasks part of the Network Connections window. (Refer to Figure 9-1.) Clicking that item runs a wizard that assists in setting up a network, which is worth a try if you're having trouble connecting your network.

✔ The information in this section is general, and applies to peer-to-peer networks.

✔ Refer to Chapter 6 for information on how to get to the Network Connections window, as well as to the System Properties dialog box.

Figure 9-3:
Revealing
the
computer's
networking
names.

Adding and removing your laptop to and from the network

After the network connection has been made, and everything is set up, you can connect your laptop to the network simply by plugging in the network cable. There is no need to turn off the laptop or restart Windows. Plugging in the cable instantly causes the network to be recognized. You're in!

Similarly, when you need to disconnect from the network, simply unplug the network cable. The networking hardware and software recognize that the cable is no longer there, and that the network is no longer accessible. No problem.

Finding other computers on the network

All the computers on the network love to share and love each other. They're all friends. Of course, sharing is optional. But still, the computers are all friends. And their clubhouse in Windows XP is a location called My Network Places.

Open the My Network Places window. (Refer to Chapter 6 on how to get there.) But before you wander around, click the View Workgroup Computers link located under the Network Tasks pane on the left side of the window. This displays the computers attached to your network — those belonging to the workgroup you've set up.

In Figure 9-4, you can see the contents of a cozy, two-computer network I created. This network was made by attaching an Ethernet cable to my desktop and laptop computers. (Directly; no hub or switch.) Both computers show up as icons, labeled with their computer names. The Workgroup name, Cat, appears in the Address bar and atop the window.

Figure 9-4:
Computers
in your
workgroup.

LAN party!

Thanks to the popularity of the film *Animal House,* toga parties were the rage on college campuses throughout the 1980s. Today's version of the toga party is just as popular, but far more geeky: It's the LAN party!

LAN parties can be planned, but they're mostly spontaneous. A group of laptop computer users suddenly find themselves together, and they create a small network, or LAN (Local Area Network). After working out the protocols and other network nonsense (covered in the main part of this chapter's text), the LAN partiers go at it. No, they don't sit around, sing "Kumbaya," and share resources. They play games! Violent, network games!

Normally you need access to the Internet or contact with some remote game server to do online games. But with a LAN party, you can have anywhere from half a dozen to hundreds of computer users networked together playing games. So the next time you're in a coffee shop or high-tech bistro, and someone looking like John Belushi shouts out "LAN party!," you'll know exactly what to do.

If your laptop has joined a network with more computers, they'll appear in the list as well. You might even see printers and modems in the list — whatever is attached to the workgroup or network.

Seeing computers displayed in the workgroup window is a sure sign of success that the network is up, connected, and ready for action.

Click the Back button to return to the My Network Places window from the workgroup window.

What you see in the My Network Places window are *shared resources.* These are disk drives, printers, or even modems connected to the network or made available to the network for access. In Figure 9-5, resources from any computers are shown as available.

Accessing network resources is covered in the next two sections. And also note that resources must be *shared,* or made available to the network, before they appear in the My Network Places window.

- Refer to the previous section for more information on computer and workgroup names.

- The steps you need to take for sharing resources are listed later in this chapter.

- If you don't see any computers in the workgroup window, then there is a problem. Either the network cable isn't connected, or it's bad. The network interface is bad. Or the computers do not share the same workgroup name.

✔ Printers shared on the network appear in the Printers and Faxes window.

✔ Modems on the network may not appear in the My Network Places window, especially if the Internet connection sits behind a firewall or router.

✔ Also note that connecting a Windows XP laptop to another version of Windows may require more work than is mentioned here.

Figure 9-5:
Shared resources on the network.

Getting into another computer's disk drives

Accessing another computer's disk drives over the network is cinchy. To be more specific, however, you don't really access the entire disk drive. No, only specific folders on the drive are up for sharing. And even then your access may be restricted by password, or to only read and not write or modify any files in that folder.

No matter what, if a computer user is foolish, er, smart enough to share a folder on the network, that folder shows up in the My Network Places window, as shown in Figure 9-5. To access a specific folder, double-click to open it just as you would any folder on your own hard drive.

If the folder isn't password-protected, then its contents appear in a window, just like any other folder on your hard drive. But remember that the folder is not on your hard drive; it's a folder elsewhere on the network.

If the folder is password-protected, you'll be asked to provide a password for access to the folder.

Once open, you can access files in the network folder just as if they were on your own computer. Note that some folders may be shared as read-only, in which case the files and folders cannot be renamed, deleted, or their contents modified.

It is polite network etiquette to close a network folder when you are done using it. If you forget, and don't close the folder, then a connection still exists between your computer and the one sharing that folder. If so, an error message may appear if the network connection goes down or if that other computer disconnects from the network.

Accessing network printers

Another joy: In Windows XP, any printers up and available on the network automatically appear in the list of available printers, either in the Printers and Faxes window or from any Print dialog box.

- ✔ To use the network printer, simply select it from the list of printers shown as available in the Print dialog box.

- ✔ Network printers have "plumbing" below their icons.

- ✔ The network printer is named using the form "Printer on Computer," where Printer is the printer's name or model number and Computer is the network name of the computer to which the printer is connected. For example, `Lexmark X6150 on Brutus`.

Sharing a folder on your laptop

Just like any stolid, unmovable desktop computer, various folders on your laptop's hard drive can be shared for others to use on the network. Just plug it in! And then follow these steps:

1. **Browse to find the folder you want to share.**

   For example, start in the My Documents folder, or open the Shared Documents folder from the My Computer window. Then keep opening folders until you find the folder you want to share.

2. **Right-click the folder's icon and choose Sharing and Security from the shortcut menu.**

   A Properties dialog box for the folder appears.

   If you haven't yet set up your laptop for sharing folders, then you have two options, as presented in the dialog box:

Network Setup Wizard. Choosing this option runs the wizard, which is probably unnecessary, especially if you've followed my advice in this chapter.

If you understand the security risk . . . blah blah blah. Scary, huh? But if your network is already set up (you've made a connection to other computers in the workgroup, as I describe in early sections of this chapter), then — despite the warning — choosing this option is the fastest.

    A. Choose the second option!

    B. In the next dialog box, select the Just Enable File Sharing option.

    C. Click OK.

The Properties dialog box should now resemble what's shown in Figure 9-6.

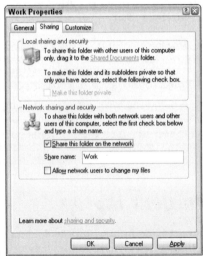

Figure 9-6:
Folder kinder-garten, your place to share.

3. **Select the Share This Folder on the Network check box.**

4. **The folder's name appears in the Share Name text box. Enter a new name if the name shown is vague.**

5. **Ponder over the Allow Network Users to Change My Files check box.**

    By selecting this check box, you're allowing others on the network to delete, rename, move, or modify the contents of the files (and the folders and those files) in the folder you're about to share. Is this what you want? If so, check the box.

6. **Click OK.**

    After some grumbling, the folder is put up for grabs on the network.

Shared folder icons appear with a little *serving hand* image beneath them. That's your visual clue that a folder has been shared.

On the network, the shared folder appears in other users' My Network Places windows. This happens only when your laptop is connected to the network, and when the laptop is up and running. (You cannot access files on a computer that is off.)

- ✔ Only share folders.

- ✔ You cannot share individual files, only the folders they live in.

- ✔ Don't share programs. Actually, I don't think that you can share programs and run them across the network (unless, of course, they're designed to do that in the first place).

- ✔ Do not share entire disk drives. This is a gross security violation. Gross, I tell you!

- ✔ For security reasons, I would also recommend against sharing the entire My Documents folder.

- ✔ Yes, that Shared Documents folder would be nice to share. Hmmm. It has the word "share" in it, doesn't it. Then you could just drag things into that folder, the things you want to share. Sounds interesting. (Hint, hint.)

- ✔ Other computers cannot access folders on your laptop when your laptop is in Stand By mode.

- ✔ You can continue to share folders, even when your laptop is on the road. That is, you don't need to unshare a folder just because the computer is disconnected to the network. The folders will become available to others when the network is reconnected.

Unsharing a folder

When you turn selfish, you can remove sharing from a folder. It's a snap: Just repeat the main steps from the previous section, but *remove* the check mark from the Share This Folder on the Network check box in Step 3. Then you can click OK, and the folder is, once again, private.

Networking with No Strings Attached (Wireless Networking)

The latest craze in computers is wireless *everything*. At the heart of the wireless mania is wireless networking, which has been heralded as the biggest boon to computers since keyboards replaced the old telegraph input device.

Then again, wireless networking can also be a real pain. It's not that easy to set up. It's a bear to maintain. And wireless security is questionable. Despite that, wireless networking remains a craze, so I thought I'd devote a few lucid moments to jotting down some worthwhile tidbits to share.

The ABGs of 802.11

Computers are just full of standards. You may have heard about a few: ANSI, ISO, IEEE, and other famous acronyms. The standard for wireless networking doesn't have a celebrated acronym. Instead it has an illustrious number: 802.11, which is properly pronounced, "Eight oh two dot eleven" or, to save time, you can omit the *dot*: "Eight oh two eleven."

As time marches on, newer and better wireless standards based on 802.11 come about. The first was 802.11a. Then came 802.11b, which is still popular, though the most current standard is 802.11g. There are even higher letters available, though 802.11g is the most renowned as this book goes to press.

The point to all this alphabetical nonsense is that in order to put the "work" into wireless networking, all the network devices must share the same standard. For example, the wireless adapter in your laptop, desktop, and wireless hub must all be 802.11g. That works best.

If your laptop uses 802.11b and the desktop uses 802.11g, then you're not totally out of it. The 802.11g standard will recognize the older 802.11b standard, but the speed will not be as good as if both were 802.11g. And if either system has a dual standard, you're doing even better. But, truly, for everything to work best, all the wireless networking devices must be of the same flavor 802.11.

- ✔ I haven't seen any 802.11a devices in a while, so I think it's safe to say that they've all gone bye-bye.

- ✔ 802.11b was the main standard, but it quickly is being overtaken by 802.11g. If you're just starting into wireless networking, get 802.11g.

- ✔ There are wireless adapters that span the alphabetic spectrum. I paid a little extra for my laptop's 802.11a/b/g adapter. It can scan and use all three standards, which gives me a broader range of connectivity options out there in the real world.

- ✔ I think I should be shot for writing, "a broader range of connectivity options." It means I've been reading too much computer sales literature lately.

Wireless networking hardware

To do the wireless thing, you need wireless networking hardware. An existing Ethernet port on (or NIC inside of) your computer just doesn't cut it. You need a specific, wireless networking gizmo. Further, you need a gizmo that supports whatever standard any existing wireless network uses: 802.11a, 802.11b, or 802.11.g.

If your laptop didn't come with the wireless network adapter, then it's a snap to add one. Either by using the USB port or a PC Card, you can attach wireless hardware to your laptop in a jiffy. Plug it in, install the software (if any or even if necessary), and you're ready to go.

I recommend getting a wireless adapter with an external antenna. For some reason, the antenna makes picking up the wireless signal easier — especially if the antenna is directional (that is, it can be moved).

If your laptop doesn't have an antenna, don't sweat it.

As with the wire-bound universe, setting up a wireless adapter in Windows XP is similar to setting up a wire-based Ethernet connection. Basically, Windows does all the work. All that's left to do is connect to the wireless network. That topic is covered in the next two sections.

Connecting to a wireless network

A laptop equipped with a wireless networking card can connect to any compatible wireless network. The first step is to find any available networks. The second step is to connect. And the final step is to use the network and the goodies it provides.

First, try to find an available wireless network. Take these steps:

1. **Open the Network Connections window.**

2. **Right-click on the wireless network connection's icon.**

   This icon represents the hardware and software needed to get a wireless networking going. You have to finish the job by connecting to a wireless network.

3. **Choose View Available Wireless Connections from the pop-up menu.**

   The Wireless Network Connection dialog box shows up, depicted in Figure 9-7. This dialog lists any and all wireless networks within range of your laptop and which are compatible with your wireless networking protocol.

Figure 9-7:
Desperately
scanning for
available
wireless
networks.

> **Wireless Network Connection**
>
> The following wireless network(s) are available. To access a wireless network, select it from the list, and then click Connect.
>
> Available wireless networks:
>
> | i KITTY |
>
> This wireless network requires the use of a network key (WEP). To access this network, type the key, then click Connect.
>
> Network key: ••••••••
>
> Confirm network key: ••••••••
>
> ☐ Enable IEEE 802.1x authentication for this network
>
> If you are having difficulty connecting to a network, click Advanced.
>
> [Advanced...]   [Connect]   [Cancel]

If your wireless networking gear supports more than one protocol, then you'll see every matching protocol appear in the window.

In Figure 9-7, one network shows up available. Its name is KITTY. The name is officially known as the SSID, or *Service Set Identifier*. That's the mumbo-jumbo term for the wireless network's name.

4. **Select the wireless network's name (if there is more than one).**

   Sometimes, you'll see a whole host of names. Sometimes you won't see any names — but don't think that means nothing is available. In fact, there is a hidden name in Figure 9-7; refer to the section, "What if you don't know the SSID?" later in this chapter, for more information.

5. **Enter the password.**

   Note that some of the passwords can be rather lengthy, so pay attention as you type them in.

6. **Enter the dang password again, if necessary.**

   This is extremely painful for those 128-character passwords.

7. **Click the Connect button.**

   If everything goes well, you'll see the little networking buddies appear in the Notification Area, plus a bubble alerting you to the wireless networking connection, as shown in Figure 9-8. You've made it!

Figure 9-8:
A wireless
network
connection
has been
made.

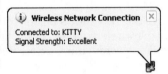

> ⓘ **Wireless Network Connection** ☒
>
> Connected to: KITTY
> Signal Strength: Excellent

Well, maybe you didn't make it. The network may require further authentication or configuration to allow your laptop to connect. Continue reading through the next few sections for some solutions to potential problems.

Also be aware that there is another location for accessing wireless networks. If you right-click on the Wireless Network Connection icon and choose Properties, you'll see the Wireless Networks tab of your network connection's Properties dialog box, as shown in Figure 9-9.

Using the Wireless Networks tab may be necessary when switching from one wireless connection to another. The bottom part of the dialog box (titled Preferred Networks) is used to store connection information about various networks so that you don't have to toil with the same connection information again and again.

✔ The wireless network must use the same 802.11 protocol as your laptop's wireless networking hardware.

✔ Some wireless networks may not be password protected, so in Step 5 of the preceding step list there may be no password required. Even so, Windows XP does not like this situation, and you may find it more difficult to connect to such an unsecured network.

✔ There is a distance and interference issue with wireless networking, and the picture isn't as rosy as the brochures claim. Basically, the best way to connect with a wireless network is to be in the same room with the hub, switch, router, or other computer that is broadcasting the signal. Things such as walls greatly reduce the potency of a wireless connection.

✔ Refer to Chapter 6 for more information on finding the Network Connections dialog box.

Figure 9-9:
Manually
doing the
wireless
thing.

Scanning for wireless networks

Any wireless network available shows up in the Wireless Network Connections dialog box (refer to Figure 9-7). If the network doesn't show up, then it's just not available, or the signal isn't strong.

Most wireless network adapters come with simple scanning tools, often much better than what Windows XP offers. For example, Figure 9-10 illustrates one such tool. Other tools are similar.

In Figure 9-10, you can see that more networks are available than Windows XP displays. That's because one of the networks is hiding its SSID name as a security precaution.

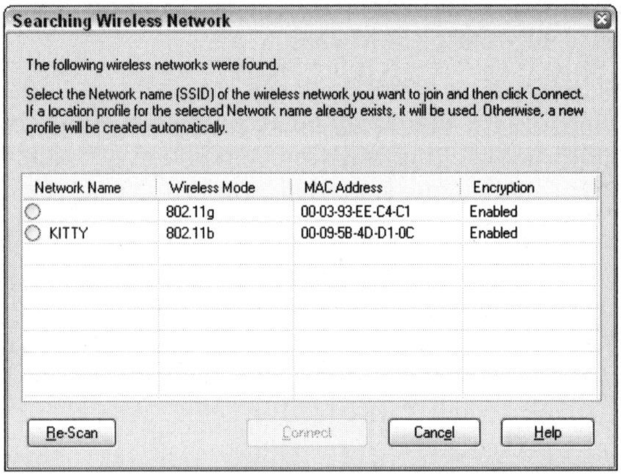

Searching Wireless Network

The following wireless networks were found.

Select the Network name (SSID) of the wireless network you want to join and then click Connect. If a location profile for the selected Network name already exists, it will be used. Otherwise, a new profile will be created automatically.

Network Name	Wireless Mode	MAC Address	Encryption
○	802.11g	00-03-93-EE-C4-C1	Enabled
○ KITTY	802.11b	00-09-5B-4D-D1-0C	Enabled

Re-Scan   Connect   Cancel   Help

Figure 9-10: All the available wireless networks.

✔ Look in the Notification Area to see if your laptop's wireless networking hardware came with such a utility.

✔ Note that such wireless utilities can also be used to scan for and connect to available wireless networks. Often these utilities are far easier to manage than what Windows offers.

✔ These wireless scanners usually sport an icon in the Notification Area. The icon generally offers feedback regarding the signal strength of the wireless network.

What if you don't know the SSID?

When the wireless network's SSID doesn't show up, as shown in Figure 9-10, then you need to ask for it. The network manager or whatever human is in charge of wireless network at your location should be able to divulge that information. When you know the SSID, follow these steps to connect to that network:

1. **Open the Network Connections window.**

2. **Right-click on the wireless network connection's icon and choose Properties from the pop-up menu.**

3. **Click the Wireless Networks tab.**

4. **Click the Add button found near the bottom of the dialog box.**

   In the Wireless Network Properties dialog box that appears (shown in Figure 9-11), you can manually configure the connection to the unknown wireless network.

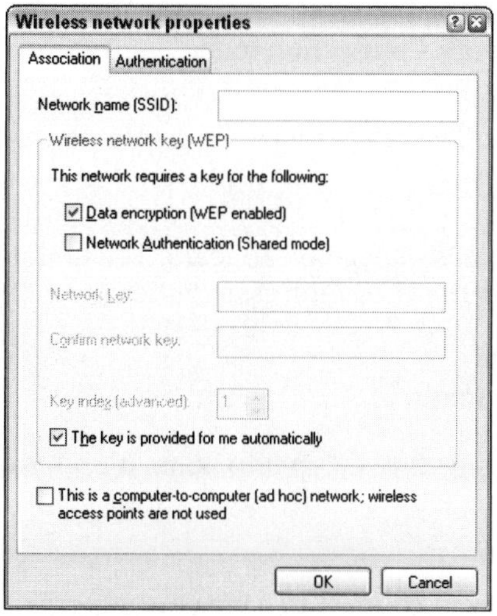

Figure 9-11:
Fill in this dialog box to connect to a wireless network.

5. **Type in the SSID.**

6. **Enter the network key or password.**

   If the network key box is disabled, as shown in Figure 9-11, then another dialog box may appear, prompting you to input the password.

7. **Click OK.**

At this point, the network should show up as available in the list. You can then connect to it by clicking on its name. (Refer to Figures 9-7 and 9-9.)

A great thing about Windows XP here is that it remembers the wireless networks you've connected to. So when you return to the same wireless location, the network information is made available and even fetched automatically for you. As long as the network password doesn't change, reconnecting to the same network is automatic.

What is the computer's MAC Address?

Some wireless networks restrict access to only those computers they know. Not having eyeballs, a network needs some other piece of identification to recognize computers it knows from utter strangers. That piece of ID is the wireless networking hardware's *MAC Address*.

A MAC Address is a unique number assigned to every networking adapter on planet Earth. No two numbers are identical, and the MAC Address is very difficult to fake. So by using the MAC Address, a wireless network can restrict access to only those computers known and registered.

Follow these steps to get your wireless network adapter's MAC Address:

1. **Open the Network Connections window.**

2. **Open your Wireless Network Connection icon.**

    This displays a Status window.

3. **Click the Support tab.**

4. **Click the Details button.**

    A Network Connection Details dialog box appears. The first item is the Physical Address, which is the MAC Address number.

5. **Copy down that number.**

6. **Close the various dialog boxes.**

The MAC Address is 12 digits long, broken up into pairs. It's a base-16 value (also called *hexadecimal*), so the letters A through F are also considered to be numbers.

If the MAC Address is necessary to connect to a specific network, then hand it over to the network manager or human in charge. He or she will add that address to the list of allowed computers, and soon you can use the network.

Renewing your lease

To keep the goofballs out, some networks only let you use their services for a given amount of time. This time allotted is referred to as a *lease*.

What may happen, especially if you use a wireless network for a great length of time, is that your lease may expire. To renew it, you need to disconnect from the network and then reconnect.

The instructions for disconnecting from a wireless network are offered later in this chapter, but for now, the simplest way to renew a lease is simply to restart Windows. Refer to Chapter 4.

Accessing a pay service wireless network

Not everything is free. Some people out there have the gall to actually charge you for using their wireless service. Imagine! Darn those capitalists!

I've seen pay wireless access work two ways:

- ✔ The first way is that you pay a cashier, and then he or she hands you a slip of paper with the SSID and a password to use. Then follow the steps from the section, "What if you don't know the SSID?" earlier in this chapter, for instructions on connecting to the network.

- ✔ The second way is more devious. The signal appears to be strong and available, and connection is not a problem. But when you go to the Internet, the only Web page you see is a sign up page. Until you fork over your credit card number, you can't go anywhere else on the Internet or access any other service (such as e-mail).

Yep. If it's a pay service, you gotta pony up!

Disconnecting the wireless connection

The main way I disconnect from a wireless connection is to close my laptop's lid. By putting the laptop into Stand By mode, the network connection is broken automatically. Opening the laptop's lid (assuming I'm within range of the wireless hub) re-establishes the connection.

Likewise, you can also turn off the laptop to disconnect from the network.

But if you must manually disconnect, you need to follow these steps:

1. **Open the Network Connections window.**

2. **Right-click on the wireless network connection icon.**

3. **Choose Disable from the pop-up menu.**

And the device is disabled, the connection is gone.

To re-enable the connection, repeat the steps, but choose Enable from the pop-up menu in Step 3.

If your laptop is in one location all the time, and you rely upon the wireless connection for your Internet or other network access, then there is no reason to disable the wireless connection.

Chapter 10

Laptop to Internet, Hello?

· ·

In This Chapter

▶ Arming yourself for Internet access

▶ Using the network to get on the Internet

▶ Connecting to a DSL or cable modem, or to a router

▶ Accessing the Internet through a dial-up connection

▶ Configuring the dial-up connection

▶ Managing multiple connection options

▶ Dialing into the Internet

▶ Disconnecting a modem connection

· ·

*I*t was the laptop computer, not the desktop, that pioneered the notion of online communications. While the first portable computers may not have come with internal modems, most of the proto-laptop computers were blessed with such hardware. After all, being portable meant being on the road. And that implied that at some point, communications were necessary.

When Ethernet became the PC networking standard, its circuitry joined the modem in being a standard feature on a laptop — long before such things became standards on desktop computers.

This chapter covers the most common of all online connections, the Internet. The topic here is how to connect. Other chapters in Part III offer tips on using your laptop on the Internet, online security, as well as using the internal modem.

What You Need to Get on the Internet

The Internet is not a computer program. Nor is the Internet a single large computer somewhere. No, the Internet is thousands and thousands of computers, all connected and all sharing information. It's more of a concept than a thing.

You need five things in order to access the Internet:

 ✔ A computer
 ✔ A device to connect to the Internet
 ✔ Software to access and use the Internet
 ✔ An Internet Service Provider (ISP)
 ✔ Money

The computer you already have. That's easy. And if it's a modern computer, then you probably have both of the common methods of connecting to the Internet, either the built-in modem or the built-in Ethernet connection (wired or wireless). Two down!

Windows XP comes with all the Internet software you need. There is special software to connect to the Internet, then software to use various resources on the Internet: the World Wide Web, e-mail, and other mysterious things and bewildering acronyms. Three down!

You connect to the Internet through an ISP. Or to put it another way, to connect your computer to the Internet, you must find a computer already connected to the Internet, and then connect to the Internet through that computer.

The Internet isn't a single computer, but rather a multitude of computers all connected and sharing information and resources.

The ISP can be your office, where Internet service is provided by your company, the government, or whatever crime syndicate you're indebted to. It can be the university you attend. Or it can be a third-party service, as described in the next section.

Finally, you need moolah to get the Internet from an ISP. Like phone service or cable TV, the ISP extracts a given monthly amount in exchange for Internet access. You have to find this money on your own.

 ✔ Free Internet access is available in most community libraries, though you must use their computers.

 ✔ If you connect to the Internet at work, then that connection is also considered more-or-less free. Though do be aware that many companies heavily filter their Internet access.

> ✔ For more information on selecting an ISP, refer to my book *PCs For Dummies*. It also contains more basic information on using the Internet, should you be new to this.

Bonus Laptop Goodies Your ISP Can Offer

Unless you specifically selected your ISP with portable computing in mind, you probably missed some of the handy and often necessary features laptop computers need when accessing the Internet. Here's my list:

Getting ISP access from all over the country

Internet access is available all over. But if you need to specifically access your own ISP, then it's preferable to have either a local access number or a toll-free number.

These suggestions are for dial-up Internet only:

> ✔ Many of the national ISPs, such as AOL, EarthLink, or NetZero, have access points all over the country. Before you leave, check to see if there are any local access numbers for your destination. That way, you can use your laptop's modem to connect with your ISP just as you do at home.

> ✔ In addition to local access, your ISP might also offer a toll-free phone number to connect. Note that there may be a surcharge for accessing this feature.

When you're lucky enough to find an Ethernet Internet connection while you're away, then there is no need to use the modem or dial in to your local ISP. As long as your computer is connected to the Internet, you can access your e-mail or browse the Web just as you would normally.

Check for Web-based e-mail access

Some ISPs know that you'll be away, so they offer a form of Web-based e-mail. This system allows you to access your e-mail through any computer connected to the Internet. Just navigate to your ISP's Web e-mail page and log in as you normally would. You can then read your e-mail on the Web instead of using an e-mail program.

Also refer to Chapter 13 for more e-mail tips and such.

Connecting Your Laptop to the Internet the Ethernet Way

To access the Internet from your laptop, you need both a hardware and software connection. The best resource here is whatever information your ISP handed you when you first signed up for the account. Those instructions detail exactly what you need and what information is necessary to fill in the various blanks.

The Ethernet connection

Any laptop configured to access a local area network is also primed and ready to access the Internet. All you need to do is connect to a network that already has an Internet connection. When your laptop is on such a network, it too can access the Internet directly from that network.

For example, if you add your laptop to an existing network, as described in Chapter 9, and that network is connected to the Internet via a DSL or cable modem, then your laptop is suddenly on the Internet. Nothing is easier. At that point, you can use your Internet software; browse the Web, pick up e-mail, launch nuclear missiles — or whatever your pleasure.

The same deal holds true for connecting to a public network, such as in a hotel with high-speed Internet access in the room, or connecting to a wireless network in a public place, or anywhere Internet access is offered.

Getting on the Internet

You don't need to do anything special to connect to the Internet. Providing that your computer is connected to a network on the Internet or directly to the Internet, then you're done. Just open any Internet application — Web browser, e-mail, and so on — and you're ready to go.

Further, you don't need to officially log off or disconnect from the Internet, though you will be disconnected from it when your laptop falls asleep (is in Stand By mode), is turned off, or when you yank out the Ethernet plug.

Connecting your laptop directly to a DSL or cable modem

When it's just you, your laptop, and a DSL or cable modem, the laptop connects directly to the modem using an Ethernet cable and your laptop's Ethernet connection.

The specific configuration is either done directly by your DSL or cable provider, or the information on making the connection is provided in a pamphlet.

If you're on your own, please refer to the information that came with the DSL or cable modem for the specifics.

If necessary, you run the New Connection Wizard to assist with setup. Choose Start⇨All Programs⇨Accessories⇨Communications⇨New Connection Wizard. Follow the wizard's instructions, clicking the Next button as necessary. You most likely want to select these options:

- Connect to Internet.
- Set up my connection manually.
- Connect using a broadband connection that is always on.

That should help you get started. The rest of the information that you need comes from your ISP.

Connecting to a router

Very often a device called a *router* sits between the DSL or cable modem and your computer or the rest of the network. The router is designed to interface between the Internet and your local network. It takes care of most of the more confusing networking options for you, plus the better model routers provide *firewall* protection between the computers on your network and the rest of the wild, nasty Internet.

Physically, the router is situated between your computer and the Internet connection or broadband modem, as shown in Figure 10-1. In this setup, your laptop would connect directly to the router, not to the modem. (In fact, all computers on the local network connect to the router, not directly to the modem.)

Yea, verily, even in a wireless setting, the connection is the same. In fact, a wireless router connects by wire to the high-speed modem. Then the rest of the computers on the wireless network connect wirelessly to the router. Figure 10-2 illustrates the shocking, wireless difference.

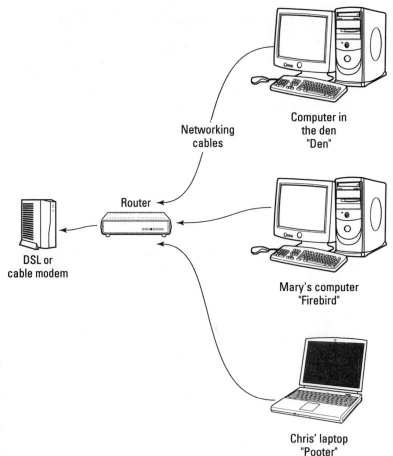

Networking
cables

Computer in
the den
"Den"

Router

DSL or
cable modem

Mary's computer
"Firebird"

Figure 10-1:
Handy
router
placement
diagram.

Chris' laptop
"Pooter"

✔ Router rhymes with *chowder*. Do not pronounce it *ROO-ter*.

✔ Broadband means "high speed."

✔ A firewall is a form of protection, guarding your computer from unwanted access by other computers on the Internet. See Chapter 12 for more information.

✔ I highly recommend setting up your computer network for sharing an Internet connection as shown in this section. Use a router. Get a good one that offers firewall protection. Connect the router to the modem, and then all the computers on the network to the router.

✔ If you use a router as I recommend, then you don't have to mess with the Windows XP Internet Connection Sharing feature.

✔ Routers are configured by logging in to them. The router will have an IP address, and you use your Web browser software, such as Internet Explorer, to connect to the router, log in, and set the configurations. Instructions for doing this come with the router.

✔ Refer to Chapter 12 for more information on Internet security.

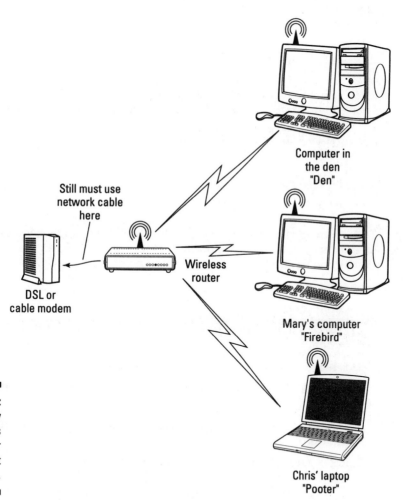

Still must use
network cable
here

Wireless
router

DSL or
cable modem

Computer in
the den
"Den"

Mary's computer
"Firebird"

Chris' laptop
"Pooter"

Figure 10-2:
Handy
wireless
router
placement
diagram.

Dial-Up Internet

Even if you're gotten used to the warm, comfy waters of high-speed Internet access, there might be a time when you need to pull out that old modem and use a 19th century technology to access the 20th century Internet on your 21st century laptop. It happens.

For more information on using your laptop's modem, please refer to Chapter 11.

Configuring a dial-up connection

If you've not yet configured your laptop for dial-up access, then run the New Connection Wizard. Before you start, you need to know the following items:

- ✔ Your ISP's name (used to identity the dial-up connection)
- ✔ The connection's phone number
- ✔ The username for your ISP account
- ✔ The password for your ISP account

This information is provided by the ISP, or whichever outfit is giving you Internet access. When you know these tidbits, you can configure the New Connection Wizard to complete the setup process. Here's how that goes:

1. **Choose Start⇨All Programs⇨Accessories⇨Communications⇨New Connection Wizard.**

2. **Quickly ignore all the printed text on the screen and click the Next button.**

3. **Select the Connect to the Internet option and click the Next button.**

4. **Select the Set Up My Connection Manually option and click the Next button.**

5. **Select the Connect Using a Dial-up Modem option and click the Next button.**

6. **Enter your ISP's name, then click the Next button.**

   It doesn't have to be your ISP's name. This name is used to identify the connection's icon. You can use any name you like, proper or profane.

7. **Enter the phone number to connect to your ISP.**

   This is the connection phone number, not its office or help line.

8. **Enter your account's username.**

   This is the name supplied by your ISP. This isn't the logon ID you use for Windows XP (though they could be the same).

9. **Enter your account's password, first in the Password text box and then again in the Confirm Password text box.**

   I have no idea why they do this.

10. **Click the Next button.**

11. **Click the Finish button.**

    Windows churns. Windows chugs. And the wizard goes away.

What? You were expecting more? Be thankful. I've known wizards that go on for weeks. In any event, the dial-up connection has been set. The next step is to use it.

✔ Don't worry about being fancy with the phone number now. Enter the phone number as you need to dial it. If modifications are necessary, such as when you're on the road, you can make them later. This book shows you how in Chapter 11.

✔ If you're using more than one ISP, you will need one dial-up connection icon for each.

✔ AOL uses its own system to connect to the Internet. Please refer to the AOL documentation for information on setting it up; I do not cover AOL in this book.

Finding the connection

 The dial-up Internet connection is located in the Network Connections window. It floats in there as an icon, shown here in the margin.

If you need to modify the connection information, right-click the connection icon and choose Properties from the pop-up menu.

Note that only one connection can be the *default,* the connection automatically made whenever your computer needs to hop on the Internet. To set the default connection, right-click a dial-up network connection icon and choose Set as Default Connection from the menu.

Default connections sport the black circle and check mark icon.

The little padlock means that the firewall security software is enabled. Flip over to Chapter 12 for more information on firewalls.

See Chapter 6 if you need help finding the Network Connections window.

Making the dial-up connection

Unlike an Ethernet or wireless connection, which is always on, you must manually connect to the Internet if you're using dial-up.

First, ensure that your computer is properly wired to the phone jack. The cord must plug in to the modem hole on your laptop and into a phone jack on the wall or piggy-backing onto some other telephonic device.

Second, run an Internet program, or some program that requires an Internet connection. For example, open your Web browser software, Internet Explorer.

You can also connect to the Internet manually by opening the Network Connections window and double-clicking the dial-up Internet connection icon that you want to use.

In some instances, you see the Connect dialog box as you attempt to dial out to the Internet, as shown in Figure 10-3. Click the Dial button to make the connection.

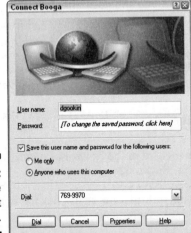

Figure 10-3:
The Connect dialog box.

After the connection has been made, the little modem buddies appear in the Notification Area, as shown in Figure 10-4. That's your clue that you're connected to the Internet. You can now use any Internet software.

> ✔ Yes, the connection speed you see may be much lower than what your modem is capable of. The speed depends upon the quality of the connection and the phone lines connecting your laptop to the ISP.

> ✔ Rarely, if ever, have I connected at any speed higher than 49 Kbps.

✔ Rumor has it that the phone company only guarantees connection speeds of 14.4 Kbps. In some areas, that's as good as it gets.

✔ Do not plug your modem into a digital phone system! It will fry your modem's gizzard! Digital phone systems are common in hotels and medium-to-large businesses. When in doubt, ask!

Figure 10-4:
The modem buddies happily report that a connection has been made.

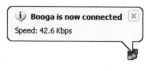

Dialing a specific connection

When you have more than one connection to choose from, you need to open the Network Connections window and double-click on whichever dial-up connection you want to use.

Windows XP uses whichever connection you've identified as the default. When you want to use another connection, you must manually select it.

Refer to the earlier section, "Finding the connection," for more information on setting the default connection.

Don't forget to disconnect the dial-up connection!

If you're used to an always-on broadband connection, then you should especially remember that dial-up connections must be disconnected manually when you're done with the Internet.

To disconnect, right-click on the little modem guys in the Notification Area. Choose the Disconnect command from the context menu.

You can also just double-click on the modem guys, which displays a Status dialog box, similar to what's shown in Figure 10-5. From there you can click the Disconnect button to end your Internet session.

Figure 10-5:
Connection
status, trivia
and stuff
like that.

✔ I often keep the Status dialog box open for reference purposes. Not only does it remind me that I'm on a dial-up connection, but it also has a timer so that I don't spend too much time online when I'm stuck using a long-distance connection.

✔ Windows automatically sets a timeout of 20 minutes for your dial-up Internet connection. If the computer thinks you haven't touched the keyboard or moved the mouse pointer in 20 minutes, it believes you to be absent, comatose, or dead, and so the Internet connection is broken, and the computer hangs up the modem.

✔ To reset the timeout, right-click on your dial-up connection icon in the Network Connections window and choose Properties from the context menu. In your connection's Properties dialog box, click the Options tab. The timeout value is set by using the Idle Time before Hanging Up drop-down list.

✔ If you set the idle time to Never, then the computer won't automatically hang up the modem for you.

Chapter 11

A Very Merry Modem

In This Chapter

▶ Adjusting the modem in Windows XP

▶ Using an external modem

▶ Configuring the dialing and area code rules

▶ Setting modem and connection timeouts

▶ Sending and receiving faxes

*P*ortable computing and modems go hand-in-hand. Long before modems were popular on desktop computers, they were required equipment on laptops. The modem provided necessary communications between the desktop and laptop. It was that vital umbilical cord between the remote system and the mothership.

Even now, as modem hardware is once again slipping from the desktop radar screen, the device is still considered an unquestionable part of core laptop technology. You may never use it. You may use it all the time. Either way, this chapter covers all the merry modem nonsense you need to know.

The Modem Hardware

Modems can live externally to your laptop, such as a DSL or cable modem, but the most common type of modem is the telephone, or dial-up, variety. This modem exists as part of your laptop's internal hardware, most likely integrated into the laptop's main circuitry.

The only part of the modem you're likely to see is the hole, or *jack,* into which the phone cord plugs. Refer to Chapter 4 for information on locating the thing.

✔ Some laptops may have two modem holes or jacks. One is used to connect the laptop to the phone jack on the wall. That's the *line* jack. The second hole can be used to connect a phone. That's the *phone* jack. That way you can still use the phone without having to unplug the modem.

✔ No, you cannot use the phone while the computer is online.

✔ The computer makes phone calls just like a human does: It dials a number, then it screeches its unmelodic tones at the other computer, which also screeches back.

✔ Long-distance charges apply to modem calls just as they do regular phone calls. Hotel surcharges apply as well.

✔ Some countries charge extra for modem-made phone calls. When you're traveling overseas, be sure to inquire about any extra fees before you use the phone.

✔ You can buy modems on PC Cards.

✔ Modem is a contraction of *modulator-demodulator*. The electronic (digital) signal from the modem is modulated into an audio (analog) signal for the phone line. Likewise, a modulated analog signal is demodulated by the modem back into digital information for the computer. Or something like that.

Where the Modem Dwells in Windows

You may not be able to locate the modem's hardware inside the laptop, but in Windows, the modem's location is painfully obvious: Open the Control Panel and open the Phone and Modem Options icon.

In the Phone and Modem Options dialog box, click on the Modems tab. There, you see a list of any modem(s) installed in your computer, as shown in Figure 11-1.

By selecting your modem and clicking the Properties button, you can make further adjustments to the modem, some of which are covered in the sections that follow.

Setting the modem's volume

Most people like to hear the modem make its noise as an online connection is being made. Some folks dislike the noise. And others can't even hear the noise. All three of these issues are addressed in the same location in Windows. Heed these steps:

1. **Open the Control Panel's Phone and Modem Options icon.**

2. **Click the Modems tab in the Phone and Modem Options dialog box.**

3. **Click your modem to select it from the list.**

4. **Click the Properties button.**

   The modem's Properties dialog box appears.

Figure 11-1:
Hello,
modem.

5. **Click the Modem tab.**

6. **Use the slider to set the volume, as shown in Figure 11-2. Loud is on the right. Soft is toward the left. Off is all the way over on the left.**

7. **Click OK to close the various dialog boxes.**

The new volume setting takes effect the next time that you use the modem to dial out.

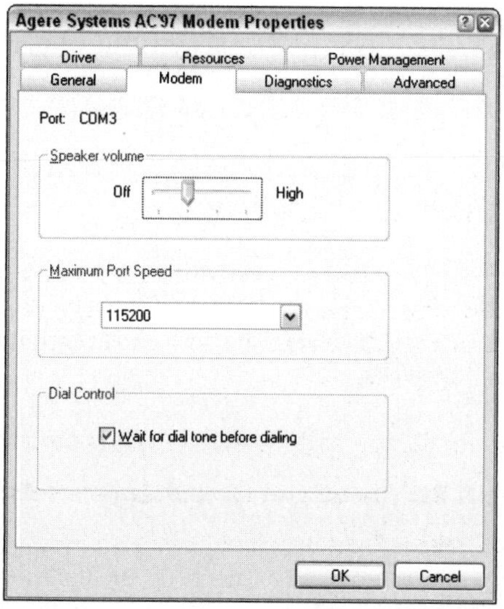

Figure 11-2:
Putting a
sock in it.

Adding special modem command settings

Some ISPs may require you to give the modem special commands. This is done to improve the connection or often to troubleshoot a bad connection. When you're directed to do so, follow these steps to give the modem its new commands:

1. **Open the Control Panel's Phone and Modem Options icon.**

2. **Click the Modems tab in the Phone and Modem Options dialog box.**

3. **Select your modem from the list and click the Properties button.**

4. **In the modem's Properties dialog box, click the Advanced tab.**

   You see a text box there (shown in Figure 11-3) where you can input the command characters given. For example, if you're told to use the command ATS58=33 then you type that text into the box *exactly* as written.

5. **Click OK to close the various dialog boxes.**

Most of the time, you can leave the command settings alone. Even if you change ISPs or locations, you don't need to reset the special command strings or use other commands unless some wise computer guru instructs you to do so.

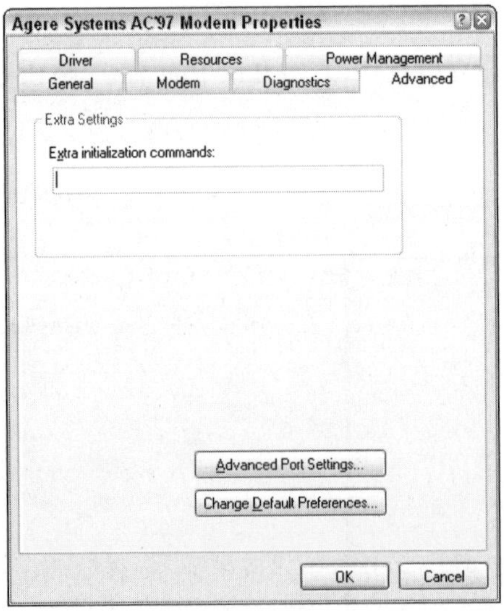

Figure 11-3: Add bonus modem commands here.

Options for disabling the modem

Because I don't often use my modem, I like to turn it off or disable it. That way the computer isn't supplying power to a device that I don't use. You can arrive at this solution in several ways.

First try this:

1. **Open the Control Panel's Phone and Modem Options icon.**

2. **Click the Modems tab in the Phone and Modem Options dialog box.**

3. **Select your modem from the list and click the Properties button.**

4. **In the modem's Properties dialog box, click the Power Management tab.**

5. **Select the Allow the Computer to Turn Off This Device to Save Power check box.**

   Whether this item is available or not depends on your modem's smarts. (On my laptop, the option is dimmed.)

6. **Un-check the Allow This Device to Bring the Computer out of Standby check box.**

   Standby is sleep mode. If you leave this item checked, then the modem can wake up the computer when it receives an incoming call. That might be what you want, but I leave this option un-checked.

7. **Click OK to close the various dialog boxes.**

Another trick you may want to try is simply to disable the modem completely. Doing so instructs Windows to utterly ignore the modem's hardware. Here's how that happens:

1. **Open the Control Panel's Phone and Modem Options icon.**

2. **Click the Modems tab in the Phone and Modem Options dialog box.**

3. **Select your modem from the list and click the Properties button.**

4. **If necessary, click the General tab in the modem's Properties dialog box.**

   Down at the bottom of the dialog box is an item titled Device Usage.

5. **Choose the Do Not Use This Device (Disable) option from the drop-down list.**

6. **Click OK to close the various dialog boxes.**

When the modem is disabled, you cannot use it. You cannot connect to the Internet, you cannot receive or send a fax.

To enable the modem and use it again, repeat the above steps but choose the Use This Device (Enable) option from the drop-down list in Step 5.

Adding an External Modem

Long ago, modems were of two types: trustworthy and frustrating. In addition to those two types, there were also the internal and external modem models.

Internal models were installed inside the computer. The external models existed in their own boxes outside the computer, connected by a serial cable.

Though external modems are rare, you may have to use one someday. Unlike most devices you add to your computer system, you have to manually install and set up the external modem. Here's how:

1. **Don't use the modem!**

   Quit your modem programs. Ensure that the modem is on, but not using the phone line.

2. **Attach the modem to your computer.**

   Plug it into the proper port, such as the serial port. You need a serial port cable to make this happen. (Refer to the notes at the end of this section.)

   If your modem came with a setup CD, then use it right now instead of trudging through the following steps.

3. **Open the Control Panel's Phone and Modem Options icon.**

4. **In the Phone and Modem Options dialog box, click the Modems tab.**

5. **Click the Add button.**

   The Add Hardware Wizard, special modem edition, begins.

6. **Select the Don't Detect My Modem; I Will Select It from a List check box.**

   Believe me, this is much faster.

7. **Click the Next button.**

   Again, if you have a CD, use it now; click the Have Disk button in the wizard and follow those instructions instead of what's printed here.

8. **Choose the modem manufacturer, as shown in Figure 11-4.**

   If your modem manufacturer isn't shown, then it means that it didn't pay Microsoft the appropriate bribe. Instead, choose "(Standard Modem Types)" from the list. See the sidebar, "Connecting anything but a modem."

9. **Choose your modem's model from the Models list.**

   If you chose the Standard Modem Type, then choose your modem based on its speed.

10. **Click the Next button.**

11. **Choose Selected Ports.**

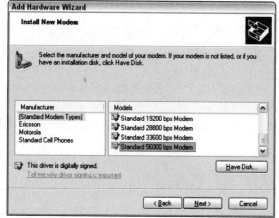

Figure 11-4:
Choosing
your modem
in the
wizard.

If your laptop has more than one serial port available, then be sure to
specify the proper port number to which the modem is attached. This
can be COM1 or COM2, depending on how many ports your laptop (or
its port replicator) sports.

12. Click to select the proper port.

13. Click the Next button.

After Windows finishes its exotic modem setup dance.

14. Click the Finish button.

The modem you just installed now appears in the Modem tab list inside the
Phone and Modem Options dialog box. (Refer to Figure 11-1.)

To use the modem, you simply need to specify it inside Windows or
whichever program requires the modem.

- ✔ Not all laptops have serial ports.

- ✔ Some laptops can be blessed with a serial port by adding a port replicator.

- ✔ Refer to Chapter 5 for more information on serial ports.

- ✔ The laptop has a 9-pin serial port, but external modems sport either a 9-
  pin or 25-pin serial port. So you need either a 9-pin to 9-pin Male to
  Female serial cable, or a 9-pin Female to 25-pin Male serial cable.

- ✔ If the modem is only being installed temporarily, then you can remove it
  when you're done. In the Phone and Modem Options dialog box, Modem
  tab, select the modem and then click the Remove button. Click the Yes
  button to confirm. The modem is gone.

Connecting anything but a modem

If you're observant, then you'll note that the Add Hardware Wizard you use for adding a modem is also where you can add various and exciting non-modem devices to your laptop as well. For example, you can add an Infrared modem, a Bluetooth cell phone, or a compatible modem cell phone. Peruse the list in the wizard's dialog box to see what's available.

Setting Up Dialing Rules

Strange hotel rooms. Dank coffee shops at 4:00 a.m. The so-called "business" lounge in the Kinshasa airport. Even the Hyatt in downtown Indianapolis. No, these aren't places frequented by some dashing young spy. They're places you may find yourself with a laptop trying to make a phone call.

The laptop's portability implies that you may find yourself in a different environment every time you use it. Sometimes those locations will be unique. Sometimes they may be the same, such as that bargain-basement Vegas hotel you keep returning to for the annual footwear convention. Regardless, Windows has these needs anticipated and easily addressed. Keep reading.

Location, location, location

Just like real estate, location plays an important role when you use a laptop. Even if your location never changes, it helps to inform the laptop of what's necessary to dial the phone. Follow these steps:

1. **Open the Phone and Modem Options icon in the Control Panel.**

   The main tab is titled Dialing Rules. It's used to list the locations where you use your laptop.

   If you haven't yet set things up, then you see New Location listed, and probably with your proper area code (which Windows knows because it's clairvoyant).

   The remaining steps describe how to properly configure your current location with the necessary dialing rules.

2. **Highlight the New Location in the Dialing Rules tab.**

   You can also use these steps to fix any entry shown in the box. Just choose that entry instead of New Location.

3. **Click the Edit button.**

   The Edit Location dialog box appears, shown in Figure 11-5. It allows you to customize the way the modem dials the phone, depending on your location.

4. **Enter a name for your current location.**

   For example, "Home" or "The Office" or wherever your laptop is right now.

5. **Select whichever country you're in now.**

6. **Enter the area code.**

7. **Fill in the dialing rules area.**

   You can leave these items blank if none are required.

   If your hotel requires you to dial an 8 before making a local call, and a 9 for making a long distance call, then put those numbers into the appropriate boxes.

8. **To disable call waiting while the modem is online, select the To Disable Call Waiting Dial check box. Then select the proper code sequence from the drop-down list.**

   The call waiting signal disconnects an active modem connection. You check this box to disable call waiting on a per-phone-call basis.

9. **Finally, select whether or not your connection requires tone or the old-fashioned pulse dialing.**

Figure 11-5:
Interesting
phone stuff
about your
location.

You need to select the Pulse option only if your area is limited to Pulse dialing. You'll be painfully aware of this annoyance; otherwise, you can choose Tone.

10. **Click OK to save the settings.**

This information is used by Windows whenever you use the modem. It may seem silly to enter this information now, but eventually, you'll have a whole collection of Locations. You can save time using that information instead of having to input it over and over again when you travel.

✔ You don't need to disable call waiting if you don't want to. Various software programs and hardware gizmos are available that will monitor incoming calls and alert you to them without disconnecting the modem. Check out the following:

```
www.catchacall.com
www.buzzme.com
www.callwave.com
```

✔ If you use AOL, check out AOL Call Alert.

✔ Don't worry over inputting the area code. The section, "Area code madness! To dial or not to dial," later in this chapter, describes how and when you can direct the modem to automatically dial an area code for you.

Creating a new location

Say you're off again in that cheesy Vegas hotel for a convention. Or you're at your summer place. Or you're away at college. Any time you set up shop in a new location, you need to tell the laptop's modem about it.

Note that this information need only be input if you're using the modem. If you're using an Ethernet connection to access the Internet, then don't bother! Otherwise, create a new location.

To set up a new location, use the Phone and Modem Options dialog box as I describe in the previous section: Start with Step 3 and click the New button instead of the Edit button. Then continue on with the steps, inputting the information as necessary for your new location.

Click the OK button when you're done. Then, in the Phone and Modem Options dialog box, be sure to click by this new location so that Windows uses that location's dialing rules.

Area code madness! To dial or not to dial

For each location you set up, there will be various dialing rules. There will also be various headache-inducing area code rules.

Don't sweat it! You need only input area code rules if you need to use area codes when you dial your modem. When you're calling only one number and it's local to wherever you are, then you can forget about the area code rules.

But when you call several numbers, and some require you to dial the area code while others do not, you can let Windows manage the hassle of when to dial the area code or when to dial the number as you've input it.

To make area code modifications, obey these steps:

1. **Choose your current location in the Phone and Modem Options dialog box.**

2. **Click the Edit button.**

3. **In the Edit Location dialog box, click the Area Code Rules tab.**

4. **Click the New button to create a new rule.**

   The New Area Code Rule dialog box appears, as shown in Figure 11-6. Here's how this works:

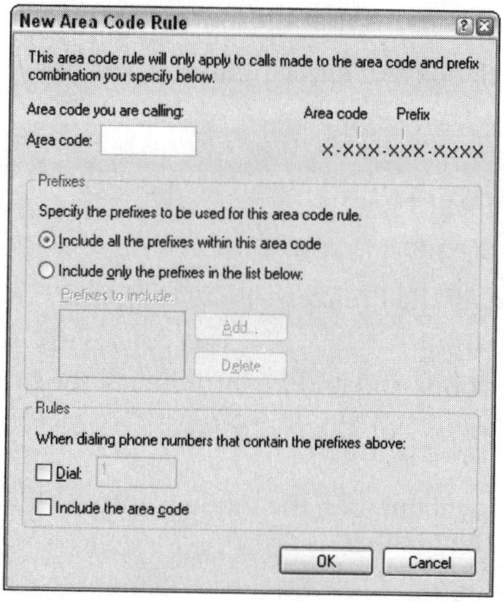

Figure 11-6: Making up a new area code rule.

If you're calling into another area code and you must always dial 1 plus that area code, then fill in the dialog box like this:

A. Enter the alien area code.

B. Choose the Include All the Prefixes within This Area Code radio button.

C. Click the check box by Dial and enter 1 into the box.

This assumes you dial 1 before dialing into another area code.

D. Select the Include the Area Code check box.

If you're calling locally and you only need to enter the area code for certain prefixes — the so-called "local long distance," or when you live in a large area covered by one area code and certain prefixes are long distance, fill in the dialog box like this:

A. Enter your own area code.

B. Choose the Include Only the Prefixes in the List Below radio button.

Don't open the phone book and enter all the prefixes! Enter only those you have to dial. For example, in my area code, prefix 334 is local long distance, and I have to dial the area code.

C. Click the Add button.

D. Type one or more prefixes into the box and click OK.

You need input only those prefixes that the modem will be dialing.

E. Select the Dial check box and enter 1 into the text box.

F. Select the Include the Area Code check box.

Finally, if you have to always dial the area code, do this:

A. Enter your own area code.

B. Choose the Include All the Prefixes within This Area Code radio button.

C. Select the Dial check box and enter 1 into the text box.

D. Select the Include the Area Code check box.

Every time you dial any local number, the modem automatically prefixes 1 and your area code to the number.

5. **Click the OK button to add the new rule.**

6. **Repeat Steps 4 and 5 to create as many rules as necessary.**

To put these dialing rules into effect, you need to select the Use Dialing Rules check box whenever you input a new phone number for the modem to dial.

Yes, it is possible to ignore and forget about all these things! You merely type in the full number to dial every time you set up a new modem connection. But if you're dialing a lot of numbers in different locations, setting up the rules can make things far easier.

Automatically using a calling card

The final tab in the Edit Location dialog box is for entering calling card information. What this does is allow Windows to automatically blast out the calling card information as the modem connects, for example, allowing you to charge a specific call at a business center to your company's credit card.

To enter calling card information, edit the Location information as described in the previous sections. Click the Calling Card tab, and you see a bunch of options similar to what's shown in Figure 11-7. Fill it in!

✔ If your card isn't listed in the Card Types list, click the New button and you can use the quite detailed dialog box that appears to input information about your credit or calling card.

✔ Yes, this is obviously sensitive information. Refer to Chapter 17 for information on laptop security.

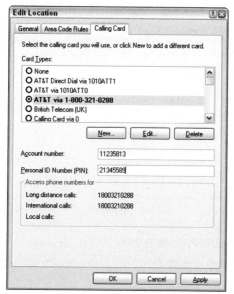

Figure 11-7:
Setting up
for a credit
card call.

Finding the Various Disconnect Timeouts

One of the sorrows of using a modem is that it occasionally decides to hang up on you. This could be for a multitude of reasons: noise on the line, call waiting, or it could be a timeout value set in Windows.

Windows uses the timeout values to ensure that people who fall asleep when they're online don't continue to tie up the phone lines. Ditto for people who die online. The timeout senses that no activity has taken place for a spell, and then it simply up and disconnects the modem.

You have two places to check modem timeout settings. The first is on the modem itself. The second is for the connection you've made. Having two settings means that you can set different timeouts for each connection, but also have a general timeout.

The general timeout

The general modem timeout value is set in a place you can find by following these steps:

1. **Open the Control Panel's Phone and Modem Options icon.**

2. **Select your modem from the list in the Modems tab, and click the Properties button.**

3. **In the modem's Properties dialog box, click the Advanced tab.**

4. **Click the Change Default Preferences button.**

5. **Select the Disconnect a Call If Idle for More Than check box and input a timeout value into the text box.**

   Yes, if you leave this item unchecked, there will be no general timeout.

6. **Click OK and close the various open dialog boxes.**

Timeouts for each session

Timeouts are also set for each connection you make with the modem. Here's how to modify the timeout for an Internet connection:

1. **Open the Network Connections window.**

2. **Right-click on the dial-up connection that you want to modify.**

3. **Choose Properties from the pop-up menu.**

4. **Click the Options tab in the Properties dialog box.**

5. **Set the timeout by the item Idle Time before Hanging Up.**

6. **Click OK and close the various open dialog boxes and windows.**

This is a situation where you might consider setting a timeout value for a long-distance or per-hour connection. No point in spending money if you're not doing anything, or "idle," while you're online.

Putting the Fax into Fax/Modem

Your modem may be called a mere *modem,* but its secret identity is *fax/modem.* Since the early 1990s, modem manufacturers discovered that it was devilishly easy to put standard fax technology into a computer modem. The result is a device that not only lets computers chitty chat, but which can chitty chat with fax machines as well.

✔ There's no need to confirm anything! Trust me, your laptop's modem can send and receive faxes.

✔ The following sections describe how to use the faxing facility inside Windows XP. Other faxing programs are available that you might find easier to use and manage than what Windows offers. Refer to your local Software-O-Rama for the variety.

✔ The faxing facility described in this chapter might be available only if the Microsoft Office suite of programs has been installed on your laptop. I'm not really sure about this, seeing how I can't find a laptop without Office installed to verify it.

✔ Faxes are a bit antique when you think about it. The e-mail attachment has supplanted the fax as the standard way documents are sent about these days. Even so, I recognize that the legal and medical communities continue to use faxes. So it's obvious that I just can't wiggle out of writing about this stuff.

✔ Refer to Chapter 13 for more information on e-mail.

Setting up the fax modem

This is a lot easier than it sounds. Providing that your laptop has a modem inside or somehow attached, follow these steps to setup faxing:

1. **Open the Printers and Faxes window.**

   Refer to Chapter 6 for help.

   2. **Locate the Printer Tasks panel on the left side of the window.**

   3. **Select the task named Install a Local Fax Printer.**

   4. **And you're done.**

Whew! That was tough!

The fax now appears as an icon in the window. But you don't really need to use that icon to send a fax. That subject is covered in the next section.

To send a fax

Faxing works just like printing, though the printer is a fax machine you connect to by using your laptop's modem. So sending a fax starts with the standard printing operation. Do this:

   1. **Prepare the document you want to fax.**

      You can fax from any application that has a Print command on the File menu.

   2. **Choose File⇨Print.**

      Do not click the Print button on the toolbar! That often just prints the document on whatever "default" printer you've selected. If the default printer is the fax machine, fine. Otherwise, beware!

   3. **Choose the Fax modem as your printer.**

      If you don't see the Fax machine sitting there, then it hasn't yet been set up. Refer to the previous section.

   4. **Make any other selections as needed in the Print dialog box.**

      For example, set which pages to print, the number of copies, and other options as they're available in the dialog box.

   5. **Click the OK button.**

      Normally, the document would print at this point, but instead, you see the Send Fax Wizard appear.

      If you haven't yet sent a fax on your laptop, then the Fax Configuration Wizard appears first (before the Send Fax Wizard). Use the Fax Configuration Wizard to enter contact information about yourself or whoever is sending the fax.

   6. **Click the Next button.**

      The next part of the wizard is used to input the name and fax number of the human who is receiving your missive.

7. **Click the Address Book button.**

   No matter what, I recommend that you create or modify an Address Book entry for each fax you send. It saves time later!

8a. **Click the New Contact button to create a new contact, or**

8b. **Locate a contact in your list and click the Properties button to edit that entry.**

   Either way, you're editing the contact's information inside a Properties dialog box.

9. **Create the new entry or confirm that the proper fax number exists for an entry.**

   Don't worry about filling in all the information about a contact; just the name and fax number are all that's needed for this operation.

10. **Click the OK button to close the contact's Properties dialog box.**

   Back in the Address Book window . . .

11. **Choose the contact from the list of contacts and click the To button.**

   This adds that contact to the recipient list for the fax.

   These Steps (8 through 11) may seem a bit much for just sending a fax, but the idea is to create a database of contacts that you can use again and again. The second time through, it won't be as time consuming.

12. **Click the OK button.**

   The contact's name now appears in the Send Fax Wizard dialog box window, as shown in Figure 11-8. But you're not done yet!

13. **Click the Next button.**

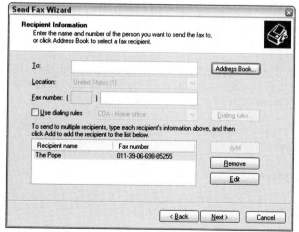

Figure 11-8:
The fax
recipient is
selected.

14. **Mess with a cover template, if you are so inclined.**

    The cover is prefixed to whatever you're sending. Don't worry — you get a chance to preview everything before the fax is sent.

15. **Click the Next button.**

16. **Choose when to send the fax.**

    I'm a Now person myself, but you can elect to send the fax at a specific time.

    Check to ensure that the laptop's system clock matches the time for whatever location you're faxing from. To set the clock, double-click on the time display in the System Tray.

17. **Click the Next button.**

    A summary screen is displayed.

    You can click the Preview Fax button to see what the fax looks like.

18. **Click the Finish button to prepare the fax.**

    The fax is sent according to the time that you scheduled in Step 16.

Lo and behold, when you send a fax, or one is pending, the Fax Monitor window appears, as shown in Figure 11-9.

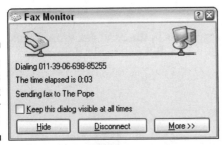

Figure 11-9:
Look ma! It's
the Fax
Monitor
window!

Fax Monitor

Dialing 011-39-06-698-85255
The time elapsed is 0:03
Sending fax to The Pope
☐ Keep this dialog visible at all times

[Hide]   [Disconnect]   [More >>]

You can click the Disconnect or Cancel button to stop the fax. This button changes to read Answer Now so that you can immediately receive an incoming fax. (That's assuming that you know one is coming.)

Clicking the More button displays more detailed information about faxes previously sent or pending.

Click the Hide button to make the Fax Monitor go buh-bye.

Fax Central

To observe all the fast-paced, thrilling fax action as it happens (or even after the fact), you need to visit Fax Central in Windows XP. This is done by opening the Printers and Faxes window. If you're lucky, you'll see a Printers and Faxes icon on the Start menu. Choose it to display the window, and then double-click to open the Fax icon. The Fax Console appears, as shown in Figure 11-10.

You use the Fax Console to review and confirm sent faxes, to receive faxes, and to control pending faxes.

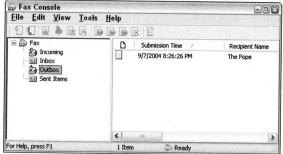

Figure 11-10:
Okay, it's not really called "Fax Central."

Canceling a pending fax

To change your mind and stop a fax from sending, heed these steps:

1. **Open the Fax Console.**

   Refer to Figure 11-10.

2. **Click on the Outbox folder on the left side of the window.**

3. **Select the fax that you want to cancel.**

   It appears on the right side of the window.

4. **Press the Delete key on your keyboard.**

5. **Click the Yes button to zap the fax to kingdom come.**

This trick works best to stop a pending fax. If a fax is in the process of sending, you have to resort to the old-fashioned Unplug the Phone Line technique. Then open the Fax Console and remove any remnants.

Receiving a fax

When you're aware of a looming fax speeding your way, summon the Fax Console (see the earlier section, "Fax Central"). Make sure that the modem is connected. Wait for the ring (if you have another phone attached to the incoming line). Then choose File➪Receive a Fax Now from the menu.

As the fax is being received, the Fax Monitor keeps track of its progress, as shown in Figure 11-11. Sit and wait.

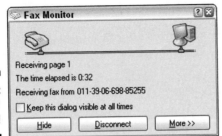

Figure 11-11:
Oh, boy!
A fax!

 After the fax has been received, a pop-up bubble may appear, or you may notice the little Pending Fax Guy in the Notification Area. That's your clue that a fax has come in.

You can also find an incoming fax by viewing the Fax Console. Any fax received appears in the Inbox — just like e-mail. To view the fax, double-click on its icon, or you can select the fax and then click the View button on the toolbar. The fax is displayed in a special window, from which you can print, save, or mess with the fax.

✔ Faxes are received as *image* files. Specifically, they're TIFF images. You cannot edit the files as text documents. Faxes are *images*.

✔ You can also answer an incoming fax by clicking on the Answer Now button in the Fax Monitor window.

 ✔ The Answer toolbar button in the Fax Console can be clicked to answer an incoming fax.

Chapter 12

Online Security

In This Chapter

▶ Using a firewall

▶ Protecting your laptop from viruses

▶ Avoiding virus risks

▶ Understanding spyware

▶ Determining what is and is not spyware

▶ Thwarting the hijacking of your Web browsing

*W*hen those few noble scientists (and Al Gore) sat down years ago to design the Internet, they did not say, "Hey! What can we do to be lax about security so that our invention can induce terror, frustration, and heartache into its millions of users?" No, they probably said, "Hey! This is cool!" You see, unlike on television, scientists in the real world are not evil, and rarely do they go, "Bwaa-ha-ha!"

The Internet was designed to work and to survive a nuclear attack. But because it was designed by well-intentioned, ethical, and honest folks, they didn't anticipate the full impact that humanity and its rabble would inflict upon their innocent invention. Today, the words Internet and Security go together like Nuclear and Terror, Corrupt and Politician, and Hollywood and Vine.

If you're using your laptop as a doorway to the Internet, then be prepared to get a nice, heavy door and some solid, reliable locks. This chapter covers the ins and outs of online security.

Setting Up a Firewall

Keyword: Firewall

What it does: Filters Internet traffic both incoming to your laptop and outgoing from your laptop.

What it protects against: Internet worms and special programs designed to find your laptop, gain control, and use your computer system to carry out evil deeds.

The background: Your computer is actually connected to the Internet in dozens of ways. Each connection is referred to as a *port.* Each of those ports is designed to communicate information in a specific way or for a specific type of program.

The problem with a standard Internet connection is that all the ports are left hanging open. And just like leaving all the windows open in your house, eventually a bad guy is going to come waltzing into the unprotected environment.

Just like a real firewall, a computer firewall either closes off specific ports completely, or it allows computers that you specify to access and use the ports. That's the good news. What's better is that Windows XP comes with firewall software to help protect you. And what's better than that is that you can easily find software from other sources that works even better than Windows XP's firewall.

- ✔ Without a firewall in place, your computer is wide open to attack from any number of nasties on the Internet.

- ✔ No, it is not up to your ISP to protect you from such things.

- ✔ The "survival time" of an unprotected, non-firewalls Windows computer on the Internet averages just 20 minutes. After that time, your laptop *will be* infected and overrun by nasty programs sent from the Internet.

The Windows XP firewall

Windows XP comes with firewall software. The original version of Windows XP had a rather limited firewall; Windows XP Service Pack 2 comes with a more robust firewall, but still one limited in its ability to detect and filter *outgoing* Internet traffic. (A good firewall should filter both incoming and outgoing traffic.)

To adjust the Windows XP Internet Connection Firewall (the one before SP2), dutifully obey these steps:

1. **Open the Network Connections window.**

2. **Right-click on your Internet connection icon.**

   For dial-up networking, click on your connection, or ISP's name. For broadband (DSL or cable), right-click on the LAN or High-Speed Internet connection icon.

3. **Choose Properties from the pop-up menu.**

   A Properties dialog box appears.

4. **Click the Advanced tab in the Properties dialog box (shown in Figure 12-1).**

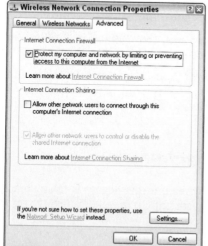

Figure 12-1:
Configure
the firewall
here.

5. **In the Internet Connection Firewall section, select the check box (the only check box).**

   That starts up the firewall.

6. **Click OK to close the Properties dialog box, and then close the Network Connections window as well.**

   You're done.

In Step 5, you could click on the Settings button, but there is really nothing to do there unless you're an advanced user who wants to activate some Internet features on your laptop. People like that probably don't need this book. Then again, those people probably are running Linux on their laptops, anyway.

Things are very similar for setting up a firewall when using Windows XP with the Service Pack 2 installed. After Step 4 (in the preceding step list), there is a Settings button that you click to display the new Windows Firewall dialog box. When you're there, click the On button, then click OK. That sets up everything for you.

While I highly recommend using a firewall, and the Windows XP firewall is better than nothing, it's just not good enough. Please consider using a third-party firewall, such as Zone Lab's Zone Alarm or the Norton or McAfee firewall and Internet security products.

✔ Refer to Chapter 6 for more information on finding the Control Panel as well as the Network Connections window.

✔ See Chapter 10 for Internet connection information.

✔ Zone Alarm is available from www.zonelabs.com. It offers a free version of its firewall for personal use, and I highly recommend it.

✔ You need only one firewall for your computer. Running multiple firewalls merely clogs up the system. So if you opt to use something other than the Windows XP firewall, turn that firewall off.

Monitoring the firewall

An ideal firewall lets you know when Internet access is taking place. This is what Zone Alarm does: It displays a pop-up message alerting you to some program that's attempting to access the Internet.

In Figure 12-2, you see a warning about a program on your computer trying to access the Internet. If this is okay, you can click the Yes button. In this instance, the "Generic Host Process" is something Windows uses to help it resolve a Web address.

How can you tell which programs should be allowed to access the Internet? You can't. You can click the No button, and if your Internet programs don't work, then you know you should click Yes next time. And if you keep clicking Yes, then put a check mark in the Remember This Answer the Next Time I Use This Program check box (see Figure 12-2) so that you're not bothered by that program again. After a few days of that, the firewall should run by itself without bothering you.

If an incoming program tries to access your computer, and you have no idea what it is, then click the No button!

✔ The firewall in Windows XP does not display pop-up warnings about Internet access.

✔ Generally speaking, when you're trying to use the Internet, expect the firewall to alert you. Only after you've trained it should the firewall stop alerting you as much.

✔ It's also possible to set up the firewall so that it permits access to your computer from other computers with a specific IP address — you know, those dotted numbers such as 10.0.0.5. That way, your computer can continue to interact with other computers on your network.

Another major weakness: Internet Explorer

Windows comes with a Web browser called Internet Explorer. If you believe Microsoft's court testimony, then Internet Explorer is an integral part of Windows, like a hand in a glove. But fortunately, it's not a hand you need to use for browsing the Web. Especially given that Internet Explorer carries many security flaws with it, and it is generally behind the curve as far as Web browsers software are concerned.

While uninstalling Internet Explorer may be a task for the über-geeks, you can install and use (and thoroughly enjoy) an alternative Web browser. I can recommend three:

✔ My IE, from www.myie2.com

✔ Opera, from www.opera.com

✔ Mozilla Firefox, from www.mozilla.org

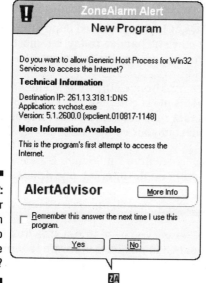

Figure 12-2: Is it okay for this random program to access the Internet?

Setting Up Antivirus Software

Keyword: Antivirus

What it does: Prevents certain malicious programs from infecting your computer.

What it protects against: Viruses, worms, Trojan Horses. These are the names for programs that set up operation on your computer, doing a number of nasty things, such as:

- Destroying random files on your hard drive.
- Storing pornography on your hard drive and using your computer to distribute those images.
- Scanning your hard drive for valuable information, such as passwords, bank account numbers, or credit card numbers.
- Taking over your computer to launch viral attacks on other computers on the Internet.
- Taking over your computer to be used by spammers to spew out bulk e-mail.
- Any number of other nasty, horrible things!

The background: In the olden days, it took an infected floppy disk or CD to give your computer a virus. That may still happen today, but most likely a virus will infect your computer through an e-mail attachment.

What happens is this: You get an e-mail from kindly Aunt Maude with a file attachment. The message says, "This file is cute!" And so you open the attached file, which is a program that runs and may in fact do something cute. But the program has also infected your computer.

The message may or may not have come from kindly Aunt Maude. It most likely came from an infected computer on the Internet, one designed to spread the virus. Aunt Maude's name was picked at random — as was yours — by the virus' ability to replicate itself.

To protect yourself against this scourge, you need to run antivirus software. You need to run it all the time. You need to use this software to protect your computer.

Scanning for viruses

Windows XP doesn't come with its own virus scanner. You have to get a third-party virus scanner, such as the Norton AntiVirus or McAfee's VirusScan. Other antivirus programs to consider as well are

- Avast! Antivirus, www.avast.com
- AVG Anti-Virus, www.grisoft.com
- Kaspersky antivirus protection, www.kaspersky.com

These programs can be used in two ways, actively and passively.

To actively scan for viruses, the antivirus program does a complete scan of memory, then the hard drive, then files on the hard drive. Everything is checked against a database of known viruses.

The passive virus scan is done as files are received into your computer. Each file coming in is individually scanned and then checked against the virus database.

- Antivirus programs typically have a tiny icon sitting in the Notification Area, such as the one for Norton AntiVirus shown in the margin. Double-click that icon to gain access to the antivirus program and control its settings.

- Obviously, each antivirus program does things differently. You'll have to refer to the documentation that came with your antivirus software program to see how things work.

- Generally speaking, I recommend turning off the active virus scan after it's done once. Try to configure your antivirus software so that it scans incoming e-mail, e-mail file attachments, and any downloads you collect from the Internet. That should keep you safe.

- Another tip: Sometimes it helps to have and run *two* antivirus programs. Not at the same time, but perhaps run one first, then shut it down, then run a second antivirus program. The second one may catch some things that the first one misses.

- Yes, some antivirus programs require a paid subscription. You don't pay for the program, but rather for accessing and updating the antivirus database. Believe me, the cost of the subscription is *worth it!* Do not delay in updating your antivirus database!

- The virus database needs frequent updating, which is done by synchronizing the database on your computer with a master database on the Internet.

- Another term for the information in the virus database is a *signature* file. Each virus has its own unique signature, by which various strains and families of viruses are identified.

- Though I'm certain most of the Web-based virus-scanning utilities are legitimate, I would avoid using them. Only if you're darn certain that the software is okay would I tell you to trust it; otherwise, who knows what kind of program you're letting into your computer?

Shutting down your antivirus program

Sometimes, you're asked to turn off your antivirus software. For example, sometimes when you install a new program, it suggests turning off the antivirus software. This helps the installation go smoothly and doesn't alarm the antivirus program, making it believe a new virus and not a new program is being installed.

To temporarily disable your antivirus software, locate its icon in the Notification Area. Right-click the icon and choose a Disable, Exit, or Quit option. That temporarily shuts down the antivirus software, allowing your new software to be installed.

When the software installation is done, restart your computer. That also restarts the antivirus software.

Good advice to help protect you from the viral scourge

Viruses happen to good people, but they also happen to idiots who don't heed good advice, such as:

- Do not open unexpected e-mail file attachments, even if they appear to be from someone you know and trust. If you weren't expecting anything, don't open it!

- Especially avoid any file attachment with the suffix, or filename extensions: BAT, COM, EXE, HTM, HTML, PIF, SCR, VBS.

- A plain text e-mail cannot contain a virus. But there can be a virus in an e-mail signature or attachment!

- Odds are good that if you don't open the attachment and just delete the message, your computer will not be infected.

- If your e-mail program automatically saves e-mail file attachments, then delete them from the folder they're saved in.

- Microsoft's Outlook Express is particularly vulnerable to e-mail viruses. Consider getting an alternative e-mail program, such as Web-based e-mail (see Chapter 13) or another program such as Eudora (www.eudora.com).

- The best protection against nasty programs in e-mail is to use antivirus software.

Running Anti-Spyware Software

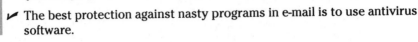

Keyword: Spyware

What it does: Spyware monitors where you go on the Internet, which Web sites you visit, which products you buy.

To fight it: Anti-spyware software removes those programs and tools that are used to monitor your Internet activities. In some cases, anti-spyware software is the only way to fully remove those programs.

The background: Spyware is a relatively new category of evil computer software, also known as *malware*. It sounds innocent: The software monitors your activities on the Internet in order to target you with better, more appropriate advertising. In fact, many people willingly sign up for such a service.

The problem is that spyware is often installed without your permission or knowledge. Often the spyware is disguised as some other program, computer utility, or cute little game. It purports to do one thing, but secretly it's monitoring your Internet activity.

The worse case of spyware consists of programs I can't mention here because the program developers are very litigious. These programs just cannot be uninstalled or removed from your computer. You try, and they come back. Again and again and again. Only by using effective anti-spyware software can you get rid of such nasty pests.

- Your antivirus software may not check for nor remove spyware programs. You may need specific, anti-spyware software.

- Your firewall cannot protect against spyware. That's because you typically invite spyware into your computer (whether you're aware of it or not). The firewall does, however, detect when the spyware uploads its vital information back to its mothership; a good firewall will stop such activity from taking place.

Protecting yourself from spyware

The best way to protect yourself from spyware is to be very, very cautious about what you download from the Internet and which Web pages you visit. Sites that cater to children, to music-swapping fiends, and pornography sites are full of means and devices for delivering spyware directly into your computer. If you can avoid such sites, do so.

In your Web browser, it helps to eliminate third-party cookies from being deposited on your computer. Third-party cookies come from advertisements on Web pages. This type of cookie is often totally unnecessary to using the Web page you're viewing, so it's perfectly acceptable to turn it off.

In Windows, follow these steps to disable third-party cookies for Internet Explorer:

1. **Choose Tools⇨Internet Options.**

   The Internet Options dialog box appears.

2. **Click the Privacy tab.**

3. **Click the Advanced button.**

4. **In the Advanced Privacy Settings dialog box, select the Override Automatic Cookie Handling check box.**

5. **Under First-party Cookies, select the Accept option button.**

6. **Under Third-party Cookies, select the Block option button.**

   See Figure 12-3.

Figure 12-3: The proper anti-spyware setup for Web page cookies.

7. **Select the Always Allow Session Cookies check box.**

8. **Click the OK button and close the various other dialog boxes and windows.**

Blocking third-party cookies helps, but to really fight the spyware plague, you're going to need software help. Keep reading in the next section.

Anti-spyware software

You can find many good anti-spyware programs out there. Heck, you might even have one included with your Internet firewall or antivirus program suite. Be sure to check!

Some free and nearly free programs are available on the Internet to help fight spyware and clean the spyware crud from your laptop. Here are my favorites:

  ✔ Ad-Aware, from www.lavasoft.de

  ✔ Spybot Search & Destroy, from www.safer-networking.org

  ✔ SpywareBlaster, from www.javacoolsoftware.com

Any of these will do the job. They're easy to install and figure out. Download and run one just to see what evil lurks on your laptop's hard drive!

How to tell if something is really spyware

Spyware is pervasive. It's often hard to tell if a well-meaning program is just that or if it is, in fact, spyware in disguise. It also doesn't help that fierce competition occasionally leads companies to accuse rival companies' programs of being spyware simply to discourage sales.

The best way I've found for determining if a program is legitimate or spyware is to visit Google (`www.google.com`) and do a search for the program name and the word "spyware."

The results that Google displays should list some online reviews, commentary and public forum feedback regarding the product. If it's spyware, there will be an overwhelming amount of evidence that it is so. If the program is legitimate, there may be a few queries, but also obvious signs the program in question is not spyware.

Avoiding a Hijack

Keyword: Hijack

What it does: Redirects you from one Web site to another, usually a site that is either offensive, trying to sell you something, or which pops up so many other windows that you can't stop the dang thing!

To fight it: Anti-hijacking software helps restore the Internet to normal operation.

The background: Some people are so desperate for attention that they actively invade your computer and redirect your Web browsing selections from where you want to go, to where they think you need to go. Why some folks feel this is a good way to sell you something is beyond me.

By using antivirus and anti-spyware software, you should be able to avoid a hijacking situation. Some anti-spyware software will even remove the malicious hijacking programs.

For specific software, I can recommend HijackThis, available from `www.spychecker.com`.

Chapter 13

Handy Web Browsing and E-Mail Tips

In This Chapter

▶ Saving Web pages to your hard drive

▶ Reading e-mail on the road

▶ Using Web-based e-mail

▶ Forwarding e-mail to another account

▶ Saving time reading e-mail on the road

▶ Disabling automatic connections

▶ Leaving e-mail on the server

▶ Skipping large messages

*L*ife is so much better today for the laptop-toting human than it was in years past. For example, this book lacks a chapter on how to disassemble a telephone wall jack and use spare wires, clamps, and a pair of tweezers to hack into a hotel's computer unfriendly phone system. (I've done that.) Most of the places you'll tote your laptop today are very friendly and forgiving to your circumstances.

Despite all the well-wishing, there may be times when you have to get on the Internet, specifically to access vital e-mail, when you're working from battery power. In those cases, it helps to be swift and efficient. Therefore, I gathered a bunch of swift and efficient Internet tips and tricks and stuffed them into this chapter — for those rare times when Internet access is necessary and timing is critical.

This goes without saying: If you're using Windows XP on a laptop with today's Internet, you're a fool if you don't use antivirus software and make sure that it's regularly updated. Refer to Chapter 12 for more information about antivirus software and online security.

Web Browsing When You're Out and About

I have only one suggestion for Web browsing on the road, especially if you're away from an Internet connection for some time (such as on an airplane): *Save your Web pages!*

For example, before you go, leaving behind your beloved high-speed Internet connection, go to a few of your favorite Web pages and quickly browse around. As you do, save those Web pages to your hard drive for offline reading while you're away.

The only furry thing you get into when saving a Web page is to properly choose which format to save. After choosing File➪Save As from Internet Explorer's menu, you notice four options for the Save As Type, shown in Figure 13-1.

- ✔ **Web Page, Complete (*.htm, *.html):** This option saves everything on the Web page, including graphics, sounds, and fun stuff like that. It takes up quite a bit of hard drive space, creating a special folder to hold all the graphics and non-text items referenced by the Web page.

- ✔ **Web Archive, Single File (*.mht):** This option saves the Web page itself, but uses the Internet storage cache to supply the images. This method takes up the least amount of hard drive space, and I recommend it, especially for reading.

- ✔ **Web Page, HTML Only (*.htm, *.html):** This option saves only the bare Web page; that is, just the text — no graphics or multimedia. Not recommended for offline reading.

- ✔ **Text File (*.txt):** This option saves the Web page for editing purposes that don't apply here.

So choose the Web Archive, Single File option for reading. Only if the Web page has graphics you want to peruse later should you choose Web Page, Complete.

- ✔ Go through your regular Web page perusing schedule. Don't stop to read! Just choose File➪Save As and collect those Web pages on your hard drive for offline reading.

- ✔ You can open any saved Web page just as you open any other file on your hard drive. The Web page opens in your Web browser, and you can read it just as you would on the Web.

✔ None of the links on the Web page you save will be active. Only when you reconnect to the Internet does clicking on the links actually lead somewhere.

✔ If you use the Web Page, Complete option, then some of the images may not appear on the Web page.

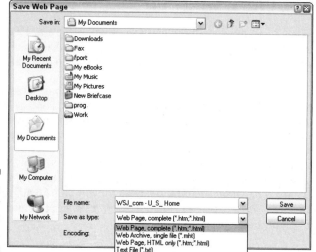

Figure 13-1:
Options for
saving a
Web page.

E-Mail Away from Home

Picking up e-mail on a laptop is not problem — until you start to think about it. After all, you're one person. You may have one or more e-mail accounts, but now you're stirring into the mix an extra computer — your laptop. That brings up a multitude of questions, many of which are answered in the sections that follow.

Accessing e-mail on the road

Picking up your e-mail on the road works exactly like picking it up from the desktop computer. You configure your e-mail program. You connect to the Internet. *Voilà!* You have e-mail!

✔ Refer to Chapter 10 for more information on your laptop and the e-mail connection.

✔ Your laptop picks up e-mail just like the desktop system.

> ✔ Refer to Chapter 11 for information on using a modem in strange and wonderful places away from home.

> ✔ If you need to dial into your ISP directly, then check to see if it has a toll-free number.

Reading your e-mail on the Web

Normally, you pick up your e-mail by using an e-mail program. That program, such as Outlook Express, connects to your ISP's mail server, which then divvies up any pending e-mail. But there is another way to do e-mail: the Web.

Before you leave, check to see if your ISP has a Web page-based e-mail system. This isn't the same as getting a Web-based e-mail account, such as a Yahoo! or Hotmail account (covered in the next section). Instead, it's merely an alternative way to check your e-mail when accessing the ISP's e-mail server directly isn't possible (or incurs an extra expense).

In Figure 13-2, you see my own ISP's preview and pickup page. After logging into this Web page, I can see all e-mail pending for me. (It's all spam in Figure 13-2.) I can click on a message to read it, click on a link to view an attachment, or just delete the messages.

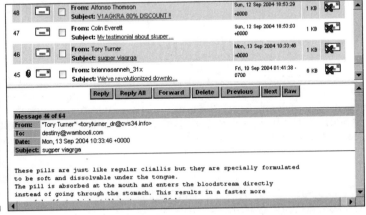

Figure 13-2:
An ISP's Web-based e-mail preview and pickup page.

Note that any mail you do not delete remains on the ISP's server for later pickup. That can be handy if you would rather wait until you're back at the desktop computer to pick up some e-mail.

> ✔ Be sure to check with your ISP to see if this type of service is available.

> ✔ Some national ISPs, such as AOL, offer a Web-page system for picking up and previewing e-mail.

Getting a Web-based e-mail account

You can find many free Web-based e-mail services that you can subscribe to. By creating a free Web-based e-mail account, you can access your e-mail anywhere you have Internet access.

For example, you can get a free account on Yahoo! Mail and either tell everyone to send your mail to that account when you're on the road, or you can have your regular mail forwarded to that account. (Forwarding e-mail is covered later in this chapter.)

Some people even use their Web-based e-mail account as their main account and keep their main account secret or for private e-mail. That way, the main account remains relatively spam-free. And when the public Web-based e-mail account becomes overwhelmed with spam, it can be discarded and a new free Web-based e-mail service used.

✔ You can access Web-based e-mail from any computer that has Internet access. You have nothing further to set up.

✔ Unlike e-mail software you must run on your computer, Web-based e-mail stays on the Web until you delete it. That way, you can keep messages in your Web e-mail inbox and have them still waiting there when you return home and use your desktop computer.

✔ Web-based e-mail is available from the following providers. This is by no means a complete list:

```
http://mail.yahoo.com

www.hotmail.com

http://mail.myway.com

http://gmail.google.com
```

✔ Most of those free, Web-based e-mail accounts have a size limit. You have to occasionally delete your old e-mail to keep the account from filling up.

Accessing your e-mail from a friend's computer

I don't think Miss Manners covers this at all. What do you do when you're visiting friends or relatives and the urge to check your e-mail hits you?

If you have a laptop, and your friends or relatives have their own network, then it's easy to hook into their network and use your laptop that way. (And that's assuming that they're open to the idea.)

They may offer to set up a personal account for you on their computer. That's nice, and a good thing to do for security reasons. But all you really need in order to pick up your e-mail is a computer with Internet access. Then you can use your ISP's Web-based e-mail system to peruse your mail, or visit any mail waiting for you on a Web-based e-mail system (Hotmail, Yahoo!, and so on).

- ✔ I do not recommend setting up your own e-mail account on a friend's or relative's computer. It's just too much of a security risk.

- ✔ The very best option is to pray that your friends or relatives have a wireless connection, and then use your laptop's wireless network adapter to hook into their network for full Internet access.

- ✔ If Internet access is disallowed, then keep in mind that you still have the library as an option. There are also cybercafés and coffee houses with wireless access that you could consider.

Forwarding your e-mail

E-mail servers have the option of forwarding all incoming e-mail if you know that you're going to be away for a while and would like to pick up your e-mail at another address. This is known as e-mail forwarding, and your ISP may offer it as a free service, or your company or business may have it available as a feature.

For example, if you know you're going to be out for three weeks, you could have your e-mail forwarded to your Web-based e-mail account for that time. Any e-mail coming into your regular account is immediately redirected to that other account. That way, you don't miss a thing.

There is, sadly, a problem with forwarding your e-mail, which is why you may not find it available as an option. Occasionally, e-mail gets stuck in the space-time continuum, in what's specifically called an endlessly forwarding loop. Your mail gets forwarded to you, which then reforwards the mail back to you, which then repeats the process. Eventually the system becomes clogged with e-mail, and when the IT guys figure things out, they just delete your e-mail account to fix things. That's bad.

So if e-mail forwarding is an option, look into it. But be careful to ensure that e-mail is being forwarded to a real account and not just lost in a loop. In, fact, test things by forwarding all your e-mail a day or so before you're set to leave so that you can ensure everything works.

And don't forget to stop forwarding your e-mail when you return.

A forwarding mail rule for Outlook Express

Mail Rules are a special way to control and manage the e-mail received in Outlook Express. (Other e-mail programs may call them *filters* or *procedures.*) Folks craft various Mail Rules to organize their e-mail, flag specific messages, or to help eliminate the scourge of spam. Another way you can use a Mail Rule is to help forward your incoming e-mail to another mailbox. This is shown in Figure 13-3.

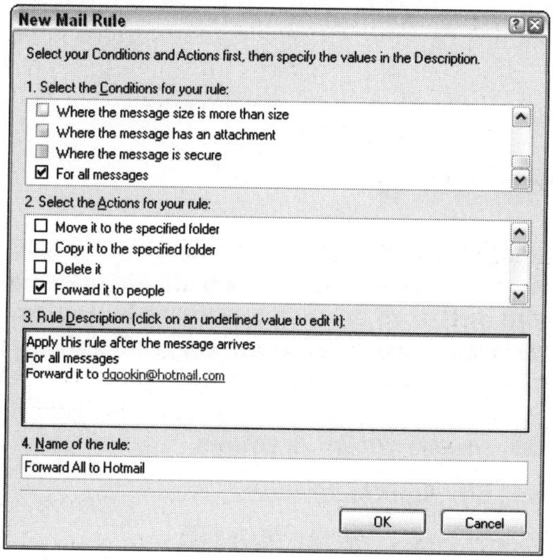

New Mail Rule

Select your Conditions and Actions first, then specify the values in the Description.

1. Select the Conditions for your rule:
   - ☐ Where the message size is more than size
   - ☐ Where the message has an attachment
   - ☐ Where the message is secure
   - ☑ For all messages

2. Select the Actions for your rule:
   - ☐ Move it to the specified folder
   - ☐ Copy it to the specified folder
   - ☐ Delete it
   - ☑ Forward it to people

3. Rule Description (click on an underlined value to edit it):

   Apply this rule after the message arrives
   For all messages
   Forward it to dgookin@hotmail.com

4. Name of the rule:

   Forward All to Hotmail

   [OK]   [Cancel]

Figure 13-3:
A mail rule for forwarding your messages.

To set things up in Outlook Express, choose Tools⇨Message Rules⇨Mail. Then fill in the dialog box as shown in Figure 13-3, though be sure to enter the real e-mail address to forward your messages in Step 3. (Note that the Hotmail address in Figure 13-3 is bogus.)

Give the rule a notable name, such as "Forward All to Hotmail" as shown in Figure 13-3. Click OK when you're done. Then close the New Mail Rule dialog box.

✔ Similar rules and filters can be set up or configured for other e-mail programs.

✔ Your computer must be on, the mail program running, and it must regularly check for mail so that the mail rule works.

✔ You may want to make more complex rules which, for example, do not allow for the forwarding of spam or other unwanted e-mail.

E-Mail Options Worthy of Consideration

Deep within the bosom of your e-mail program lies many complex and puzzling options. The reasons for these options may seem obscure or unnecessary — until you understand how they can be used, and specifically how those options can be an advantage to the laptop user away from home or desperately low on battery juice.

The following sections cover some of those strange e-mail options that have a rightful purpose and place for the laptop on the road. Note that this information is specific to Outlook Express. Other e-mail programs have similar features.

Omit your password

Having Windows remember your Internet and e-mail passwords is handy for a desktop — a desktop in a secure location or one with adequate password protection. But even with password protection on your laptop, do you really want your e-mail password to be kept inside the computer? If not, here is how to suppress it if you're using Outlook Express:

1. **In Outlook Express, choose Tools⇨Accounts.**

   The Accounts dialog box reports for duty.

2. **In the Accounts dialog box, click the Mail tab.**

3. **Click to select your ISP's mail server in the list.**

   If more than one server is listed, you'll have to repeat Steps 4 through 7 for each of the ISPs.

4. **Click the Properties button.**

   Your ISP's e-mail connection Properties dialog box appears.

5. **Click the Servers tab.**

6. **Erase your password from the Password text box and deselect the Remember Password check box.**

   See Figure 13-4.

7. **Click OK to make the change.**

8. **Click the Close button to dismiss the Internet Accounts window.**

Note that by removing your e-mail password, you will be prompted for it each time you go to pick up e-mail. A dialog box appears. Just enter your password, and then you can pick up your mail.

Also refer to Chapter 17, which covers laptop security in more detail.

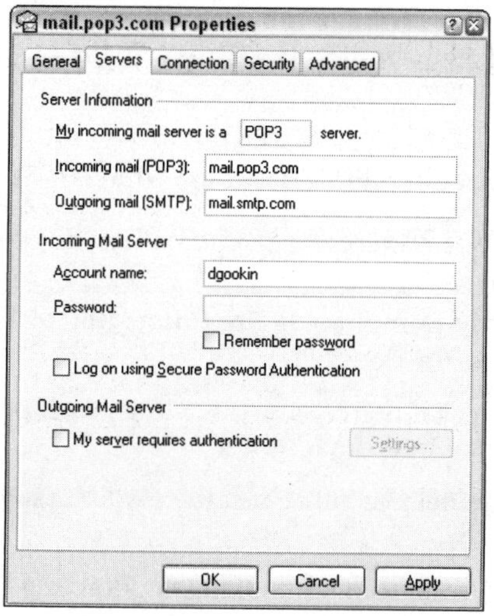

Figure 13-4:
Removing
your
password
from the
Internet
e-mail
account.

Disconnect after picking up e-mail

You don't need to be connected to the Internet while you read your e-mail. Especially given how much power the modem draws, I recommend having your e-mail program immediately hang up (or disconnect) after sending or receiving e-mail. Here's where to check those settings in Outlook Express:

1. **Choose Tools⇨Options.**

   The Options dialog box duly appears.

2. **Click the Connection tab in the Options dialog box.**

3. **Select the Hang Up after Sending and Receiving check box.**

4. **Click OK.**

You might also want to disable automatic checking, as covered in the next section.

Disabling automatic checking

When you're connected to the Internet all the time, especially at the office, you probably have your e-mail program configured to check for new messages every so often. On a laptop, however, that may mean that you're faced with a sudden panic as you realize that your computer is, once again, dialing out of the hotel during peak hours to pick up new e-mail.

Rather than having to worry about skillfully removing the phone card, just disable the automatic mail checking feature. Here's how it goes:

1. **Choose Tools⇨Options.**

2. **In the Options dialog box, click the General tab (if needed).**

3. **Un-check the Check for New Messages Every [blank] Minutes check box.**

4. **(Optionally) From the If My Computer Is Not Connected at This Time drop-down list, choose Do Not Connect.**

   Setting this option ensures that merely starting your e-mail program doesn't cause it to try to dial into the Internet.

5. **(Optionally optional) Deselect the Send and Receive Messages at Startup check box.**

   This prevents Outlook Express from immediately contacting the Internet when you first start the program. That way, you can read pending messages and then connect with the Internet when you're ready to.

6. **Click OK.**

 To connect with the Internet and send or receive messages, click the Send/Recv button, or use the keyboard shortcut Ctrl+M.

Sending everything in one batch

As you peruse your e-mail, you read messages, reply to messages, and then click the Send button to send those messages. But rather than cause your e-mail program to dial-in, connect, send, then disconnect over and over, I recommend sending all your e-mail messages at once in a single batch. To do this, you tell Outlook Express to queue the messages as opposed to sending them individually. Here's the lowdown:

1. **Choose Tools⇨Options.**

2. **In the Options dialog box, click the Send tab.**

3. **Deselect the Send Messages Immediately check box.**

4. **Click OK.**

The messages will now sit in the Outbox and wait until you connect again.

To pick up or leave on server

When I leave for a conference or on vacation, I typically lie and tell people that I will not be checking e-mail. That sort of keeps away most of the trivial messages, but occasionally something important floats in. So I want to check my e-mail, but I still want to keep it all available for the desktop computer when I get home.

Rather than try to coordinate incoming e-mail between my laptop and desktop, I use a different solution: I keep all my e-mail on the ISP's e-mail server. That way, I can read my e-mail, respond if necessary, and then trust that the same e-mail will be waiting for me when I return.

Here is how to set up the "leave on server" e-mail option for Outlook Express:

1. **Choose Tools⇨Accounts.**

2. **Click the Mail tab in the Internet Accounts dialog box.**

3. **Choose your ISP's mail server from the list, then click the Properties button.**

4. **In the Properties dialog box, click the Advanced tab.**

5. **Select the Leave a Copy of Message on Server check box.**

   That way, even after you've picked up your e-mail on the road, it's still available for pickup from the server later.

6. **(Optional) Select the Remove from Server when Deleted from 'Deleted Items' check box.**

   That way, if I answer and delete a message, it's also deleted and won't appear again later when I pick up my mail back at the office.

7. **Click OK, and then close the Internet Accounts dialog box as well.**

For me, this solution solves the problem of wanting to receive important e-mail on two different computers — and without the bother of trying to coordinate Inbox files at a later date.

   ✔ As an alternative to this approach, consider using Web-based e-mail instead. That way, you can continue to read all your e-mail at home or away without worrying about coordinating e-mail between a desktop and laptop system.

   ✔ Do be aware that your ISP may have a size limit on what can be stored in your inbox. I used this exact technique on a protracted vacation once, only to discover that after 14 days, my e-mail account was full and all new incoming mail was being rejected. The solution there is just to pick up and deal with your e-mail when you're away and not bother leaving it on the server.

   ✔ You just can't escape technology!

Skip messages over a given size

If your remote e-mail connection must be made over the modem, then you probably don't want to waste time downloading those huge files. For example, a 500K e-mail attachment may take a blink of an eye to receive at your office, where high-speed Internet is the norm. But on the road with a lousy 28.8K connection at the Dubuque Motel 3 1/2, it just won't cut it.

Some e-mail programs have a settings option that lets you skip over e-mail of a given size. For example, in Eudora, the message text is downloaded, but the attachment isn't; you're alerted to the presence of the large attachment and given the option whether to download it now or later.

In Outlook Express, you must create a Mail Rule to specifically skip over messages of a certain size. Here are the steps to take:

1. **Choose Tools⇨Message Rules⇨Mail.**

   A New Message Rule window appears.

2. **In area 1, scroll through the list and select the Where the Message Size Is More Than Size check box.**

3. **In area 3, click on the word Size.**

4. **Enter a size in kilobytes (KB).**

   Short files seem to be okay, and I often expect files in the 70KB to 120KB range. So I set the value at 200KB.

5. **Click OK.**

6. **In area 2, choose the Do Not Download It from the Server option.**

7. **In area 4, name the rule something descriptive, such as, "Skip 200KB messages."**

8. **Click OK to create the rule.**

9. **Click OK to close the other dialog box as well.**

The sad part about this approach is that you'll never know that any huge messages are pending for you. When you return to the desktop, or any e-mail system that lacks the "Skip 200KB messages" (or similar) rule, then you'll discover and download the big messages. (Unlike Eudora, Outlook Express doesn't let you know that the big message is pending and give you the option of downloading it.)

Chapter 14

The Desktop-Laptop Connection

. . . .

In This Chapter

▶ Getting your laptop and desktop connected

▶ Using a direct connection

▶ Keeping files up to date between desktop and laptop

▶ Using the Briefcase

▶ Synchronizing files with Briefcase

▶ Accessing the desktop remotely

. . . .

*I*f you're a laptop junkie and you don't have a desktop computer, then this chapter doesn't apply to you. You live and breathe and play on your unbound laptop. Take it with you anywhere, and all your stuff is with you. But when your primary computer is a desktop and you're only an occasional road warrior, you most likely want your laptop to be the portable extension of your desktop. That means you have to do one of the most complex, involved, and technical operations in all of computing: Getting two computers to talk with each other.

This chapter is about the desktop-to-laptop connection. It's getting your desktop and laptop computers connected so that information can be exchanged and shared. This chapter covers the connection as well as the sharing part.

Connecting Desktop and Laptop

Exchanging files between two computers is as old as computers are themselves. It can be done with wires, but also by using disks. The term *sneaker net* once referred to folks exchanging files by using floppy disks and walking (in their sneakers) from one computer to another.

Floppy disks (and CD-Rs) can still be used to exchange information from two computers — provided that the two still use floppy disks. Oh, you can *burn* a CD-R and use it for exchanging files between your desktop and laptop. But — hey folks! — this is the 21st century. The real way to connect your desktop and laptop is by using wires. Or if you're really slick, wirelessly! The following sections explain how.

The easy way: Over the network

The simplest way to connect between laptop and desktop is to place them both on the same network. Configured and connected properly, you can share and access either the desktop or laptop's hard drive to easily exchange files and whatnot.

✔ This is the preferred way to connect two systems together. Even if all you have is a desktop and a laptop, I highly recommend getting networking hardware to make connecting the two a snap.

✔ Refer to Chapter 9 for more information on networking your desktop and laptop, both with and without wires.

That ugly wire thing

Before a networking standard appeared, computer users would connect their desktop and laptop computers by using both systems' serial or parallel ports. To accomplish this, an ugly wire cable was used, similar to what's shown in Figure 14-1.

The ugly wire cable has both serial and parallel (printer) port connections on both ends, providing for a variety of ways to connect a desktop and laptop system.

Merely connecting the two computers isn't enough, however; you also need software to help make the connection happen. The software comes in two parts, one for the laptop and another for the desktop. Both parts must be running simultaneously for the dang thing to work. Refer to the section, "Toiling with Windows Direct Connection," later in this chapter, for more information.

✔ You need software to drive the ugly wire thing connection. See the next section.

✔ Printer port = parallel port. It might also be called the LPT or PRN port.

✔ Serial port = RS-232C port (though it's not really the RS-232C port any-more, the old term lingers).

✔ Between the serial and parallel connections, the parallel one is faster.

✔ Some cables are serial-to-serial only, which may seem confusing because they have both 25-pin and 8-pin connectors (as shown in Figure 14-1). So if you want a parallel-to-parallel connector, be sure to read the label.

✔ Your laptop may not have a serial port. See Chapter 5. If the laptop lacks a serial port, get a port replicator.

✔ Not any old cable will work for a direct connection. I recommend buying a cable setup designed specifically for connecting two computers, such as the one shown in Figure 14-1. A standard printer or serial cable just won't work.

✔ Yes, the cable type must be considered a *null modem*.

✔ The old NEC UltraLite (see Figure 1-6 in Chapter 1) lacked a floppy drive, but it had a serial port. It was through that port and a cable that the system was connected to a desktop for exchanging files. (This was years before Ethernet became a networking standard.)

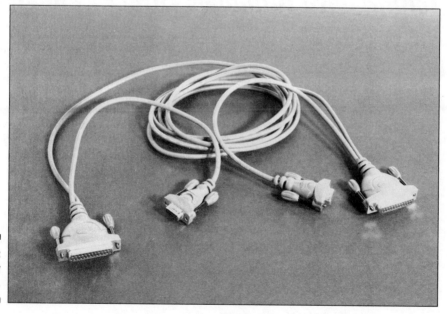

Figure 14-1:
The ugly
cable thing.

Using the infrared port

If both desktop and laptop have an infrared (IR) port (which is doubtful, but I have to write about it anyway), you can use that port to beam information between the two systems.

The best thing to do is to orient the laptop and desktop so that the IR ports are doing a Mexican Standoff with each other, eye-to-eye as it were. That way nothing comes between them to break the connection.

✔ Refer to the next section, "Toiling with Windows Direct Connection," for more information on completing this setup.

✔ I know of hardly any desktops with an IR connection, though it's not unheard of. I think a few IBM models sport that feature.

✔ Ensure that the IR port is enabled before you proceed. Check with Chapter 17 for more information. (Chapter 17 covers laptop security, and an enabled IR port is considered a security risk. Though enabling the IR port for this type of file transfer is okay.)

Toiling with Windows Direct Connection

If you're connecting your desktop and laptop by using serial or parallel ports, or the infrared port, then you need to configure Windows for a direct connection. That sounds well and good, but in practice it's not that easy to set up and even harder to get going. So if you have the stamina for it, here are the steps to take. First comes the desktop computer:

1. **Open the Control Panel's Networking Connections icon.**

   This displays other Network Connections window.

2. **Click the Create a New Connection task over in the Network Tasks part of the window (on the left).**

   Or you can choose File➪New Connection.

   The New Connection Wizard rears its boring head.

3. **Click the Next button.**

4. **Choose the Set Up an Advanced Connection option.**

   Why this is considered "advanced" is beyond me.

5. **Click the Next button.**

6. **Choose Connect Directly to Another Computer.**

7. **Click the Next button.**

8. **On the desktop computer, choose Host. On the laptop computer, choose Guest.**

   It doesn't matter which is which, but one computer must be the host and the other the guest.

9. **Click the Next button.**

   The remainder of the rules here apply to the Host computer. The steps for the Guest computer appear later in this section.

10. **From the drop-down list, choose the port you're using to connect.**

    This depends on the cable, but also on which ports are available. Be sure to choose the right one! Most desktop systems have two serial ports, labeled COM1 and COM2.

    Note that this is also how you set up the infrared connection by choosing that port from the drop-down list.

11. **Click the Next button.**

12. **Choose the user(s) allowed access to your computer.**

    Select the login name from the list.

13. **Click the Next button.**

14. **Click the Finish button.**

    A new icon appears in the Network Connections window. For the Host computer, the icon is named Incoming Connections.

After completing these steps for the Host computer, you must do the same on the Guest computer. Here goes:

1. **Complete Steps 1 through 9 in the preceding list, and then continue to Step 2 in this list.**

2. **Type in a name for this connection, such as** Desktop.

   This is merely the name applied to the icon that appears in the Network Connections window. For example, you could give the icon the same name as the desktop computer.

3. **Click the Next button.**

4. **Choose the port you're using to connect to the desktop computer.**

   Serial ports are labeled COM1 and COM1, the parallel (printer) port is LPT1. The infrared connection, if available, can also be chosen from the list. Choose the port that you'll be using based on the way that you're connecting the two systems.

5. **Click the Next button.**

6. **Click the Finish button.**

   Well . . . you really aren't finished yet.

7. **Click the Cancel button to close the Connect Desktop dialog box.**

Windows is eagerly jumping the gun here. Anyway, the connection icon appears in the Network Connections window. Now you're ready to run through a direct connection.

When both computers are configured, you can then connect them. Plug in the connecting cable to the proper ports. Then to make the connection from the laptop, double-click the desktop computer's connection icon in the Network Connections window. (The *guest* connects to the *host.*)

Fill in the Connect dialog box with your account name and password for the desktop computer. Click the Connect button. The desktop computer should answer and create the connection. After it's set, the two computers are "networked," and you can use standard networking methods to access each system's resources. (Refer to Chapter 9.)

To disconnect the guest machine, you can revisit the Network Connections window, right-click the connection icon, and choose Disconnect. Or you can just rip out the cord, though I think the computer enjoys itself more when you disconnect properly.

And now the bad news: This doesn't work as best as it could. The chances of making a successful connection are iffy at best. A few third-party programs are available, such as PC Anywhere, and they can do a better job. (Some programs even come with their own cables.) But there are just so many variables and adjustments necessary to make Windows Direct Connection workable that it can be a nightmare.

✔ When the direct connection has been established, the Host computer displays an icon indicating the guest's connection, as shown in the margin.

✔ Any other network connections the Host computer has will also be shared with the Guest computer.

✔ Note that regular Ethernet networking is about a jillion times faster than direct connection. Don't be surprised when you discover this is a slow way to keep your laptop updated.

✔ If you've tried and this really doesn't work, then I highly recommend you avoid the frustration of troubleshooting the connection and instead get the Ethernet cable and network your desktop and laptop PCs the "real" way.

✔ Chapter 9 discusses setting up an Ethernet connection as well as how to share resources, such as folders and printers, between two networked computers.

Synchronizing Files between the Desktop and the Laptop

After the desktop-to-laptop connection is made, the next step is most likely some type of file transfer. Specifically, what you want to do is synchronize the files between your laptop and desktop system.

For example, you may want to carry with your laptop some files to work on while you're away. When you return back to the desktop, you want to ensure that only those files you worked on are updated on both computers. How can you tell?

Never mind! Let the computer do the work, thanks to the handy *Briefcase*. The following sections cover the details.

Creating a Briefcase

To make a Briefcase, the starting point for sharing files between two computers, open any folder window on your desktop computer. For example, open the My Documents window.

 Choose File⇨New⇨Briefcase. The Briefcase icon appears, named New Briefcase. That's all you need to do.

To use the Briefcase, refer to the next section.

- ✔ Only one Briefcase icon needs to be created on your desktop computer. Later sections in this chapter tell how to get that desktop Briefcase onto your laptop, but you do not need to create a Briefcase icon on your laptop using the steps described in this section.

- ✔ The Briefcase works kind of like a folder, but it's not really a folder. It's a storage unit you can use to shuttle files between two computers.

- ✔ Feel free to rename the Briefcase icon if you wish. Click the icon to select it, press the F2 key, and then type in a new name.

- ✔ Renaming the Briefcase icon is a nifty idea if, for example, you have two laptops. Create two Briefcase icons and name each of them after your two laptops.

- ✔ Refer to Chapter 6 for information on finding the My Documents window.

- ✔ In older versions of Windows, the Briefcase was one of the standard desktop icons. In Windows XP, it's no longer standard, and you can place it in any location you want (not always the desktop).

Populating the Briefcase with stuff

After you have created a Briefcase, the next step is to copy over to it those files and folders and documents you want to take with you on the laptop.

You add anything to the Briefcase just as you would copy files in Windows: You can drag the icons to the Briefcase icon. You can copy the files, and then open the Briefcase icon and paste things in. Or you can use any of the other 4,999 ways to copy files in Windows.

The Briefcase folder itself holds duplicates of the files you copy into it, listing the file's original location and its status, as shown in Figure 14-2.

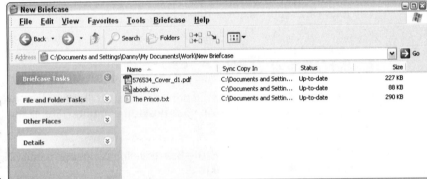

Figure 14-2:
The New
Briefcase
window.

 If a file has been changed after sitting in the Briefcase, you see the text "Needs updating" appear in the status column. That means the file's copy out on the hard drive has changed. To update the file, select it, and then click the Update Selection button on the toolbar. Obey the instructions on the screen.

Close the Briefcase window when you're done with it.

After filling the Briefcase with files and stuff you want on your laptop, the next step is to copy the Briefcase file over to your laptop. That's covered in the next section.

✔ Only copies of files are kept in the Briefcase.

✔ When you open the Briefcase folder, you may see a Welcome to Windows Briefcase window displayed. I have no idea how to stop that, but clicking the Finish button does make it go away.

Moving the Briefcase over to the laptop

To take those files from your desktop to your laptop, you need to move the Briefcase icon from one computer to the other.

 First, check the list of all the files in the Briefcase to ensure that they're up to date. You can do this quickly by opening the Briefcase and clicking on the Update All button. That will tell you if anything needs updating or not.

Second, connect your laptop and desktop. Various methods for this are covered in the earlier sections in this chapter. (I still say networking is the best.)

Third, ensure that your laptop has a shared folder, one that allows you both read and write access. I share a Work folder in the My Document folder on my laptop. The Work folder is specifically for sharing Briefcase icons.

Fourth, drag the Briefcase icon to the shared folder on your laptop. Or you can copy and paste, or otherwise copy the Briefcase icon over.

Note that this is actually a *move* operation; the Briefcase is moved entirely over to the laptop computer; it's icon and files are no longer available on the desktop system. But that's exactly what you want.

 If you already have a Briefcase on your laptop computer, it must have a different name than the Briefcase you're moving in. Yet another good reason to rename your New Briefcase folders.

Using Briefcase files on your laptop

With the Briefcase icon, and all its contents, copied over to the laptop, you're now ready to go on the road and continue working on your files.

Keep the files in your Briefcase icon. Just open them as you would any other files, saving them back to the Briefcase.

And any new files you create, put them in the Briefcase icon/folder as well.

Synchronizing the files

When you return with your laptop and modified files, you need to synchronize things between your desktop and laptop systems. You want to ensure that those files you modified on your laptop are now modified on the desktop system as well.

First, connect the laptop to the desktop.

Second, copy the Briefcase from the laptop to the desktop. Just use the reverse procedures for when you originally moved the Briefcase to the laptop. Note again that this actually *moves* the Briefcase from one computer to the other, moving all the files along with it.

 Third, open the Briefcase on your desktop. To update any files you changed or modified on your laptop, click the Update All button. Use the Update dialog box to preview which files need to be updated or changed.

Close the Briefcase window when you're done.

- ✔ Any new files added in the Briefcase must be manually copied from that folder to another folder on the desktop. You'll notice that these new files are flagged as "Unchanged in Briefcase."
- ✔ Deleting files in the Briefcase folder does not affect the originals elsewhere on your hard drive.

Accessing the Desktop from Elsewhere

One final desktop-laptop trick is something really amazing: The ability to access your desktop computer from your laptop (or any other computer) and use it just as if you were sitting at the desktop computer in person.

 This type of remote access is really something, but it's also really a security risk. Do you really want every creep on the Internet using your desktop? It may happen! Therefore, I strongly advise that you try the following tricks only with a well-established firewall in place, specifically one designed only to let in your laptop and not any other computer system. (This may take the abilities of a computer security expert to set up, but that's good. This is not something to try lightly.)

Avoiding Windows XP Remote Desktop

Windows XP comes with a Remote Desktop feature, one that allows you to connect to your computer from another computer on the network (or over a direct connection), or another computer system on the Internet. Sounds nifty. And when it works, it can be fun.

Golly by gosh, the Windows Remote Desktop feature is truly a royal pain to configure. I counted over 50 odd steps when I did it and, honestly, between Windows Remote Desktop and the VNC program, covered in the next section, it just isn't a contest. I don't want to waste your time: Use RealVNC as covered next.

Real Virtual Network Computing

A fine company in the U.K. called RealVNC produces a free product that lets you access and use your computer from any other location on the Internet. Yes, again, the product is free. It's easy to install and use, beating the pants off of Windows Remote Desktop. Here's the low-down:

Go to the Web page at www.realvnc.com. Read a bit about virtual network computing (VNC), and then download the viewer for your laptop, and both the viewer and server for your desktop.

The viewer doesn't require any installation; you simply run the program.

The server requires a bit of installation, but it's cinchy to follow the instructions on the screen.

 To set things up on the server, right-click on the VNC icon in the Notification Area. This displays the VNC Server Properties (Service-Mode) dialog box. In the Authentication tab, select the VNC 3.3 Authentication, No Encryption option. Then click the Set Password button to choose a system password.

If you know the IP address from which you'll be connecting to the desktop, enter it in the Connections tab, as shown in Figure 14-3. In the Access Control area, click the Add button, and then enter the IP address. That limits access to your desktop from only that IP address. (Further, you need to modify the Internet firewall protecting the desktop computer to allow access through port 5900. It's best to have an expert help you set this up.)

Click the OK button to close the dialog box when you're done.

To make the connection, run the viewer program on your laptop. In the dialog box that appears, enter the network name or IP address of your desktop computer, and then click the OK button. Enter the proper password, and the other computer's desktop appears in a window on your screen, similar to what's shown in Figure 14-4.

When you move the mouse on the laptop, the mouse moves on the desktop. Open a window. Run a program. What you see on the laptop is happening over the network on the desktop.

Figure 14-3:
Only IP
address
123.45.67.0
can access
this
computer
remotely.

When you're done, just close the other computer's window on your laptop. That breaks the connection.

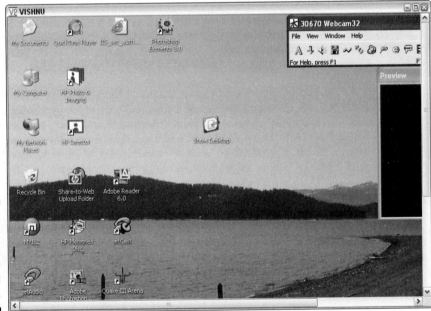

Figure 14-4:
Another
computer's
desktop
appears in
a window.

Firewall advice

I do not recommend that you leave your computer wide open for full access over the Internet. Even without running a remote desktop, your Windows XP desktop computer is one of the most vulnerable computer systems on the Internet. You need protection! Get a firewall!

Firewalls don't just block all incoming traffic. They can, when configured properly, allow in specific types of traffic. For example, to use virtual network computing (VNC), you can tell your firewall to allow all traffic in through port 5900 (which is what VNC uses). If you're using a router or central firewall for a network, you can direct all traffic through port 5900 to a specific computer on the network. And if you know the IP address of the remote system, you can even configure the firewall to only allow traffic from that IP address into port 5900 on the local computer.

Is this driving you nuts? That's why there are network security experts who can help you set up and configure a firewall, which is what I recommend. Never leave your computer open for attack. So if you're in doubt about any of this, do not use remote access.

Part IV
On the Road Again

In this part . . .

For me, one of the sheer joys of having a laptop is knowing that when I'm utterly sick of my surroundings, I can make them change in a blink. Sure, I've used a laptop on an airplane — and even done real work up there! I've used my laptop in coffee houses, diners, midnight cafés, parks, in my car, at the library, and even when I was pulling technical duties in the local theater and it was 90 minutes between light cues. Laptops can go anywhere.

If you haven't yet hit the road with your laptop, then it's high time that you do! This chapter covers lots of on-the-road topics in several nifty little chapters. Read them. Enjoy them. And take your laptop on the road!

Chapter 15

Before You Hit the Road

In This Chapter

▶ Selecting a laptop case

▶ Preparing for a trip with your laptop

▶ Packing your laptop case

▶ Taking your laptop to the airport

▶ Dealing with airport security

▶ Using your laptop on an airplane

There are two types of people. Well, unless you count in binary, and then there are ten types of people. But I digress. One type always leaves the house in a hurry, dashing out to the car in a Technicolor blur, grabbing kids, keys, coats, and whatever else in a massively chaotic fast-forward ballet of noise and panic. The second type of person takes much longer to leave, plodding along, checking coat pockets, and maybe even referring to a list. The second type starts earlier, so these people get to the end location at the same time (or often earlier) than the first type.

No matter which type of person you are, it helps to check a few things before you hit the road with your laptop. If you're the first type of person, then get and pack a useful, ready-to-go-and-grab laptop case. Have it standing ready by the door. For the second type of person, do the same thing! Either way, you have all the stuff you need to make your road warrior experience fully enjoyable.

The Proper Laptop Case

You need a proper laptop case, not because carrying a laptop computer by itself makes you look like a nerd, but more because the laptop is only one part of a larger collection of stuff you'll be taking on the road. Further, the laptop needs a comfy storage place to protect it from damage and disguise it from thieves. Getting the proper laptop case is just a darn good idea.

- ✔ Your laptop needs a case.
- ✔ Suggestions about the stuff you should pack into your case are covered in Chapter 23.

Avoid the manufacturer's case

Many laptop manufacturers provide a case for their laptop systems as a bonus or extra. Generally speaking, such a case is probably the worst choice you can make.

Manufacturers generally give you a case in either of two extremes. First, they provide you with something that they call a "case" but is really little more than a zippered pouch. That's just cheap and shameful.

Second, manufacturers provide you with too much case. They go overboard on size and give you something hulking and huge. Figure 15-1 shows a manufacturer's case that's just too bulky to be useful — despite its "luxurious leather." The case shown in Figure 15-2 is also from a manufacturer, but it's too boxy and actually includes extra padding to keep the laptop from sliding around. Who wants something extra to tote around in a laptop case?

Figure 15-1:
A computer manu-facturer's bulky, yet luxurious leather case.

Figure 15-2:
Another manufacturer's case.

The bottom line with manufacturer's laptop cases is that they just don't give you any choice. Unless you've researched laptop cases and the manufacturer happens to offer one of the brand-name cases that agrees with you, just set aside any notion of getting a name-brand computer manufacturer's case.

Things to look for in a case

I always look in a new case to see if there is any money in it. That's one thing to look for in a case. But seriously, the title of this section deals with features to look for when buying a laptop case. Here's a list:

✔ Does your laptop fit into the case? This doesn't imply that the case needs a compartment designed to fit your specific laptop. Instead, you want to ensure that your laptop does fit comfortably inside the case and that the case can zip up or close easily with the laptop inside.

✔ Actually, you *don't* want a case with a compartment designed to fit your specific laptop. You may not be using the same laptop years from now, but it's nice to keep using the same case.

✔ Get a soft case, not something hard like the traditional briefcase. I think the soft cases hold the laptop more securely, whereas a laptop does tend to jostle around inside a hard case.

✔ Does the case have plenty of pouches? You need pouches for storing accessories, office supplies, discs, manuals, Altoids, year-old receipts, and other things you plan on carrying around with you.

- ✔ I recommend a case that opens to display two large and separate areas. You can slide your laptop into one and put paper, notepads, or computer accessories into the other area.

- ✔ Extra pouches, clips, and such are good for holding various office supplies. They can also be used for smuggling.

- ✔ Zippers are preferred over snaps, buckles, or latches.

- ✔ Having an easy-access pouch on the case's outside helps with storing important documents and other information you need to grab quickly.

- ✔ A carrying handle is a must, but also consider a shoulder strap.

- ✔ A backpack can also make a great laptop carrying case. The bonus here is that shouldering the backpack keeps both your arms and hands free. That way, you can hold your boarding pass in one hand and slap-up the airport counter help with the other.

- ✔ If you know you'll have to carry lots of stuff, say extra material for your job or perhaps something heavy like a printer or video projector, consider getting a laptop case with wheels and a retractable handle.

- ✔ Keep in mind that the bag needs to fit beneath the seat in front of you on an airplane! Don't get something too big.

- ✔ The idea behind your laptop bag is to safely carry and protect the laptop while you're traveling, plus it needs to carry all your laptop toys and other related goodies. Go nuts on the extra features if you must. But, honestly, if you can find a solidly made case, bag, or backpack that does what you need, you're set.

Recommended brands

I've been using an Eddie Bauer soft briefcase as my laptop bag for the past 15 years. The same nylon bag is shown in Figure 15-3. It has plenty of pouches, zippers, and storage compartments, plus room left over for me to toss in magazines and books or even a box of chocolates to take home. That bag has been all over the world with me.

Here is a list of brand name bags I can recommend or that have been recommended to me. If you have an outlet or location near you, pay the place a visit and peruse the stock. Don't forget to take your laptop with you for a test fitting!

- ✔ www.ebags.com
- ✔ www.eddiebauer.com
- ✔ www.targus.com
- ✔ www.thenorthface.com

Figure 15-3:
My trusty
old Eddie
Bauer soft
case.

I'm Leaving, on a Jet Plane Check List

You may not be jetting across the country. Perhaps you're just walking over to the neighborhood coffee bistro. Either way, consider the next two sections your laptop check list.

Things to do before you go

Here are some things you should consider doing before you venture out with your flat PC:

- ✔ Charge the battery! In fact, this is probably something you want to do well in advance before you leave. For example, I typically charge my laptop batteries the night before I leave on a trip.

- ✔ If you're lucky enough to have a spare battery, charge it as well.

- ✔ Synchronize with your desktop. Refer to Chapter 14 for more information on using Briefcase.

- ✔ Back up your important files. The easy way to do this, if your laptop has a CD-R/RW drive, is to drag a copy of the My Documents folder from the laptop's hard drive to the CD-R/RW drive, and then burn that disc. Keep the disc in a safe place (such as a fire safe).

✔ As an alternative backup program, consider Retrospect Backup from Dantz. Norton Ghost can also be used.

✔ Remove any CDs or DVDs from the drive. This avoids having the drive spin into action when you start up on battery power. It also helps to put that disc with your other discs so that you don't forget about it or neglect it.

✔ Go online and save a few Web pages to your hard drive for offline reading while you're away. (See Chapter 13.)

Things to pack in your laptop bag

A good laptop case is useful for holding more than just the laptop. Otherwise it would be called a laptop *cozy* and not a case. So when you're at a loss as to what to put into your laptop case, consider this list for inspiration.

✔ Two words: office supplies. Pens. Paper. Sticky notes. Paper clips. Rubber bands. Highlighter. And so on.

✔ Pack the power cord and AC adapter!

✔ Bring any extra batteries you should have.

✔ Bring along your cell phone, though many prefer to keep that clipped to a belt or in a purse.

✔ When you're traveling overseas, remember to bring along a power conversion kit or overseas power adapter.

✔ Bring a phone cord if you plan on using a modem.

✔ Bring a 6-foot Ethernet cable if you plan on using a network.

✔ Bring headphones if you plan on listening to music or watching a DVD.

✔ If you're making a presentation, don't forget the presentation! If you need your own video projector, pack it too!

✔ Pack any necessary peripherals: mouse, keyboard, PC cards, external storage, and so on.

✔ Ensure that you have some screen wipes.

✔ A deck of cards. (You need something to play with after the battery drains.)

✔ If you're taking a digital camera along, don't forget the camera's computer cable or a memory card reader. It's nice to be able to save those digital images right to the laptop when you're away.

Also take a look at Chapter 23 for more goodies you may want to take with you.

Looming Questions at the Airport

Taking a laptop onboard a commercial airliner today is about as normal as bringing onboard a newspaper and cup of coffee. That's good news. It means that bringing your laptop with you on a commercial airline flight is not unusual and that the airlines are willing to accommodate your needs and not consider you as some oddball exception.

Is your laptop case one carry-on bag or half a carry-on bag?

Sadly, your laptop's case is often your only carry-on luggage. Some airlines let you carry the laptop case plus the typical overnight bag — the same kind of bag many folks try to jam into the overhead bins. Other airlines are more strict.

Do not check your laptop as luggage! You don't want to subject the laptop to the kind of torture most checked bags suffer. You do not want your laptop to be in the sub-zero cargo hold. And you do not want to risk your laptop being stolen. Do not check the laptop!

When the plane is full, and you've tried to sneak on too much carry-on luggage, check the luggage, not the laptop.

If you absolutely must check the laptop case, keep the laptop with you; just check the case.

Laptop inspection

Thanks to the take over of airport inspections by the TSA, the security screening procedures for laptop computers are pretty standard all over the United States. Here's what you need to do:

1. **Before you get into the inspection line, remove your laptop from its carrying case.**

   Yes, this means you'll be burdened with stuff for a few moments. You have to carry your boarding pass, picture ID, laptop case, coat, and carry-on bag — plus any small children, coffee, croissant, and whatnot. But it's only for a few moments.

2. **When you get to the X-ray machine, place your laptop in its own container and put the container on the conveyer belt.**

   You might want to alert the baggage screeners to the laptop's presence.

Do not put your coat over the laptop. Don't toss your car keys into the same bin. Like a fat guy on a roller coaster, the laptop wants to enjoy the ride by itself.

3. **Mind your laptop through the X-ray machine.**

4. **Pick up your laptop on the other end of the X-ray machine.**

After the ordeal, you can put everything away, replacing the laptop back into its case, and storing all the other stuff that was disassembled or removed during the screening process. Then you're on your way to the gate.

✔ Mind your laptop! The X-ray machine is a popular spot for thieves! Refer to Chapter 17.

✔ The X-ray machine will not harm the laptop.

✔ You may be asked to turn the laptop on. That's a good reason to have the batteries fully charged. If they're not, then be sure to pack the power cord; most of the X-ray stations have a wall socket that you can use.

All aboard!

When you get into the plane, find your seat. Try to store the laptop under the seat in front of you. It's okay to put it in the overhead storage, but I prefer the under seat storage, which is easier to get to and avoids the peril of having latecomers jamming their steamer trunks and body bags into the overhead bins and crushing your laptop.

Keep the laptop in its carrying case! Wait until the announcement comes that it's okay to turn on your electronic devices before you whip out the laptop.

✔ Obviously, it helps to avoid the bulkhead seats, which lack under-seat storage.

✔ I prefer window seats for computing aloft. That way, I can control the window blind, shielding my laptop's screen from the sun. Plus it's easier to angle the laptop toward me and away from prying eyes in other seats.

Up, up in the air

After the announcement is made allowing you to use your electronic devices in the plane, you can whip out your laptop and . . . do whatever with it.

Of course, the real conundrum is trying to find a place for the thing. Some seats are so close together that it's nearly impossible to open the laptop while it's sitting on your tray table. And when the guy in front of you lowers his seat, computer time is over!

When you can get the laptop open and running, the real choice becomes: Do you get work done or play games? Or perhaps watch a DVD movie? Hmmm.

How long you have to use the laptop depends primarily on the battery life, but also on the flight duration. When the announcement comes to shut down electronic devices, shutdown Windows and turn off (or hibernate) your laptop.

✔ The airlines have been toying with supplying power for laptop users. I don't know the status of this situation, but I do believe that such a service is available only in business or first class.

✔ There is also a flirtation with supplying live Internet access during certain flights. The only information I have on this is that it is available in a few places, but it's just so expensive that it's silly.

✔ Refer to Chapter 4 for more information on hibernation.

The secret 747 exit wall socket

I'm sure I'm going to be Banned For Life from all air travel for revealing this, but a secret wall socket is in most 747 Jumbo Jets. It's located near the exit door, and my guess is that it's where they plug in the vacuum when the plane is being cleaned.

Anyway, the socket is 110 volts, and it's powered on during the flight. If you can finagle a seat near this socket, then you can plug in for some AC-powered laptop luxury during the entire flight! From Los Angeles to Sydney, that can be quite a period of laptop computing!

Chapter 16

The Road Warrior (Or Computing in the Strangest of Places)

In This Chapter

▶ Taking your laptop on the road

▶ Setting up the laptop in a café or bistro

▶ Finding wall sockets

▶ Using your laptop in a hotel room

▶ Obeying the low-battery warning

▶ Keeping the laptop cool

O, I remember the bad old days of laptop computing! I remember having to hack into a hotel's phone system using lamp cord and a pocket knife! I remember taking my laptop behind the old Iron Curtain and hot swapping in strange Soviet batteries. I remember crowing over getting a 300 bps connection up and running from London to San Diego! You ain't got nothin' on me today!

If you haven't been out in a while, then relax and know that taking a laptop on the road is no longer considered odd, unusual, or even noteworthy. It happens all the time. In fact, it's unusual *not* to see someone camped out with a laptop in a coffee house. Most of the time, you see several people; sometimes it's *everyone*. Would you like to join them? Keep reading!

Café Computing

It used to be that you'd go into a coffee house, order a cappuccino, sit around with artsy folks dressed in black and discuss Marxism. Today, you go to the coffee house, order your double-tall-decaf machiatto, sit around with frustrated people dressed in "Friday casual," and discuss how to connect to the café's Wi-Fi. The gal sitting next to you may still be a Marxist. But so what? If she knows the SSID and WEP, you can have a conversation.

The following sections mull over a few of my observations while café computing:

- It doesn't have to be a café. In fact, there was a park in a major U.S. city that soon became a hub of activity with all sorts of people using their laptop computers. The reason? The new business next to the park set up a wireless network *without security*. So the laptop users were "borrowing" the free Internet access.

- You see one other difference between the cafés of yesterday and today: Where a Marxist could sit in a café all day, laptop users eventually get up and leave when the battery juice runs dry.

Where to sit?

Before visiting the counter to order your beverage and under-cooked bread snack, scout out the entire café for a good place to sit.

You want a table, unless you think it's fun to balance a laptop on your knees while you sit on a sofa or an old sack of Columbian coffee beans.

You want to grab a table that is either away from the windows or facing the windows. You want to avoid having that bright light from the windows reflecting on your laptop screen and washing everything out. (You can tilt the screen to avoid the glare when there's nowhere else to sit.)

Another suggestion: Be mindful of high windows and skylights. As a sunny day grows long, the sun will sweep a slow swath of bright light across some tables. You don't want to be sitting at a table that's in the path of that moving shaft of light. (The voice of experience is speaking here.)

When you really want to get work done, find a spot away from the door and away from the sales counter. Do the opposite if you prefer to be social.

Be a socket sleuth

Another important factor in determining where to sit is the presence of wall sockets. Without trying to look like you're scanning for bombs, duck down and look under some tables or up against walls for a helpful AC power source.

When you find a power source, great! Grab that table.

If you want to be moral about things, enquire at the counter if it's okay to plug in. Otherwise, just sneak a cord over the socket as nonchalantly as possible.

Note that not all the power sockets will be on. My favorite coffee house in my home town has a row of very obvious wall sockets next to some nice tables. Those wall sockets, sadly, are usually turned off. You can tell this when you plug in: Your laptop will not alert you to the AC power presence and continues sucking down battery juice.

When you do manage to plug in, try to arrange the power cord so that no one will trip over it. If someone does trip over your cord, expect expulsion.

Other tips 'n' stuff

It's always good to buy things when you're computing in a coffee house, diner, or café. Get a cup of coffee. Have a biscotti. Get a snack. The management at some places may enjoy having you there as it adds to the atmosphere, but these places are also in the business of making money. So buy something!

In my book *PCs For Dummies* (Wiley Publishing, Inc.), the rule is simple: No beverages near your computer! That goes double for the laptop, where the keyboard and computer are in the same box. But who am I to deny you a nice, delicious, warm cup of Joe? If you want to drink and compute, get your beverage in a heavy, hard-to-topple, ceramic mug. But also grab yourself a nice thick wad of napkins Just In Case.

Never leave your laptop unattended! If you have to go potty, close down the laptop and put it away, or maybe even bring it with you. But never leave the laptop sitting by itself at the table. It will be stolen. (Also see Chapter 17.)

Don't forget to pack a mouse in your laptop bag! When I work on the road, especially in a spot where I'm setting up shop for a few hours, the external mouse is a blessing.

There are times when you may be asked to leave or relocate, especially if you don't buy anything or you're taking up an entire booth all by yourself. Be knowledgeable about this in advance. If you see the place filling up, try to move to a smaller table or just pack up and leave.

Laptopping in Your Hotel Room

Most of this stuff is review from other chapters in this book:

 ✔ If you're using a modem, be sure to create a location and a set of dialing rules for the hotel. Especially if you plan on returning, creating the location and rule set now saves you time in future visits. See Chapter 11.

Beware of magnets

Should you be paralyzed with fear over the thought of exposing your laptop to a magnet? Perhaps.

Magnets aren't really the problem. No, the problem is with the *fields* the magnet generates. If you recall from when you slept through high school science class, an electromagnetic field is generated by magnets, electric motors, stereo speakers, and the planet Jupiter.

In the olden days, computer users avoided magnets because even the slightest magnetic field would scramble the data on a floppy disk. Floppy disks are now part of the past, but those magnetic fields are still around and should be avoided. Something like a blender could generate a magnetic field that might interfere with a laptop right next to it.

It's a good idea to avoid leaving your laptop near appliances with electric motors or large stereo speakers, and definitely don't take the laptop to Jupiter. Or even Saturn.

✔ Many hotels have broadband, or high-speed, Internet access. You pay for this. An Ethernet cable is usually provided, though I recommend you remember to pack your own. Upon connecting the cable, you open your Web browser, then follow the instructions on the screen to set things up.

✔ Beware of digital phone lines! Do not plug your modem into anything other than a hole properly labeled "modem."

✔ The inexpensive printer: Send a fax to the hotel's fax machine. See Chapter 11.

✔ It is a security risk to leave your laptop set up in the hotel room. It's not that the housekeeping staff will steal it; they probably won't. It's more likely that an information thief will get a hold of your laptop to cull out passwords and credit card numbers. See Chapter 17 about security issues while in a hotel.

✔ Another security risk is the hotel's wireless network. Be very careful when sending sensitive data over the wireless (or even wired) network. Who knows how secure that network is or whether hackers are lying in wait nearby?

✔ Occasionally, I find that rare hotel that lacks enough power sockets by the desk. Note that if you unplug a lamp or TV in some hotels, it activates the security system. I would still consider doing that, just be braced to explain the situation to the security guy when he shows up.

Dealing with the Low-Battery Warning

Thanks to smart battery technology, your laptop can be programmed to tell you when the juice is about to go dry. In fact, you can set up two warnings on most laptops. (See Chapter 8.) The idea is to act fast on those warnings when they appear — and to take them seriously! Dally at your own risk. It's your data that you could lose!

The real trick, of course, is to ration what battery power you do have. Here is a summary of tips, some of which are found elsewhere in this book:

✔ **Be mindful of the power-saving timeouts.** Setting a Stand By timeout for 15 minutes might be great in the office, but on the road you may want to adjust those times downward. Refer to Chapter 8.

✔ **Modify the display to use a lower resolution or fewer colors on the road.** In fact, for most computing, a resolution of 800 x 600 with 16-bit color is fine. Such a setting uses less video memory, which requires less power to operate and keep cool.

✔ **Mute the speakers!** Not only will this save a modicum of power, but it also saves the ears of those next to you from hearing those silly noises that your laptop makes.

✔ **Disable unused devices.** If you're not using the modem, turn it off. If you don't need the CD/DVD drive, remove its disc. Speaking of which . . .

✔ **If your laptop's CD/DVD drive is removable, consider removing it when you go on the road.** That saves a bit on weight as well as power usage.

✔ **Save some stuff to do when you get back home or reconnect to a power source.** Face it, some stuff can wait. If that 200K file upload isn't needed immediately, then save it for when you're connected to the fast Internet line back at the office.

✔ **Going into Hibernation mode saves your stuff just as well as pressing Ctrl+S does.** When time is short, and your laptop has the Hibernation smarts, just Hibernate. (But remember to press Ctrl+S to save your stuff when you revive the laptop later.)

Mind the Laptop's Temperature

If you're a wise guy, then you will note that there is no thermometer hole in your laptop. Even so, minding the laptop's temperature is an important thing.

Today's laptops have cooling fans, mostly to keep the high-speed electronics inside cool. The typical Pentium microprocessor requires a lot of cooling to help it work. (Ideally, the electronics want things to be as cold as possible — but not wet.) Also consider that the battery generates heat as it discharges. So it's important not to let your laptop get too hot.

✔ **Avoid putting your laptop anywhere that it will be in the direct sunlight.** For example, do not leave your laptop sitting on your car's passenger seat on a sunny day in August. The heat will kill your laptop. Ditto for the trunk. Ditto for any storage location where the laptop can be exposed to external heat.

✔ **Don't let the laptop run in a closet or any closed environment where air cannot circulate.** Do not block the little vents on the laptop that help it inhale cool air and expel hot air.

✔ **As a suggestion, consider buying your laptop a cooling pad.** Chapter 22 covers this and other gizmos.

Chapter 17

Laptop Security

· ·

In This Chapter

▶ Pilfering a laptop

▶ Preventing a theft ahead of time

▶ Marking your laptop

▶ Watching for crooks

▶ Attaching a security cable

▶ Using passwords

▶ Encrypting data

▶ Making a lost laptop phone home

· ·

*L*aptops are hot! I don't mean that they're hot as in the best new technology or that they're selling extremely well. And I don't mean that they're hot in that a Pentium laptop generates enough heat to turn bread into toast. No, I mean that laptops are one of the favorite things that crooks like to steal.

Thanks to their mobile nature, not to mention that most laptops cost at least a thousand dollars, your favorite portable computer ranks high on the lust list of the common thief. Laptops are easy to lift, easy to conceal, and easy to resell. For the typical thief, that's good news. For you, it's bad news.

This chapter covers the things that you can do to help prevent your laptop from becoming yet another statistic. It covers things you can do beforehand, things you can do on the road, and even stuff that makes your laptop itself tell you when it has been the victim of a crime.

Laptops Are Easy for the Bad Guys to Steal

Unless you stole this book, you probably don't have the mind of a thief. This is good news for humanity. In fact, most of us aren't thieves and tend to be fairly trusting. Sadly, it's our trusting nature that the bad guys take advantage of.

First the good news: Most laptops are forgotten and not stolen. As silly as that sounds, people do leave their expensive laptops sitting around unattended more often than someone sneaks off with it. Despite that, consider that no laptop is ever safe. Many are stolen right out from under the eyes of their owners.

Think of the laptop as a sack of cash sitting around. To a crook that's exactly what it is. Treat the laptop as a bag full o' money, and chances are that you'll never forget it or have it stolen.

The best way to protect your laptop is to label it. Specific instructions are offered later in this chapter. But keep in mind this statistic: 97 percent of unmarked computers are never recovered. Mark your laptops! (See the next section.)

Other interesting and potentially troublesome statistics:

- ✔ Forty percent of laptop theft occurs in the office. That includes both coworkers as well as the Well Dressed Intruder, a thief in a business suit.
- ✔ Laptop theft on college campuses (from dorm rooms) is up 37 percent.
- ✔ A $2,000 stolen laptop is typically sold for about $50 on the street.
- ✔ According to police, 90 percent of laptop thefts are easily avoidable by using common sense.

What to Do before It's Stolen

Any law enforcement official will tell you that a few extra steps of caution can avoid a disastrous theft. Thieves enjoy convenience just as any shopper does; if your laptop is more difficult to pinch than the next guy's, it's the next guy who loses.

The following sections contain helpful hints and suggestions on things you can do ahead of time to help prevent theft or recover your laptop should it go missing.

Mark your laptop

This is most important: It helps with the recovery of a stolen laptop if you've marked your laptop by either engraving it or using a tamper-resistant asset tag. After all, the best proof that something is yours is your name right there on the stolen item.

- ✔ You can use an engraving tool to literally carve your name and contact information on your laptop.

✔ I know some folks who are clever and merely write their names inside the laptop, either on the back of some removable door, inside the battery compartment, or other places a thief wouldn't check. Use a Sharpie or other indelible marker.

✔ Asset tags are available from most print shops. The tags peel and stick like any sticker, but cannot be easily removed or damaged. For an investment of about $100, you can get a few hundred custom tags, not only for your computers but for other valuable items as well. (Cameras, bicycles, TVs, and so on.)

✔ The STOP program offers bar code asset tags that leave a special tattoo if removed. The program also offers a recovery system that automatically returns stolen (or lost) property directly to your door. STOP stands for Security Tracking of Office Property, though home users and (especially) college students can take advantage of the service. Refer to www. stoptheft.com for more information.

Don't use an obvious laptop carrying case

That carrying case with the emblazoned Dell logo (or IBM logo, or what have you) isn't just a proud buyer appreciation/marketing gimmick. The custom laptop case is a sure clue to the casual thief that something valuable lurks inside. This is why in the previous chapter, I recommend against getting a manufacturer's laptop case.

✔ A non-descript, soft laptop case works best.

✔ Backpacks are also good places to store laptops.

Register the laptop and its software

Be sure to send in your laptop's registration card, as well as the registration for any software you're using. If the laptop is then stolen, alert the manufacturer and software vendors. Hopefully, they'll care enough so that, if in the future, someone using your stolen laptop ever tries to get the system fixed or upgraded, it helps you locate the purloined laptop.

✔ This trick assumes that the person fencing the laptop doesn't fully erase the hard drive.

✔ Be sure to keep a copy of the laptop's serial number and other vital statistics with you, specifically in a place other than the laptop's carrying case. That way, you know which number to report to the police as well as the manufacturer.

Be mindful of your environment

They say that gambling casinos are a purse-snatcher's paradise. That's because most women are too wrapped up in the gambling to notice that their purse is being purloined. The purse can be on the floor, at their feet, or even in their lap. Thieves know the power of distraction.

When you're out and about with your laptop, you must always be mindful of where it is and who could have access to it. Watch your laptop!

For example, when dining out, put the laptop in its case beneath the table. If you need to leave the table, either take the laptop with you or ask your friends to keep an eye on it for you.

Take your laptop with you when you go to make a phone call.

Keep your laptop with you when you go to the restroom.

Secure your laptop in your hotel room's safe. If the hotel lacks a room safe, then leave it in the hotel's main safe at the front desk.

Be especially mindful of distractions! A commotion in front of you means that the thief about to take your laptop is behind you. A commotion behind you means the thief is in front of you. Thieves work in pairs or groups that way, using the commotion to distract you while your stuff is being stolen.

Places to watch out for a group of thieves pulling the distraction ploy: Airport screening stations! Just one raised voice or "the woman in the red dress" can divert your attention long enough for your laptop to be gone. Also be aware of distractions on crowded escalators, where the movement of the crowd can knock you down and someone can easily grab the laptop bag and be gone.

The old ball and chain

In Chapter 5, this book took you on a tour around your laptop's externals. One of the things I pointed out back then was the place for the old ball and chain: a hole or slot into which you could connect a security cable. That hole has an official name. It's the USS or Universal Security Slot.

The USS is designed to be part of the laptop's case. Any cable or security device threaded through the USS cannot be removed from the laptop; only the cable itself can be cut (or unlocked) to free the laptop.

Obviously, the USS works best when the laptop is in a stationery place. Like a bicycle lock, you have to park the laptop by something big and stable, then thread the cable through that big thing and the USS for the lock to work.

- ✔ The best place to find a security cable for your laptop is in a computer or office supply store.

- ✔ Some cables come with alarms. You can find alarms that sound when the cable is cut, plus alarms that sound when the laptop is moved.

- ✔ Another way to anchor a laptop is to get a docking station where the laptop can be locked into place. A thief would rather steal a laptop than a full-sized computer (or laptop in a docking station).

- ✔ It kind of tickles my fancy to read the title of this section and actually consider such a thing: Imagine a laptop chained to a 16-pound bowling ball. A thief would have to be really desperate to try and flee with such a setup!

Protecting Your Data

Passwords only protect your laptop's data, not the laptop itself. Most thieves are looking to make a quick buck, generally for drugs. They don't care about the contents of your laptop; they just want the quick cash it brings. But a data thief wants into your laptop.

Data thieves want to find your passwords. They want to locate credit card numbers, which are valuable to sell. Further, they can use your own computer to order stuff on the Internet or make transfers from your online bank account to their own.

The sad news is that password protection really doesn't stand in the way of most clever data thieves. They know all the tricks. They have all the tools. At best, you're merely going to slow them down.

The following sections offer various ways to protect the data on your laptop. This may not prevent a theft, but it will help keep the information on your computer away from the weirdoes who want it.

The BIOS password

Your laptop's setup program allows you to affix a password on the system, a password that's required well before the operating system loads. This is the first line in data defense, but I cannot recommend it because of two things:

First, if you forget your password, you're screwed. So many people march forward with this BIOS password scheme, then they end up leaving the laptop on 24 hours a day and over time, they forget the password. That's bad.

Second, it's possible to circumvent the BIOS password because so many people forget it. Just about every manufacturer has some method of overriding the password, which essentially nullifies the reason for having it in the first place.

- ✔ If your laptop manufacturer has assured you that the BIOS password cannot be circumvented, corrupted, erased, or overpowered, then feel free to use it. But do not forget the password!

- ✔ You're prompted for the password every dang doodle time you start your laptop.

- ✔ Some data crooks just yank the hard drive from the laptop so that they can steal the information from your hard drive using their own special equipment. In this instance, the BIOS password will not protect you.

- ✔ Refer to Chapter 4 for more information on the BIOS setup program, which is how you can access and change the system's BIOS password.

Use the NTFS file system

Ensure that your laptop's hard drive is formatted using the NTFS formatting scheme. This is a technical jabber-doohickey, but it's easy to confirm:

1. **Open the My Computer window.**

   Refer to Chapter 6.

2. **Click your laptop's hard drive icon to select it.**

3. **Locate the Details panel in the list of tasks on the left side of the window.**

    You may need to click the down-pointing chevrons to display the Details information.

4. **Check to see that it says "File System: NTFS" in the Details information.**

   This is shown in Figure 17-1.

5. **Close the My Computer window.**

The NTFS format is more secure than older methods of formatting a hard drive. For example, by using NTFS, you essentially hide the entire hard drive from any floppy disks that could be used to start the computer. The NTFS system also supports file encryption, which helps protect your hard drive's data.

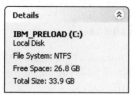

Figure 17-1:
The drive is
using the
NTFS file
system.

> **Details**　　　　　⊗
>
> **IBM_PRELOAD (C:)**
> Local Disk
> File System: NTFS
> Free Space: 26.8 GB
> Total Size: 33.9 GB

If your hard drive is not using NTFS — it's using FAT32, for example, or some other format — then you can update your hard drive to the NTFS format. This is done by running the CONVERT utility at the command prompt. I recommend that you have your dealer or computer guru do this for you.

One reason not to use NTFS is compatibility: Some older programs do not understand the NTFS formatting scheme and will not work if you convert your drive. Especially if you're using older software, check with the developer to ensure that it's NTFS compatible before you convert.

Set a password on your account

Another method of reasonable protection is to ensure that your account on Windows has a password. Now I know that elsewhere in this book I said this wasn't necessary for a single user. But if data security is important to you, definitely add a password to your account in Windows XP.

Refer to Chapter 6 for information on adding password protection to your account.

Disable the Guest account

The Windows XP Guest account allows anyone to enter your computer. Even given that the Guest account is highly limited, that's just enough for a data thief to get a foothold and start hacking away.

Refer to Chapter 6 for information on disabling the Guest account in Windows XP.

Lock Windows

Windows has a unique locking command. By pressing the Windows key (Win) and the L key, you can quickly lock the computer, temporarily logging yourself off of Windows. Only by logging in again — which requires you to type your password — can you regain access.

Use good, strong passwords

Too many passwords are easy to figure out. Do you know what the most common password is? It's "password" — believe it or not! People use their own first names as passwords, simple words, single letters — all sorts of utterly insecure things.

If you're serious about protecting your computer's data, get a serious password. The computer jockeys like to call it a *strong* password. That usually involves two unique and often unrelated words and some numbers. For example, something like `ibrake4cats`.

Two words are necessary because password-cracking programs simply skim through the dictionary and a list of common names.

Numbers are good because they add an element of unpredictability to the password.

Try to avoid using symbols other than numbers in your passwords. They may not be accepted in some instances.

When you have trouble remembering your password, write it down! Just don't keep the password list near your computer. I know folks who write their passwords down on the kitchen calendar. Random words and numbers there may not mean anything to a casual on-looker, but it's helpful if the password is forgotten.

If you plan on leaving your laptop for a moment, consider locking it: Just press Win+L. That way, even if you trust the other folks with you, they'll be prevented from doing even the most harmless of mischief.

If your laptop lacks a Windows key, press Ctrl+Alt+Delete to summon the Windows Task Manager. Then choose Shut Down⇨Switch User from the menu.

Note that on some systems, pressing Ctrl+Alt+Delete automatically locks the computer.

You can also lock up a computer by applying a password to the screen saver. This is yet another level of protection, but consider that it's easier to press Win+L to lock a computer as opposed to waiting around for the screen saver to kick in. (See Chapter 6 for information on the Display Options dialog box, which is where you'll find the screen saver settings.)

Encrypt important files or folders

Windows XP has the ability to scramble or encrypt your files, providing that your hard drive is set up with the NTFS formatting thingy, covered in the section, "Use the NTFS file system," earlier in this chapter.

The encryption is transparent: You can access the files just as you normally would. The files are decrypted as you open them and encrypted when you close them. So they're saved on your hard drive in a scrambled state — which is good.

To encrypt files or folders, follow these steps:

1. **Right-click the file or folder to encrypt.**

2. **Choose Properties from the pop-up menu.**

3. **Click the Advanced button in the General tab.**

4. **In the Advanced Attributes box, select the Encrypt Contents to Secure Data check box.**

   See Figure 17-2.

Figure 17-2: I'd like my file scrambled, please.

5. **Click the OK button to close the Advanced Attributes box.**

6. **Click OK to close the file or folder's Properties dialog box.**

   When encrypting only a file, an Encryption warning may appear. When you only want the file, and not the entire folder encrypted, choose the Encrypt the File Only option and click OK.

The file shows up with green text in its name, which is your only real clue that it's encrypted.

You can repeat these steps to remove the encryption, but seeing how encryption doesn't slow things down or otherwise hinder you, what's the point?

This feature may only be available with Windows XP Professional edition.

Why can't you just password-protect your files?

In 20 years of writing computer books, the most common question I've ever received is why can't individual files or folders have their own passwords. It makes sense. And it's a feature I wish the operating system had. People apparently want it. But yet it just isn't to be.

Of course, you're not stuck in the mud. While you cannot password-protect files, you can password-protect Compressed Folder, or ZIP file, archives. These archives are commonly used to send files and programs over the Internet. The compression allows larger files to be sent in less time. The archive also allows more than one file to be sent in a single batch.

You can choose File⇨New⇨Compressed (zipped) Folder in Windows to create a Compressed Folder. Then copy files you want to password-protect into that folder.

To set the password, open the Compressed Folder icon and choose File⇨Add Password. Enter the password twice, then click OK. That's about as good as it gets.

As a trivial aside, the ancient operating system for the early 1980's vintage TRS-80 computer had password-protected files. The operating system was called TRS-DOS. The manufacturer was a little company in Seattle called Microsoft.

Disable the infrared port

Apparently, some mysterious software out there can tunnel into your laptop via the infrared (IR) port. I was surprised by this, but I'll defer to the greater wisdom of the computer security experts.

To disable your laptop's IR port, comply with these steps:

1. **Open the Control Panel's System icon.**

2. **Click the Hardware tab in the System Properties dialog box.**

3. **Click the Device Manager button.**

   This brings up the handy Device Manager window, shown in Figure 17-3.

4. **Click the Infrared Devices item (shown in Figure 17-3) to open it.**

5. **Double-click the Infrared Port item that appears beneath the Infrared devices thingy.**

6. **In the bottom of the Properties dialog box, locate the Device Usage drop-down list and choose the Do Not Use This Device (Disable) option from that list.**

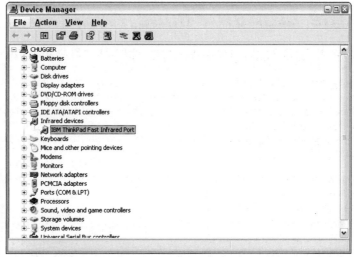

Figure 17-3:
Out, out,
infrared
spot!

7. **Click OK to close the Properties window.**

8. **Close the Device Manager.**

If no infrared item is listed in the Device Manager, then your laptop most likely lacks an infrared port. That's fine.

Refer to Chapter 6 for more information on the System icon in the Control Panel. That chapter also mentions the Device Manager.

Back up your data!

When you lose a laptop, you lose two things. First you lose the laptop's hardware. Secondly, and more important, you lose the data on the laptop. If that data means something to you, then I highly recommend that you keep a backup copy of that data.

You can back up data in many ways. The simplest is backing up over a network to a large capacity hard drive. Just drag your My Document folder to that network hard drive, and that's pretty much it. (Though this is a rather simple explanation.)

The best way to back up data is to get real backup software, stuff that will let you back up your stuff to a network drive as well as to a CD-R or DVD-R drive, should your laptop have one. I can recommend Retrospect Backup from Dantz for this task.

Having the Laptop Phone Home

This is perhaps one of the niftiest ways to protect your laptop ever. It involves having your laptop make a phone call and tell you where it is. Amazingly enough, it works.

This technique was supposedly discovered by accident. It went something like this: A laptop user programmed his system to phone his home computer every night at about 8:00. The two computers would then exchange and update each other.

One day the laptop was stolen from work. But then, a few days later, the phone suddenly rang at 8:00. The person picked up the phone and heard the sound of the laptop's modem making the call. He immediately grabbed the Caller ID of the incoming and used that information to help the police nab the laptop thief.

The laptop was recovered because it was programmed to phone home at a specific time every day. This program ran automatically, so when the thief (or whomever ended up with the stolen laptop) plugged the system in, the program continued to run.

You don't need to be a programmer to set up a similar system on your own computer. Many such programs do basically the same thing as described above: They make the laptop phone home, or often they alert a tracking service over the Internet. The end result is the same: The laptop's cry for help is heard, and the system is eventually recovered.

For more information, refer to the following Web sites of companies that offer such "phone home" services:

- ✔ www.ztrace.com
- ✔ www.computrace.com
- ✔ www.secureit.com
- ✔ www.stealthsignal.com

Your thumbprint, please

The latest trend in security devices is the thumbprint reader. It requires that you press down your thumb as a form of identification. Providing that it's the correct thumb, the reader's software unlocks the laptop and lets you proceed. Obviously, this is a far more secure method of identification than a password. I mean, who ever forgets a thumb?

Thumbprint readers are available as external (USB) devices, as part of a mouse, or some newer laptops include them as part of the laptop itself.

Chapter 18

Giving a Presentation

In This Chapter

▶ Preparing for your presentation

▶ Using PowerPoint

▶ Connecting to the video projector

▶ Using handy PowerPoint keyboard shortcuts

I suppose that, for the longest time, the main reason to lug around a laptop was to give one of those infamous video presentations. You've been there. You're in a darkened room. Warm. Too little sleep from the night before. A "presenter" talking in a droning monotone. Dull, lifeless information. Soon, you're starting to nod off. Try not to snore (or drool).

Because of the close relationship between laptops and presentations, I thought I'd throw in one more chapter just to brush up and review on the subject.

✔ These days, it's often not necessary to bring a laptop to a presentation. Merely having the presentation files on a CD-R is enough.

✔ Some handheld devices can be used to "drive" the video projectors that give presentations.

Setting Things Up

I suppose that the most nerve-wracking part about giving a presentation is ensuring that everything works. When you get everything working correctly, the speech itself should go smoothly, right? Even when well prepared, few folks enjoy speaking before a large group, especially a group of business folk who are used to — and are often unimpressed by — computer presentations.

In most circumstances, you're allowed to set up your laptop and run through a test to ensure that everything works before giving your presentation to an audience. A technician might be available and even do everything to set up for you. That's great. But it still doesn't make the situation any less nerve-wracking.

Creating the presentation

Before you leave and hit the road with your dog and pony show, you must first create your presentation. The program of choice for doing this is Microsoft's PowerPoint, which can be purchased as an individual program or as part of the Office suite of applications.

PowerPoint creates documents generically referred to as *slide shows*. Each slide can contain text, graphics, pictures, or some combination of each. You can add animations and sound effects, plus interesting fades and transitions between the slides.

All in all, PowerPoint is a fairly easy program to figure out and fun to use with enjoyable results. That may not make the subject matter more enthralling, but just keep in mind that creating your presentation isn't the worst job in the world.

✔ PowerPoint must be installed on your laptop.

✔ Microsoft does offer a PowerPoint viewer program, which lets you play, but not edit, PowerPoint presentations. This allows you to see a presentation even when you don't have PowerPoint (for example, if the laptop you're using doesn't have PowerPoint installed). This viewer program can be obtained from the Microsoft Web site (www.microsoft.com) in the Downloads area.

✔ PowerPoint is fairly easy to figure out, though you can find tutorials for it, as well as a few good books and references.

✔ One trick I've used to keep the presentation from getting too boring is to engage the audience during the show. Ask questions or have the audience fill in the blanks. Not only can that make the show more lively, but it also helps keep people awake and on their toes.

✔ Indeed, it's a good idea to complete the presentation before you leave. Even so, I'm one of many folks who work on presentations up until the minute that they're given!

✔ Yes, it is an *excellent* idea to create a backup copy of your presentation on a CD-R. That way, should you lose the laptop, or suddenly discover an incompatibility, you can use the CD-R with someone else's computer to deliver the talk.

> ✔ You might also consider running the Microsoft Office Pack and Go Wizard on your presentation, moving it into a portable format as a secondary backup. The Pack and Go format can be easily read by other computers in case something happens to your laptop.

Hooking up to the video projector

For a small presentation, showing the PowerPoint slide show on your laptop screen, sitting at the end of a table, is perfectly fine. Most of the time, however, you'll be connecting your laptop to a video projector. The video projector works like a giant monitor, displaying its image on a large screen at the end of a meeting room or convention hall.

The hook-up process is easier than it seems. In the best-case scenario, a helpful technician is there to assist you, and the connection is made and confirmed in advance. But even when there is no technician, you can generally figure things out: Connect your laptop's external video connector to the video projector.

You can use either the S-video or external monitor port.

You'll probably also need to connect your laptop's audio-out port to the projector or to the location's sound system as well.

After connecting the laptop to the video projector, check the image. In some cases, you'll see your laptop's display on the video projector and not the laptop's screen. That's great. You're set to go.

There are other times when the video projector acts as the laptop's second monitor. The laptop shows the regular laptop screen, but the presentation appears on the video projector. (That's just PowerPoint being smart.) You can confirm if your laptop has this ability by opening the Control Panel's Display Properties dialog box and clicking on the Settings tab. If you see the second blank monitor there (as in Figure 18-1), then the laptop is automatically configured to use the external monitor. You're ready to go.

What I usually do is get the PowerPoint slide show all set up, displayed on the screen, and ready to go. Then I close my laptop's lid, putting it into Stand By mode, and leave it up on the dais. When I'm ready to go, I step up, open the laptop's lid, and when it comes to life, the presentation is right there on the video projector's display and ready to go.

> ✔ Sometimes the video projector is provided at the scene.

> ✔ Sometimes you have to bring your own video projector. They're not cheap, but they're small and portable.

✔ Be sure to pack an extra bulb if you're using your own video projector. You want to be able to replace a burned out bulb quickly, and those bulbs aren't easy to find.

✔ Some laptops sport a special function (Fn) key on the keyboard, used to activate the external video port. You may need to press this key to switch the display over to the video projector.

✔ Some laptops may have dual video built in, allowing you to use the video projector as a second monitor. To confirm this, open the Display Properties dialog box and click on the Settings tab. There should already be a second monitor configured (refer to Figure 18-1). If so, you're set and ready to go.

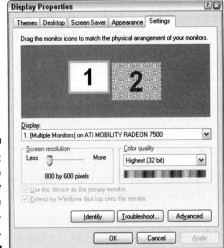

Figure 18-1:
This laptop
is ready
to make
presen-
tations.

PowerPoint Keyboard Shortcuts Worthy of Knowing

Here are a few keys you can use in PowerPoint to help save your rear in times of panic and dread.

Keys to display the next slide:

✔ Spacebar

✔ Enter

- ✔ N
- ✔ Down-arrow key
- ✔ Right-arrow key

Keys to redisplay the previous slide (or to back up through an animation sequence):

- ✔ Up-arrow key
- ✔ Left-arrow key
- ✔ P
- ✔ Backspace

Keys to display a blank screen in the middle of the presentation:

- ✔ B (black screen)
- ✔ . period (black screen)
- ✔ W (white screen)
- ✔ , comma (white screen)

Keys to cancel the show:

- ✔ Esc
- ✔ - (hyphen)

Keys to hide the pointer and navigation box:

- ✔ A
- ✔ = (equal sign)

Part V
Troubleshooting

The 5th Wave   By Rich Tennant

"I tell him many times — get lighter laptop. But him think he know better. Him have big ego. Him say, 'Me Tarzan, you not!' That when vine break."

In this part . . .

What? Trouble? With a computer? I'm shocked!

It's sad, but trouble follows a computer around like a dog follows a little kid with a dripping ice cream cone. In fact, I would venture to guess that there has been more information written about computers and what can go wrong with them than there is information written about the universal topic of parenting. (The 1991 manual listing all the error codes possible for the old MS-DOS 5.0 was over 500 pages long!)

The two chapters in this brief section cover laptop troubleshooting, as well as the topic of upgrading and repairing your laptop. For more information on the subject, I recommend my book *Troubleshooting Your PC For Dummies*, which goes into far more detail than I can cover here.

Chapter 19

Major Trouble and General Solutions

In This Chapter

▶ Understanding computer trouble

▶ Restarting Windows to fix things

▶ Using System Restore

▶ Setting a restore point

▶ Restoring your system

▶ Using Safe Mode to find problems

▶ Fixing common problems

*E*very computer is different. Not every laptop has the same hardware, the same size hard drive, memory capacity, and other options. Multiply that by the many combinations of computer software out there, and then multiply that by the number of potential configurations for the software. If you can picture that, then you can understand how everyone's computer can be so unique. And any effort to list all the potential problems for anyone's computer would be futile.

Rather than do a specific problem list with solutions, I decided to take a more general course in this chapter. Here, you find some advice about avoiding problems in the first place, followed by some sure-fire general solutions, and also some preventive measures you should take.

Soothing Words of Support for the Computer Weary

Generally, one good reason why your computer is having problems is that *something has changed.* It may seem obvious; I mean, duh! The thing doesn't work any more! But it's usually some change that took place *before* the trouble started that is to blame.

Computers are really a house of cards waiting to collapse at the slightest whiff of error. It's amazing that they run well at all. Adding new hardware, new software, or changing an existing configuration can lead to trouble. So the question you need to ask when trouble comes is simple:

What has changed recently?

Anything new? Think back a few days. Chances are good that whatever you've added to the computer, whatever you've changed or modified, is the cause of the error. Reversing the change often fixes things.

- ✔ Changing or modifying your data files (such as Word documents, MP3s, or JPEGs) is not the type of change referred to in this section. No, changing or modifying *programs* or parts of the Windows operating system is what can lead to trouble.

- ✔ When you know the trouble is related to a specific hardware or software change, contact the hardware or software developer on the Internet. Look up the Web page's support section and see if any of your issues are mentioned or solutions offered.

- ✔ Removing or undoing the change often fixes things. Also refer to the section, "The Miracle of System Restore," later in this chapter.

The Universal Quick Fix

Sometimes computers just act weird. There may be nothing wrong, though I refer to the syndrome as "tired RAM." The solution, as well as the first thing you should try at the hint of trouble, is to restart Windows.

Often times, restarting Windows unclogs the drain and allows your computer to work properly once again. At the least, it's worth a try.

See Chapter 4 for information on restarting Windows.

You don't need to reinstall Windows

Way back when, tech support was provided as a form of customer service. The developer felt it owed after-sale support to its customers. But that was then. Now, tech support seems more like an obligation, and the support offered isn't often very helpful. In fact, because the bean counters measure tech support on a per-call basis, the real desire of the support personnel is not to solve the problem but rather to get you off the phone as quickly as possible.

Industry-wide, the average call for tech support must be less than 12 minutes. When the call reaches 10 minutes, tech support people are advised to direct you simply reinstall the Windows operating system to fix your problem. Does this fix the problem? That's the issue; it fixes *their* problem in that it gets you off the phone.

I've been troubleshooting and fixing computers for years. Only a handful of times has reinstalling

Windows been necessary to fix a problem — and that's usually because the user deleted parts of the Windows operating system either accidentally or through ignorance. Beyond that, with patience and knowledge, any computer problem can be solved.

Reinstalling Windows is drastic. In the entire history of computers, only today is reinstalling a computer operating system considered "routine." It shouldn't be. The operating system is the bedrock upon which you build your computer house. Reinstalling Windows is like rebuilding your home's foundation when all you need to do is fix a leaky faucet.

When someone tells you to reinstall Windows, run. No, better: Scream, and then run. Try to find another source of help. ***Remember:*** Only in drastic situations is reinstalling Windows necessary. If you can find someone knowledgeable and helpful enough, he can assist you without having to reinstall Windows.

The Miracle of System Restore

There is so much going on with Windows that a problem can exist *just about anywhere*. To assist you, a nifty program was created to take *just about anywhere* and save it for you. That way, when a problem happens, you can restore *just about anywhere* back to the way it was before the problem. The program is called System Restore.

Enabling System Restore

System Restore is a feature that you can turn off or on. Some folks turn it off because it uses mass quantities of hard drive space molecules. My advice is that you leave System Restore on because it is a powerful and useful tool. Either way, check to confirm that System Restore is enabled by heeding these steps:

1. Open the Control Panel's System icon.

Refer to Chapter 6 for more information on both the Control Panel and the System icon.

2. Click the System Restore tab.

The System Restore information appears in the dialog box, as shown in Figure 19-1.

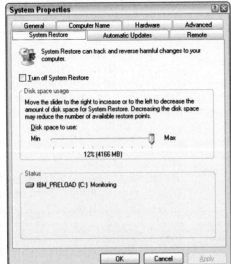

Figure 19-1:
System
Restore
control
central.

3. To activate System Restore, deselect the Turn Off System Restore check box, or disable System Restore by adding a check mark.

You can also adjust disk space usage by manipulating the slider in the middle of the dialog box.

Should your laptop have more than one hard drive, you'll have to select the drive and then click the Settings button. The next dialog box you see contains the slider.

4. Click OK to confirm your settings.

Do note that having System Restore on uses more disk space than with it turned off. In fact, it might have been turned off to save disk space. In any event, you can use the slider in Step 3 to adjust how much disk space System Restore uses.

The more disk space you allocate for System Restore, the more restore points you can set and use. See the "Setting a restore point" section, later in this chapter.

When to run System Restore

Anytime you plan on changing anything on your computer, modifying Windows, adding an update, installing new hardware, or changing a system setting, you should run the System Restore program. Specifically, you should set a *restore point.* That way, should anything weird happen, you can generally recover.

✔ The Control Panel is where you go to modify various settings in Windows. Upon opening the Control Panel, you should think, "Should I be creating a restore point now?"

✔ Create a restore point before installing new hardware.

✔ Create a restore point before removing hardware.

✔ Create a restore point before adding or updating a new hardware driver.

✔ Create a restore point before installing any programs that you download from the Internet.

✔ Especially create a restore point before you decide to toil with network configurations. That will really save your butt.

✔ If you neglect to set a restore point, don't fret! The computer automatically sets them every few days. You should be fine.

Setting a restore point

To set a restore point, follow these steps:

1. **From the Start button's menu, choose All Programs⇨Accessories⇨ System Tools⇨System Restore.**

   The Welcome to System Restore window appears. It's rather dull, so I shan't bore you with an illustration of it.

2. **Choose the Create a Restore Point option and click the Next button.**

3. **Enter a description.**

   Or type a reason why you feel the restore point is necessary. For example: "Updating video drivers," or "Adding wireless networking," and so on.

You don't need to enter the date; that information is automatically saved with the restore point.

4. **Click the Create button.**

The next screen tells you that your restore point has been created, listing the description, date, and time.

5. **Click the Close button.**

At this point, you can go on with the software or hardware change, or whatever modifications you were going to make in Windows.

Restoring your system

When the computer starts acting goofy, and given that you know it may be due to a recent change, you can make the attempt at fixing things by using System Restore. You can select a restore point from the past, and hopefully recover the system to a workable state.

To recover your system, and hopefully fix the problem, obey these steps:

1. **From the Start button's menu, choose All Programs⇨Accessories⇨ System Tools⇨System Restore.**

2. **Choose the Restore My Computer to an Earlier Time option.**

3. **Click the Next button.**

4. **Choose a restore point from the calendar displayed.**

See Figure 19-2.

Note that some days may have more than one restore point.

5. **Click the Next button.**

6. **Close any running programs.**

This is done as a precaution; you don't want to lose any data.

7. **Click the Next button.**

Windows logs you off and restarts the computer. This is necessary for some of the changes to have full effect. Just sit back and wait, or get another cup of your favorite caffeinated beverage.

8. **Click the OK button on the final screen.**

The final screen is displayed after the restore point is complete.

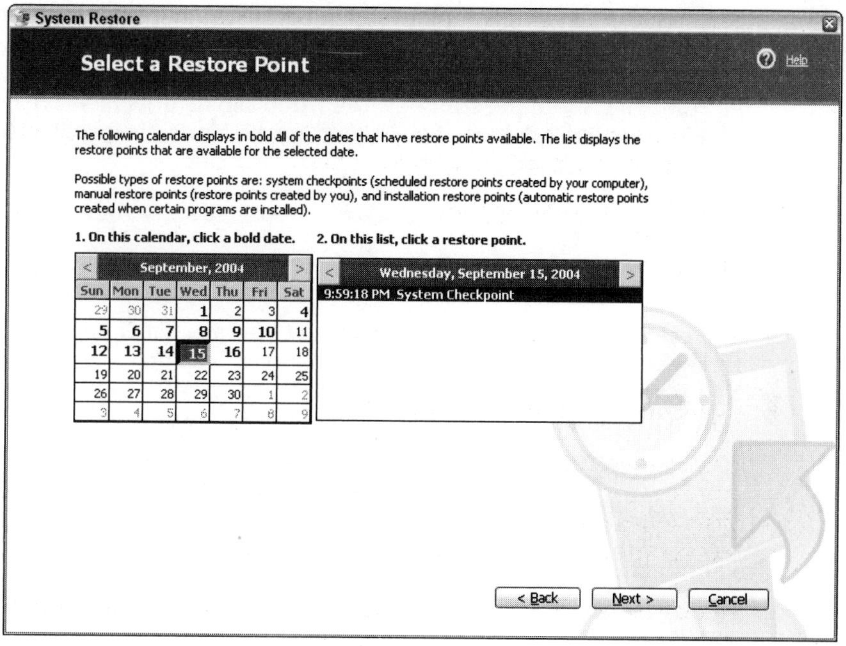

Figure 19-2:
Help me,
Mr. Wizard!

This should fix the problem, especially if it was due to a recent system change. If not, then you can try starting the laptop in Safe Mode, which is covered in the next section.

✔ Running System Restore undoes any changes you've made between now and the date and time of the restore point. Some of the changes may not have caused the problem, so don't be surprised, for example, if your screen saver changes or other parts of Windows change, parts unrelated to the original problem.

✔ System Restore only lets you reset the system back a few days or so. Attempts to use a restore point earlier than a week back generally don't meet well with success.

Safe Mode

I take exception to the name "Safe Mode." It's the Windows mode for troubleshooting and solving problems. But doesn't that imply that Windows regular mode is unsafe? But I digress . . .

Safe Mode is good for troubleshooting because it helps determine one major thing: Whether the problem is with Windows or other software. In Safe Mode, only the most basic programs required to run Windows are loaded on startup. The rest of the stuff — those troublesome drivers — are not loaded. This means that if the problem is gone in Safe Mode, the problem is *not* to be blamed on Windows.

Entering Safe Mode

You can start the laptop in Safe Mode in two ways. The first is by pressing the F8 key when the laptop first starts. If you're quick enough, you'll be greeted by a startup menu. One of the options present is Safe Mode. Choose that option to continue starting the computer in Safe Mode.

The second way to start in Safe Mode is by using the master troubleshooting tool, the System Configuration Utility, a.k.a. MS Config. This tool, shown in Figure 19-3, helps you troubleshoot startup problems by selectively disabling various startup services and programs.

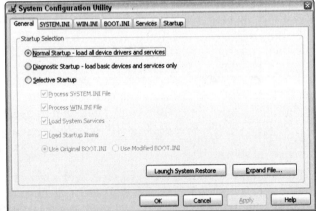

Figure 19-3:
The System Configuration Utility.

To configure the computer to start up in Safe Mode, use the System Configuration Utility as follows:

1. Choose the Run command from the Start button's menu.

Or you can press the Win+R keyboard shortcut. Either way, the Run dialog box is summoned.

2. **Type** MSCONFIG **into the text box, then click the OK button.**

   The System Configuration Utility appears, as shown in Figure 19-3.

3. **Choose the Diagnostic Startup radio button.**

4. **Click OK.**

   Wait a few seconds. The computer is "thinking."

5. **Click the Restart button.**

   Your laptop then restarts in Safe Mode.

Let the troubleshooting begin!

✔ Refer to the next section for what to do in Safe Mode.

✔ To get out of Safe Mode, repeat the preceding steps, but this time, choose the Normal Startup – Load All Device Drivers and Services option in Step 3.

✔ For more information on the System Configuration Utility, refer to my book, *Troubleshooting Your PC For Dummies* (Wiley Publishing, Inc.).

✔ Another startup menu may appear on your laptop, one that gives you the option of starting a Windows Recovery Console. Using that utility is also covered in my *Troubleshooting Your PC For Dummies* book, starting with the 2nd edition.

Testing in Safe Mode

In Safe Mode, Windows doesn't load common device drivers or extensions to the computer system. Therefore, the screen will be of a very low resolution, and some hardware features you're used to working with won't be available.

Forget about networking. Forget about the Internet.

Instead, try doing whatever it is that's causing your trouble. If the problem exists in Safe Mode, then it's most likely a Windows problem. The best way to proceed is to visit the Windows tech support knowledgebase on the Internet and look up your problem. (Remember that you'll have to restart back in normal or "Unsafe Mode" to access the Internet.) Here's the address for the knowledgebase:

```
http://support.microsoft.com/
```

When the problem doesn't exist in Safe Mode, then you can blame your computer's hardware device drivers. Most likely, the problem is with one of three different drivers: Video, Networking, or Power Management. Refer to your computer dealer's or manufacturer's Web site for how to proceed.

To restart the computer back in regular mode, refer to the steps in previous section. Be sure to choose the Normal Startup option in Step 3.

The laptop always starts in Safe Mode!

When the laptop starts in Safe Mode, it means that something is wrong. Some piece of hardware or software has told Windows that it just can't function, and so the system starts in Safe Mode to first alert you to the problem, and second, to give you the opportunity to fix things.

In most cases, the problem's description appears on the screen, and you can address the issue by reading the text displayed.

Sometimes, you may have to check with the Device Manager to look for mis-behaving hardware: Open the System icon in the Control Panel, click the Hardware tab, and then click the Device Manager button. Malfunctioning hardware appears in the Device Manager's list highlighted by a yellow circle with an exclamation point in the middle. Double-clicking on that item dis-plays the error message and possibly a suggestion for fixing things.

To restart your computer in normal mode, follow the steps in the section, "Entering Safe Mode," earlier in this chapter. In Step 3, choose the Normal Startup option.

Common Problems and Solutions

It would be near impossible for me to mention every dang doodle problem your laptop can experience. So rather than list every dang doodle one of them, or even 1,000 or even 100, I've narrowed the list down to five. Each of them is covered in the following sections.

The keyboard is wacky!

This happens more often than you would imagine, based on the e-mail I receive. The solution is generally simple: You have accidentally pressed the Num Lock key on your keyboard and half the alphabet keys on your keyboard are acting like numbers.

The solution is to press the Num Lock key and restore your keyboard to full alphabetic operation.

Making the mouse pointer more visible

 The Mouse icon in the Control Panel is a hotbed of rodent-like activity. Especially if you're having trouble seeing the mouse pointer on your laptop's screen, visit the Pointers or Pointer Options tab in the Mouse Properties dialog box. The following suggestions can help you make the mouse pointer more visible:

- ✔ In the Pointers tab, you can choose larger mouse pointers than the set normally used by Windows. In the Scheme drop-down list, choose Windows Standard (extra large) for some super-sized mouse pointers.

- ✔ In the Pointer Options tab, use two of the options in the Visibility area to help you find a mouse pointer on the screen. Specifically, try pointer trails or the Ctrl key click option.

- ✔ Pointer trails adds a comet-tail effect to the mouse in Windows, helping you locate the mouse pointer as you move it around.

- ✔ When the mouse plays Where's Waldo, you can find it with the Ctrl key click option by pressing either Ctrl key on your keyboard. A series of concentric rings surrounds and highlights the mouse pointer's location.

The laptop won't wake up

A snoozing laptop could mean that the battery is completely dead. Consider plugging in the laptop and try again.

When the laptop has trouble waking from Stand By mode — and you have to turn it off, then turn it on again to get control — then you have a problem with the power management system in your laptop. Refer to the next section.

Power management woes

When the laptop suddenly loses its ability to go into Stand By or Hibernate mode, it means that there may be a problem with the power management hardware or software.

First check with your computer manufacturer's Web page to see if you can find any additional information or software updates.

Second, ensure that both modes are activated by checking the Power Options icon in the Control Panel.

Finally, confirm that other hardware or software isn't interfering with the power management software. If so, then remove the interfering software or hardware, or check for updates that don't mess with your laptop's power management system.

The battery won't charge

Batteries do die. Even the modern smart batteries are good for only so long. When your battery goes, replace it with a new battery. When the battery goes unexpectedly, consider replacing it under warranty if it should prove defective.

Rules and laws govern the disposal of batteries. Be sure to follow the proper procedure for your community to safely dispose of or recycle batteries.

Chapter 20

Upgrading Your Laptop

- -

In This Chapter

▶ Updating your software

▶ Getting a new version of software

▶ Updating Windows

▶ Adding new hardware

- -

*L*aptops aren't designed with upgrading in mind. They're sealed units. Your laptop might have space to add an extra DIMM or two of RAM, or perhaps there's a drive bay where you can install an optional floppy, CD, DVD, or extra hard drive. But when compared to the expandability of the desktop computer, laptops are a closed and shut case, literally!

Upgrading your laptop is possible, and often advisable. But upgrading isn't limited to hardware alone. You may desire at some point in time to upgrade your software as well. This chapter covers both types of upgrades, software as well as hardware.

How 'bout Some New Software?

Generally speaking, I do not recommend upgrading software. In the olden days, upgrades were necessary to add new features and expand upon the abilities of older programs. But today's software is so advanced that even a program purchased back in the late 1990s would still serve you well today.

Upgrading your software

I recommend upgrading your software only when the newer version of the program offers features you need or fixes problems you have. Otherwise, my motto is, "If it ain't broke, don't fix it!"

I'm serious: You can avoid a lot of trouble by not upgrading. I've seen too many stable computers become unstable after a simple upgrade. I've seen printers suddenly not work. And worse yet, I've seen the chain reaction of having to upgrade more than one application just to keep things compatible. That can be expensive.

Still, upgrading can often be effortless. The newer version of the application can boost your productivity. The key is to be prepared for anything.

- ✔ Before upgrading, set a system restore point. That will help you recover things in case the upgrade doesn't work properly. Refer to Chapter 19.

- ✔ Upgrading is as easy as sticking the new program's CD into your laptop's CD drive. Everything after that should run automatically, with your input required only for a few simple questions.

- ✔ The hard part about upgrading is living with any unintended consequences. An upgrade is a change to your laptop. Sometimes changes aren't good. Refer to Chapter 19.

- ✔ You don't need to uninstall the previous version of a program when installing an update. The only exception is when you're specifically advised to uninstall any older versions.

- ✔ Refer to Chapter 6 for information on removing software from your computer.

Upgrades verses updates

Computer jargon can be confusing enough without having to deal with vague terms that also exist in English. Prime examples of this are the words *upgrade* and *update*. They may seem like the same thing, but in the computer world, they're not.

Upgrade means to install a newer version of some program you already own. For example, you upgrade from version 2.1 of a program to version 2.2. Specifically, that's referred to as a *minor* upgrade. From version 4.0 to version 5.0 is a *major* upgrade.

Update means to improve an existing program, but not change its version or release number. For example, Microsoft routinely releases security updates for Windows. These updates, or *patches,* are applied to your version of Windows to improve things, address security issues, or fix bugs. But applying the update does not upgrade the software.

In some universe somewhere else, this all makes sense.

Updating Windows

Windows is routinely updated by Microsoft as bugs are fixed or security issues are addressed. These updates can be automatically installed as your laptop accesses the Internet, or they can be manually installed by visiting the Windows Update service on the Internet or obtaining the occasional update CD directly from Microsoft.

To set up your laptop to use automatic updates, follow these steps:

1. **Open the Control Panel's System icon.**

   Refer to Chapter 6 for more information.

2. **Click the Automatic Updates tab.**

   Figure 20-1 illustrates the Automatic Updates tab.

3. **To activate automatic updates, select the proper option at the top of the dialog box.**

4. **Choose other options in the dialog box, depending on how you wish to obtain, install, and be notified of new updates.**

5. **Click OK.**

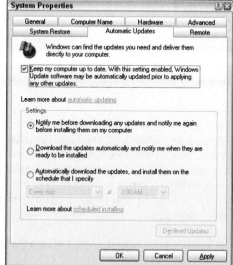

Figure 20-1: The Automatic Updates tab in all its glory.

When your computer is configured for automatic updates, Windows goes to the Microsoft update site and downloads the updates in the background every time you're connected to the Internet. As new updates are available, they'll be provided to you. Then you'll be informed of the updates and given the option to install them, depending on which settings you chose in Step 4.

You're free to disable automatic updates. If you'd rather, you can manually update Windows and choose which updates you want or need to install. This is done by choosing the Windows Update command (choose Start⇨All Programs, and look for Windows Update at the top of the All Programs menu). That connects you to a Web page where you can manually update Windows, should you choose to do so.

If you need to, you can remove Windows updates from your system. This is done by using the Add/Remove Programs icon in the Control Panel, as discussed in Chapter 6.

Another thing to consider with a laptop is using your Internet connection while you're on battery power. Do you really want to be downloading updates in such a situation? It's probably best to configure your laptop for manual updates, and update only when you're not running off the battery and connected to a high-speed Internet connection.

Upgrading Windows

I highly recommend against upgrading your laptop's operating system. Specifically, I recommend against upgrading Windows. Once upon a time, upgrading the operating system was great. But today, the improvements and changes they make to Windows are just too great to risk the stability of your computer.

Instead of upgrading Windows, the next best thing is simply to wait until you can afford to buy a new computer or laptop with the latest version of Windows preinstalled. That way, you're assured that all the hardware is compatible with the new version, and that it's robust enough to handle the new version of Windows. When upgrading an older computer, you just can't be assured of those things, so it's a risk. And I don't recommend risking the investment you have with your laptop.

Sure, if you want to upgrade Windows, go ahead. I can't stop you. But I highly recommend against upgrading Windows.

Why the author doesn't do automatic Windows updates

Some people don't do the automatic update thing. I'm one of them. Some of the updates do interfere with the computer system, making it unstable. Microsoft notoriously recalled an update years ago, one that disabled a number of computer systems. Even so, some people continue to blindly update.

Because I protect my computers with a stout firewall and antivirus software, I generally avoid many of the problems that the Windows updates address. Therefore, I choose not to update my systems. Only when I deem an update necessary do I install it. Then I use the manual method and install only the single update. Otherwise, I am just unwilling to expose my computer system to the risks of unknown automatic updates.

Giving Your Laptop New Hardware

If you're fortunate enough to have an upgradeable laptop, then by golly you should take advantage of it someday!

Internal expansion options are somewhat limited with laptops. Even so, on many laptops, it's possible to replace or upgrade the hard drive and memory (RAM). Most other things on the laptop cannot be upgraded; the microprocessor, video circuitry, networking adapter, modem, and other hardware are often all integrated into the laptop's main circuitry board, or *motherboard*. It's cheaper to buy an entirely new laptop than to try to upgrade anything on the motherboard.

If your laptop is equipped with a handy method for adding more memory, do so! Memory chips are available far and wide, though my favorite place to shop for RAM is the online memory store at www.crucial.com. The site has a configuration program that helps you select the exact memory you need. It's very handy, plus the memory chips come with good instructions on how to install them in your computer.

Some laptops allow for the hard drive to be replaced or upgraded. The easiest way to do this is when there is a drive bay option. For example, you can use a floppy drive, CD-R, DVD, or hard drive in the drive bay. So if your computer came with a CD drive and you want to replace it with a second hard drive, the operation is not only possible but relatively easy to accomplish. The bad news is that the extra drives are available only from the manufacturer and are often quite pricey.

Beyond those few basic items, your laptop is essentially a closed box, and no further upgrades are offered. But don't despair! Refer to Chapter 7 for various ways to expand your laptop's universe. With the USB standard, there is really no limit to your laptop's hardware extents.

- ✔ Instead of upgrading your laptop with an internal hard drive, consider getting an external USB 2.0 drive instead. Ditto for an extra CD, DVD, or recordable media drive.

- ✔ New hardware is recognized almost instantly by Windows. A pop-up bubble from the Notification Area alerts you to any new hardware that Windows finds.

- ✔ When new hardware isn't automatically found, open the Control Panel and open the Add Hardware icon. Run the Add Hardware Wizard to help set up and configure your new hardware.

- ✔ Some USB peripherals may not be recognized. For example, a new USB mouse or keyboard may not cause any alerts to appear or notices to show up. That's fine. Check the device to ensure that it's working and you're doing well.

- ✔ You must add external modems manually. Refer to Chapter 11.

- ✔ Joysticks must be configured manually. Use the Game Controllers icon in the Control Panel to do this.

- ✔ *Remember* to refer to the documentation that came with your hardware for how exactly to configure it. Note that sometimes the software that comes with your device (usually on a CD) may need to be installed first, before you install the hardware. Other times, it's vice versa.

Part VI
The Part of Tens

The 5th Wave   By Rich Tennant

"In preparation for takeoff, we ask that you turn off all electronic devices, laptop computers, and mainframes..."

In this part . . .

1 f you love trivia, world records, or books and Web pages containing lists, then this is the part of the book you've been waiting for. These aren't meaningless "Lists of Tens," such as Ten People Who Have Plunged to Their Deaths over Niagara Falls, Ten Otherwise Ugly People Who've Made the Successful Transition from Politics to Film, or Ten Things Easily Disguised as Fried Chicken. Instead these are interesting lists of Do's and Don'ts, suggestions, tips, and other helpful information.

Note that there won't always be ten items in each chapter, and in some cases, there may be more. After all, if one more fool died while going over the falls, why leave him off the list?

Chapter 21

Ten Battery Tips and Tricks

In This Chapter

▶ Avoiding battery perils

▶ Draining the battery

▶ Using less battery power

▶ Preventing virtual memory swapping

▶ Cleaning the battery terminals

▶ Storing the battery

▶ Understanding that the battery drains itself over time

*P*erhaps the most unique and notable thing about a laptop computer is that it has a battery. Just about everything else on the laptop is somehow related to or has a counterpart on the non-portable desktop computer. But laptops have batteries, and better than any carrying handle ever, it's the battery that makes the laptop portable.

This chapter contains ten tips and tricks to help you use your laptop and its battery in the most productive manner possible. Note that these aren't the standard battery tips. I'm assuming, for example, that you know better than to try and put your laptop's battery into your mouth. Further, that you won't suddenly desire to put your laptop's battery on a campfire "to see what happens." And finally, that you'll never go anywhere near your laptop's battery with a can opener or soldering iron — unless it's your dying wish to see your grieving relatives try to explain your stupidity to a television news crew.

Don't Drop the Battery, Get It Wet, Short It, Play Keep-Away with It, Open It, Burn It, or Throw It Away

Enough said.

Scary Lithium-Ion battery trivia

Lithium-Ion batteries are what many of us humans aspire to be: smart and popular. But there is a scary side to the Lithium-Ion battery as well. The following are some frightening Lithium-Ion battery statistics designed to literally shock you away from any thought of messing with your laptop's battery:

- One of the functions of the Lithium-Ion battery's smarts is to prevent overcharging.

- When a Lithium-Ion battery is overcharged, it gets hot. Then it explodes.

- The Lithium metal in the battery will burn inside water.

- The acid inside the battery is not only highly caustic, it's flammable.

- I'm sure the acid is poisonous as well, but — golly — the sentence above had me at "caustic."

- There is an increased risk of explosion when the battery gets too hot.

- You cannot recycle a used Lithium-Ion battery, so don't ever think of buying or using a "recycled" battery.

Every Few Months, Drain the Battery All the Way

To keep your laptop's battery nice and healthy, remember to drain it completely at least once every few months.

Most laptops use modern, intelligent Lithium-Ion batteries. Unlike the "memory effect" batteries of the past (NiCad and NiMH), you can recharge your Lithium-Ion batteries at any time, and they still maintain full capacity. Even so, it's a good idea to let the battery completely drain about once every two or three months. Then recharge the battery nice and slow, probably over night is best. That will keep your battery healthy and happy.

Turn Down the Monitor's Brightness

To save a bit on battery life on the road, adjust the brightness on your monitor down just a hair — or perhaps as low as you can stand. That definitely saves the juice.

✔ Buttons near the laptop's LCD monitor control the brightness.

✔ Sometimes the brightness is controlled by using special Fn key combinations.

✔ Your laptop's power manager may automatically dim the screen when the laptop is on battery power.

✔ Also check the Power Options dialog box (from the Control Panel), to see if there are any advanced or specific settings on your laptop for disabling or saving power used by the display.

Power Down the Hard Drives

Power is consumed in your laptop the most by motors, specifically those motors that keep the hard dive constantly spinning. Sometimes this is necessary. When you're using a program that constantly accesses the hard drive, such as a database, then it's more efficient to keep the drive constantly spinning. But when you're working on something that doesn't require constant disk access, it's a good idea to save some juice by sleeping an idle hard drive.

 To control when the hard dive sleeps, use the Power Options icon in the Control Panel. In the Power Schemes tab, set a quick sleep time for the hard drive when the laptop is under battery power. Refer to Chapter 8 for more information, in the section, "Managing Your Laptop's Power."

Add More RAM to Prevent Virtual Memory Disk Swapping

One way the hard drive conspires with the operating system to drain the battery quickly is when the virtual memory manager pulls a disk swap. The way to prevent that is to add more memory (RAM) to your laptop.

Virtual memory has nothing to do with virtue. Instead, it's a chunk of hard drive space that Windows uses to help supplement real memory, or RAM. Mass chunks of information are swapped between RAM and your laptop's hard drive, which is why you never see any "Out of Memory" errors in Windows. But all that swapping does put a drain on the battery.

Virtual memory settings are kept in the System Properties dialog box. Here's how to observe the settings, which are really buried deep:

1. **Open the System icon in the Control Panel.**

   Refer to Chapter 6 for more information.

2. **Click the Advanced tab.**

3. **Click the Settings button in the Performance area.**

   Note that there are *three* Settings buttons on the Advanced tab. Ensure that you click the right one.

4. **In the Performance Options dialog box, click the Advanced tab.**

5. **Click the Change button in the Virtual memory area.**

   Finally, you get to see your laptop's virtual memory settings. Note that the recommended values are displayed in the dialog box, as shown in Figure 21-1.

Figure 21-1: Dig deep enough, and you'll find this dialog box.

6. **Make adjustments as necessary.**

   Normally there is no need to make changes here. But if your laptop is packed with RAM, say over 1GB, assigning less or zero disk space for the cache can help reduce disk access.

7. **Keep clicking OK buttons to close the various open dialog boxes, windows, and whatnot.**

The idea isn't really to adjust virtual memory as much as it is to add more RAM to your laptop and prevent virtual memory from ever taking over in the first place.

A good amount of RAM to have with Windows XP is 256MB, though 512MB is better, and 1GB (1024MB) or more of memory is just ideal.

To see how much memory is installed in your laptop, open the Control Panel's System icon. The amount of memory installed appears near the bottom of the General tab, such as the 512MB shown in Figure 21-2.

Figure 21-2: This laptop has a paltry 512MB of RAM. The owner must be a real cheap bastard.

Refer to Chapter 20 for more information on adding RAM to your laptop.

Run as Few Programs as Possible/ Close Unused Programs

Because of Windows XP and its multitasking nature (which is good), excess power is used to keep several programs running at a time (which is bad). To optimize performance, I recommend running only one program at a time on your laptop when you're using the battery.

When you're in a situation where you're switching from one program to another, then running those two programs at once is fine. What I'm speaking about is running many programs at once, as a desktop user would. For example, you could be reading e-mail in your e-mail program, browsing the Web, have your word processor open for editing a document, keep a game of Spider Solitaire going in another window, and so on. All that is really unnecessary, and shutting down those programs that you're not using does help save battery life.

Guard the Battery's Terminals

Like a big city airport or bus station, your laptop's battery has terminals. People do not traverse a battery's terminals, but electricity does. So the terminals are usually flat pieces of metal, either out in the open or recessed into a slot.

- ✔ Keep your battery in the laptop.

- ✔ Outside of the laptop, keep the battery away from metal.

- ✔ Keep the terminals clean; use a Q-tip and some rubbing alcohol. You'll need to do this when you succumb to the temptation to touch the terminals, even though you shouldn't be doing that.

- ✔ Do not attach anything to the battery.

- ✔ Do not attempt to short the battery or try to rapidly drain it.

- ✔ The terminals appear in a different location on the battery, depending on who made the battery and how it attaches to the laptop.

Avoid Extreme Temperatures

Batteries enjoy the same type of temperatures you do. They do not like it to be very cold, and they do not like hot temperatures either.

Store the Battery If You Don't Plan on Using It

You should try to avoid letting your battery sit. If you keep the laptop deskbound (and nothing could be sadder), then occasionally unplug the thing and let the battery cycle just to keep the battery healthy. That's the best thing to do.

When you'd rather run your laptop without the battery inside, or for storing a spare battery, run the battery's charge down to about 40 percent or so, then put the battery in a non-metallic container. Stick the container in a nice, cool, clean, dry place.

- Like people, batteries need exercise! Cycle your battery every two months or so whether you're using the laptop remotely or not.

- The recommended storage temperature for Lithium-Ion batteries is 59 degrees (Fahrenheit) or 15 degrees (Celsius).

- Also refer to the next section.

- A Lithium-Ion battery has an expiration date! After two or three years, the battery will die. This is true whether you use the battery or store it.

Batteries Will Drain Over Time!

No battery keeps its charge forever. Eventually, over time, the battery's charge will fade. For some reason, this surprises people. "That battery was fully charged when I put it into storage six years ago!" Don't be one of the surprised; know that batteries drain over time.

Yet, just because a battery has drained doesn't mean that it's dead. If you've stored the battery properly, then all it needs is a full charge to get it back up and running again. So if you've stored a battery (see the previous section), anticipate that you'll need to recharge that battery when you go to use it again. This works just like getting the battery on the first day you bought your laptop; follow those same instructions for getting the stored battery back up and running again.

Chapter 22

Ten Handy Laptop Accessories

In This Chapter

▶ Getting a laptop bag or case

▶ Adding a spare battery

▶ Expanding the laptop with a port replicator

▶ Keeping the laptop cool with a cooling pad

▶ Cleaning with a mini-vac

▶ Illuminating with a USB lamp

▶ Enjoying a full-sized keyboard and mouse

▶ Adding an ID card

▶ Installing theft prevention

*O*ne thing that's kept the computer industry alive for years and years is that the computer purchase never stops with the computer itself. First comes software. Then follows more hardware and even more hardware. Peripherals! Gizmos! Gadgets! And then there are accessories like mouse pads and tchotchkes to sit atop the monitor. The computer is endlessly expandable.

Feast your eyes, dear reader, and stretch your pocket book on the following ten fun or must-have items to expand your laptop universe. (Go to Chapter 7 for more about other peripheral devices you can use with your laptop.)

Laptop Bag or Travel Case

Buy yourself and your laptop a handsome laptop bag. Chapter 15 offers some great suggestions and recommendations.

Spare Battery

Nothing cries "freedom!" to the laptop road warrior more than an extra battery. Having a bonus battery doubles the time you can compute without being tethered to an AC wall socket. Some laptops even let you hot swap from one battery to another while the laptop is still running, meaning that the total time you can use your battery greatly exceeds your capacity to do work.

Ensure that the spare battery is approved for your laptop, either coming directly from the manufacturer or from a source that is reliable and guarantees compatibility. Using the wrong battery in your laptop can meet with disastrous results.

Docking Station or Port Replicator

A docking station or port replicator helps immensely when it comes time for your laptop to serve desktop duty. For example, you can keep the big monitor, full-sized keyboard, and desktop mouse attached to the port replicator and keep that in one spot at home or in the office. Then when you're ready to go, pop off or pop out the laptop, and hit on the road.

✔ A port replicator also gives your laptop more ports and more expandability options than the laptop may come with on its own.

✔ The docking station and port replicator are specific to your laptop. You'll need to obtain them from your laptop's manufacturer or computer dealer.

Cooling Pad

The ideal accessory for any modern laptop is the laptop cooling pad. This is a device, similar to what's shown in Figure 22-1, upon which your laptop sits. The device contains one or more fans and is either powered by the laptop's USB port or standard AA batteries. Your laptop sits upon the device, and the fans help draw away the heat that the battery and microprocessor generate. The end result is a cooler-running laptop, which keeps the laptop happy.

✔ Note that the cooling pad runs from the power supplied by the USB port or from its own batteries. That means it's portable.

✔ Sadly, you cannot use a cooling pad with a port replicator or docking station that gets in its way.

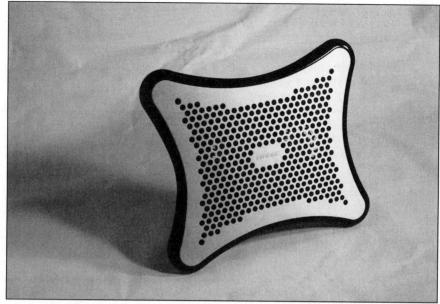

Figure 22-1:
A cool
cooling pad.

> ✔ If you're getting a USB-powered cooling pad, try to get a model that has a pass-through USB port, so that you don't lose a USB port when you add a cooling pad.

> ✔ Some cooling pads also double as a USB hub.

Mini-Vac

Handy for cleaning your laptop, especially the keyboard, is the mini-vac. These can be found in most office supply stores, and many are portable (battery powered). You'll be surprised (and disgusted) by the gunk the mini-vac can suck from your laptop.

USB Lamp

Your laptop's LCD screen is illuminated and even shows up in the dark. Sadly, however, most laptop keyboards do not light up as well. To help you see the keyboard, as well as other important things around your laptop, you can light things up with a USB-powered lamp.

The lamp plugs into a standard USB port on your laptop. It either has a stiff, bendable cord or clamp so that you can position it. Flip the switch and let there be light!

Note that some laptops may already have a built-in keyboard light. Some IBM models feature a lamp mounted atop the LCD screen. A special function key turns the lamp on or off.

Full-Sized Keyboard

While you may not want to tote one around with you, there is a certain pleasure to be had when using a laptop with a comfy, full-sized keyboard. Especially if you rely on the numeric keypad, either for numbers or cursor control, it's a joy to use a full-sized keyboard with a laptop.

There is nothing special you need to do for a full-sized keyboard, but do note that most laptops don't sport a PC keyboard port. Instead, use the USB port, or if you have a port replicator or docking station, you can connect the full-sized keyboard to it instead.

In addition to (or perhaps, instead of) a standard full-sized keyboard, you can select any of a number of fun and different keyboards for your laptop. You can find keyboards with special Internet buttons, ergonomically designed to make typing easier on the human bod, as well as wireless keyboards. Because your laptop didn't come with a full-sized keyboard, it's your buyer's paradise as far as choosing one for your laptop. Or if all you need is that numeric keypad, there are special USB numeric keypads you can get for your laptop.

External Mouse

The only problem I have with using an external mouse on my laptop is that I neglect it. I'm so trained to use the touch pad that I forget about the full-sized, comfy, and easy-to-use mouse right next to my laptop.

As with a keyboard, you aren't limited to your choice of an external mouse for your laptop. You can get a basic mouse, one of those space-age optical glowing mice, a mouse with lots of buttons, that weird mouse that you can hover in the air and use like a TV remote, wireless mice, trackball mice, those tiny laptop mice, and the list goes on and on.

While you can disable the touch pad on your laptop, I would recommend keeping it active when you use an external mouse. Often when I'm browsing the Web or just reading some document, I typically revert to the touch pad instead of using the external mouse. (I'm hard to train.)

Your laptop most likely lacks a mouse port. Get a USB mouse.

ID Card or Return Service Sticker

If your laptop wore underwear, you'd most likely want to write the laptop's name on the underwear. Fortunately, laptop's don't require underwear, so the next best thing is to create an ID card for your laptop.

It's common for business people to simply tape their business card somewhere on the inside of the laptop, such as just to one side of the touch pad.

The idea here is not only to claim ownership of the laptop, but to pray that if it's ever lost or stolen, the laptop will be recognizable as your own. A good citizen will phone you up and offer to return the laptop he or she found with your name emblazoned on an ID card.

A better solution is to use a return service and take advantage of its tamper-resistant asset tags. Refer to Chapter 17 for more information.

Theft Prevention System

The perfect gift for the laptop you love: either some type of cable to keep your laptop from walking off, or one of those annoyingly loud my-laptop-has-been-moved alarms. Ease your fears! Also refer to Chapter 17 for more information on laptop security, specifically these types of devices.

Chapter 23

Ten Things to Throw in Your Laptop Case

In This Chapter

▶ The laptop's power cord

▶ A spare battery

▶ An external mouse

▶ Something to clean the laptop

▶ Security devices

▶ Removable media

▶ A set of headphones (or two)

▶ Cables, cables, and more cables

Some people just don't know how to pack. The amateur recognizes the need to cook out in the wild, but toting around your every cast iron pot, pan, and skillet is unnecessary. After all, lightweight and resourceful camping cooking gear exists.

I suppose that it all boils down to experience. The toil and trials of toting cast iron cookware around every weekend begs for a solution. Likewise, you want to pack your laptop carrying case with what you need and no more — especially no cast iron peripherals. Plus, there may be some handy things to pack that you're utterly unaware of. To help in your education, this chapter presents ten handy, useful, and necessary things you should consider including in your laptop carrying case.

Power Cord and Brick

This is one even I forget. Sometimes I think, "Oh, I'm only going to be gone for an hour, and the battery lasts for three hours, so I don't need the power cord." Then an appointment is cancelled, and I have more time, but regret not having the power cord with me.

Always bring your power cord, and the adapter or "brick" with you in your laptop case. You just never know when a wall socket appears. Take advantage of it!

Spare Battery

If you're blessed with a spare battery for your laptop, bring it!

- ✔ Don't forget to charge the spare battery before you leave.
- ✔ Also see Chapter 8 for more information on your laptop's battery.

Mouse or Trackball

Anyone who's used to a real mouse probably won't forget to throw it in the laptop's case, but you never know. I highly recommend using a real mouse with your laptop, especially if your laptop sits somewhere on a table or desk with room for the mouse.

- ✔ The real mouse adds little weight to your laptop case.
- ✔ Get a USB mouse or use the USB connector if you have a desktop mouse. (You won't need the green-colored desktop PC mouse adapter.) Most modern laptops sport a USB port, but few come standard with a mouse port any more.
- ✔ If your laptop is Bluetooth-enabled, you can use a wireless Bluetooth mouse.
- ✔ A trackball is a special type of mouse, often called the "upside down" mouse. You manipulate a ball with your fingertips, and the ball spins in a stationary base. This is often easier to use when desk space is limited. In fact, trackball users claim that such a mouse is easier to control than the typical bar-of-soap model mouse.

Screen Wipes and Cleaner

Go the office store and get some screen wipes and a small, portable bottle of cleaner. Toss 'em in your laptop bag and keep them there. If you can find the screen wipes in a smaller, portable size, buy them. Make it a permanent part of your laptop bag.

Laptop Lock

Don't forget your laptop's anti-theft device. Be it a cable you can connect to something solid or one of those loud, loud audio alarms, you probably want to pack it in your laptop bag.

See Chapter 17 for more information on laptop security.

Removable Media

Saving your stuff to the laptop's hard drive often isn't enough. It helps to have an assortment of alternatives to get that information out of the computer, especially when your laptop isn't connected to a network for easy file transfer. Two such options are CD-Rs and USB flash drives.

- ✔ I often toss one of those ten-pack blank CD-R bundles into my laptop bag in case I need to burn a CD-R on the road.

- ✔ CD-Rs can also be used for backing up important data.

- ✔ Ensure that your laptop does have a CD-R drive before you buy the blank CD-R discs. Not every laptop comes with such a drive.

- ✔ You can also bring and use CD-RWs, though I personally just use CD-Rs. The CD-Rs are cheaper, and I rarely find myself erasing or rewriting the CD-RWs anyway.

- ✔ This same reasoning holds for DVD-R and the other DVD writable disc formats. Just ensure that you get the proper blank discs for the type of DVD drive in your laptop.

- ✔ USB flash drives are handy, key ring-sized gizmos that plug directly into one of the laptop's USB ports. Windows instantly recognizes the new drive and lets you copy stuff to it, up to 512MB or more! The drive can then be removed and its information accessed by any other computer with a compatible USB port.

✔ There is a difference between a USB flash drive and the media card used by a digital camera. The media cards require some form of card reader interface, whereas flash drives do not. But you can still use a media card as yet another form of removable storage — providing that you also pack the card reader in your laptop's carrying case.

Headphones

The computer is a musical machine! Why bring along a portable CD player, when all you really need are your music CDs, the laptop, and . . . headphones!

I prefer using headphones with my laptop because its little internal speakers are just too feeble. Yeah, I know, they try. But with headphones, you can also turn the volume way, way up and enjoy your music without annoying anyone nearby.

When I go traveling, I take two sets of headphones with me. Then I use a headphone splitter/adapter so that both sets of phones can plug in to the laptop. That way, two of us can enjoy viewing a DVD movie on the laptop during a long airplane ride.

Tools

Consider packing a small "handyman" kit with your laptop. Or include in your laptop case at least a small regular and Phillips head screwdrivers, a pair of pliers, and a small wire cutter. I would also recommend a small utility knife, however, such a thing is likely to be confiscated by airport security.

Cables, Cables, Cables

Cables are good. When you can, bring spare Ethernet, phone, USB, IEEE 1394 (also called FireWire), S-video, power, and any other type of spare cable you can muster. You may never use them, but then again, you may never know.

✔ You never know where the Internet lurks! Taking along a goodly length Ethernet cable with your laptop is always a good idea. That allows you to instantly connect to any available Ethernet network without having to wait for or (worse) rent a cable.

- A goodly length is about 6 feet long.

- Most hotels with in-room high speed Internet keep a spare Ethernet cable in the room's closet. Even so, bringing your own cable means you don't have to go hunting for it.

- Ethernet cables have other advantages as well. No, I don't mean that they make a statement as a table setting decoration. As I write this, I'm sitting in a café using a wireless Internet connection. My son's laptop lacks a wireless network adapter; however, by using the Ethernet cable, I can connect my laptop to his and share the Internet connection. Now both of us are on the Internet, thanks to that cable.

- Cables don't have to be all tangley, either. If you don't like wrapping up your cables, look for those cables that come with their own spools at any office supply store.

- Another cable to have, if it's available for your laptop, is an automobile cigarette lighter DC adapter. (Some newer cars don't even call it a "cigarette lighter" any more. No, it's the DC adapter!)

Not the End of the List

You can pack your laptop bag full of so much stuff that the bag will eventually weigh more than you do. There is only so much you can take: Portable printers, USB hubs, PC Cards, external disk drives, and the list goes on.

The items mentioned in this chapter are good to *always* have in your laptop bag. Add the other stuff as you need it. Or when you're traveling, consider putting those things in your checked luggage so that you're not toting the extra weight.

Index

• *Numerics* •

802.11 wireless standards, 28, 160
1394 port, 69, 120, 125

• *A* •

abacus, 9
AC adapter. *See* power brick
accessories, 305–309
Acrobat Writer software (Adobe), 132
activating. *See* enabling
Ad-Aware anti-spyware software, 210
Add Hardware Wizard, 186–187, 188
Add or Remove Programs dialog box, 105–106
Add Password command (File menu), 266
Address Book, faxing and, 197
administrator account, 110–111
Adobe Acrobat Writer software, 132
Advanced Attributes dialog box, 265
Advanced Privacy Settings dialog box, 210
advertisements with your laptop, 51
air travel. *See* portability; travel
airport inspections, 247–248, 260
alarms
  anti-theft, 309, 313
  low battery warnings, 139–141, 255
alkaline batteries, 134, 135
All Programs menu, 53
alphanumeric keys, 73
Alt key, 73–74
anti-hijacking software, 211
anti-spyware software
  determining if a program is legitimate, 211
  disabling third-party cookies, 209–210
  need for, 209
  overview, 208–209
  recommended programs, 210
anti-theft alarms, 309, 313
antivirus software
  disabling, 207–208
  need for, 206, 213
  overview, 205–206
  scanning for viruses, 206–207
  spyware and, 209
  tips for avoiding viruses, 208
  using two programs, 207
  Web-based utilities, 207
AOL Internet service, 171, 177, 216
Apple Macintosh computers, 2
appliances, keeping away from, 254
applications. *See* software
area code rules for modems, 191–193
arrow keys, 74
assembling your new laptop, 39
asset tags, 259
attachments to e-mail, 208, 224
automatic e-mail checking, disabling, 221–222
automatic updates, 291–293
Avast! Antivirus software, 206
AVG Anti-Virus software, 206

• *B* •

background of desktop, 51, 96
backing up, 245–246, 267
balloon tips, disabling, 103
batteries. *See also* battery life; power management
  buying a laptop and, 26–27, 135
  changing, 142
  charging, 38–39, 141–142, 245, 288
  cycling, 143, 298

batteries *(continued)*
  dead, 57, 144, 288
  determining what you have, 135, 136
  drained versus dead, 303
  Dreaded Memory Effect, 134, 135, 138
  external charging unit, 142
  finding your laptop's, 136
  future of, 17, 135
  hot, dangers of, 136
  hot swapping, 142
  introduction in laptops, 11, 12
  low battery warnings, 139–141, 255
  monitoring, 136–139
  in new laptop, 38–39
  NiCad versus Lithium-Ion, 26, 134
  portability and, 133
  removing when using AC power, 143–144
  second or spare, 142, 306, 312
  shorting to drain, avoiding, 142
  smart, 136, 139
  status indicator, 72
  storing when not in use, 143, 302–303
  terminals, 302
  tips and tricks, 297–303
  types of, 134–136
  unapproved, avoiding, 136
  won't charge, 288
Batteries.com site, 142
battery life. *See also* power management
  automatic updates and, 292
  battery won't charge, 288
  buying a laptop and, 26, 27
  cycling the battery and, 143, 298
  devices that consume power, 144
  disk swapping and, 299
  hard drives and, 144, 145, 146, 299
  LCD display and, 27, 144, 145, 255,
    298–299
  low battery warnings, 139–141, 255
  of modern notebooks, 16
  monitoring the battery, 136–139
  multitasking and, 301–302
  NEC UltraLite laptop, 15

removing battery and, 143
smart batteries and, 136, 139
spare battery and, 142, 306, 312
specifications versus reality, 19
temperature and, 302
tips for conserving, 144–146, 255, 297–303
unused hardware and, 99, 255
USB-powered devices and, 119
using two batteries and, 27
wallpaper and, 96
beverages, dangers from, 40, 253
BIOS password, 261–262
BIOS Setup program, 49
Bluetooth wireless networking, 72, 116
booting, 48. *See also* turning on your
    laptop
box
  saving, 37
  unpacking, 35–38
Briefcase folder
  copying items to, 232
  creating, 231
  moving it to the laptop, 233
  "Needs updating" in status column, 232
  renaming the Briefcase icon, 231
  synchronizing files, 233–234
  using files from, 233
broadband, 174
browser alternatives, 205
browsing. *See* Web browsing
business trips. *See* portability; travel
Buying a Computer For Dummies (Gookin,
    Dan), 21
buying a laptop
  batteries and, 26–27, 135
  communications options and, 28
  docking stations and, 29
  expansion options and, 25, 27–28
  extended warranties and, 30
  finding software first, 22–23
  further information, 21
  hardware not required, 25

hardware requirements, 24–29
laptop carrying case and, 242–243
LCD display and, 26, 27
port replicators and, 29
portability and, 25
power management hardware and, 29
price and, 22, 29, 32
reasons for, 18–19, 22
research needed for, 21
service and support and, 22, 29–31
size and, 26
steps for, 22
unpacking the laptop, 35–38
waiting for a better deal, 32
weight and, 26, 27
where to buy, 31–32

● *C* ●

cable modem Internet connection, 173
cables
  for direct connection (desktop-laptop),
    226–227, 230
  Ethernet, 150, 173
  packing, 314–315
  USB, 116, 117–118
café computing
  choosing a place to sit, 252
  finding a wall socket, 252–253
  overview, 251–252
  tips, 253
call waiting, disabling for modem use, 189
calling cards with modems, 193
canceling a pending fax, 198, 199
Caps Lock key indicator, 72
case (shell) of your laptop. *See also* laptop
    carrying case
  cleaning, 84
  closing the lid, 57, 62–63, 127
  opening the lid, 44–46
  ports overview, 68–71
Category View (Control Panel), 93–94

CD discs
  for desktop-laptop exchange, 225–226
  ejecting, 66, 91
  installing software from, 104
  packing, 313
  for presentations, 269
  removing before traveling, 246
  unpacking the laptop and, 36
CD drives
  adding a USB device, 120–122
  battery life and, 144, 145
  CD/DVD combination drives, 66
  exchangeable drives, 27, 28
  external, 294
  placement of, 66
  removing a USB device, 123–124
  removing to save power, 255
  software requirements and, 23
  types of, 66
charging batteries
  battery won't charge, 288
  before traveling, 245
  for new laptop, 38–39
  recharging, 141–142
  wall socket on planes, 249
chip. *See* microprocessor
Clarke, Arthur C. ("Into the Comet"), 9
Classic View (Control Panel), 93
cleaning your laptop, 83–85, 313
Cleansweep utility (Norton), 106
clock, alkaline battery for, 135
closing the lid of the laptop
  external monitor and, 127
  setting options for, 62–63
  Stand By (sleep) mode and, 57
cold boot, 48. *See also* turning on your
    laptop
colleges, laptops at, 20
color coding
  on keyboard keys, 74
  for keyboard port, 71, 127
  for mouse port, 71
  for ports, table summarizing, 69–70
  power cord, 40

communications. *See also* desktop-laptop connection; modems; networking
  buying a laptop and, 28
  portability and, 10
CompactFlash card reader. *See* memory card readers
Compaq computers
  Compaq 1, 10–11
  Compaq III, 12
  Compaq SLT, 13–14
compressed files or folders, 266
Connect dialog box, 178
connecting. *See also* desktop-laptop connection; Internet connection; plugging in; USB ports
  batteries, 136, 142
  external mouse, 83, 128–129
  FireWire devices, 120
  modem to phone jack, 178
  to networks, wired, 153–154
  to networks, wireless, 161–163, 165–166
  PC Cards, inserting, 124–125
  printers, 129–130
  second monitor, 127
  USB devices, 118, 120–122
  video projectors, 127, 271–272
Context key, 73–74
Control Panel. *See also specific dialog boxes*
  accessing, 93
  Add or Remove Programs icon, 104, 105
  Classic versus Category View, 93–94
  Display Properties icon, 88, 96
  as fly-out menu on Start menu, 94–96
  icon on Start menu, 54
  laptop-specific icons, 101
  Network Connections icon, 97, 228
  Phone and Modem Options icon, 99, 182, 188
  Power Options icon, 60, 62, 97, 137
  Printers and Faxes icon, 99
  System icon, 98, 266, 280, 300

  User Accounts icon, 107
  Wireless Link icon, 101
converting to NTFS file system, 263
cookies, disabling third-party, 209–210
cooling pad, 115, 256, 306–307
copying items to Briefcase folder, 232
counting board (abacus), 9
cover templates for faxing, 198
CPU. *See* microprocessor
Critical Battery Alarm, 140
Critical Battery Alarm Actions dialog box, 140–141
Ctrl key, 73–74
cursor control keys, 74, 75
cycling the battery, 143, 298

● *D* ●

DC power. *See* batteries; battery life; power management
DCIM folder, 122
deactivating. *See* disabling
dead battery, 57, 144, 288
defaults
  Internet connection, 177, 179
  printer, 100
deleting. *See* removing
Dell 320LT, power brick of, 14
desk, positioning your laptop on, 40
desktop computer, laptop as extension of, 22–23
Desktop Items dialog box, 88
desktop (Windows)
  defined, 51
  My Documents folder on, 88
  overview, 51–52
desktop-laptop connection
  accessing the desktop remotely, 234–237
  CD discs for, 225–226
  direct connection using cables, 226–227, 228–230
  floppy disks for, 225–226
  infrared port for, 228

need for, 225
network for, 226
synchronizing files, 19, 231–233
Device Manager window, 98
dialing rules for modems
  adding a new location, 190
  area code rules, 191–193
  need for, 188
  setting up a location, 188–190
  using calling cards, 193
dial-up Internet connection
  choosing a specific connection, 179
  configuring, 176–177, 180
  default connection, 177, 179
  digital phone systems and, 179
  disconnecting, 179–180
  finding the connection, 177
  firewall, 201–205
  ISP for, 171
  making the connection, 178–179
  speeds, 178–179
  Status dialog box, 179–180
  timeout for, 180, 194–195
digital cameras. *See also* memory card
    readers
  DCIM folder for images, 122
  USB port for, 115
digital phone systems, modems and,
    179, 254
digital video port, 69
direct connection (desktop-laptop),
    226–227, 228–230
disabling. *See also* enabling; turning on
    and off
  antivirus software, 207–208
  automatic e-mail checking, 221–222
  automatic updates, 292
  balloon tips, 103
  call waiting for modem use, 189
  Guest account, 110, 263
  hardware not used, 99, 255
  infrared port, 266–267
  modems, 184–185
  third-party cookies, 209–210

touch pad, 82, 83, 129
Windows firewall, 204
wireless connection, 167
disconnecting. *See also* removing;
    unplugging
  after picking up e-mail, 221
  from the Internet, 172, 179–180
  from networks, wired, 154
  from networks, wireless, 167
  to stop faxes, 198
disk swapping, 299–301
display. *See* LCD display
Display Properties dialog box, 88, 96–97,
    128
displaying. *See* viewing
disposing of dead battery, 144, 288
docking stations
  buying a laptop and, 29
  defined, 29, 71
  for non-USB keyboards, 127
  for non-USB printers, 130
  overview, 306
  port replicators versus, 71
  storing, 40
downloading, 89
drained battery, 303
Dreaded Memory Effect, 134, 135, 138
drinks, dangers from, 40, 253
drivers, 130, 281–282
DSL Internet connection, 173
DVD discs
  ejecting, 91
  installing software from, 104
  movies and LCD display size, 27
  packing, 313
  removing before traveling, 246
  unpacking the laptop and, 36
DVD drives
  adding a USB device, 120–122
  battery life and, 144, 145
  CD/DVD combination drives, 66
  external, 294
  removing a USB device, 123–124
  removing to save power, 255

• E •

EarthLink Internet service, 171
Eddie Bauer laptop case, 244, 245
Edit Location dialog box, 189–190, 191, 193
802.11 wireless standards, 28, 160
Eject command (File menu), 66, 91
ejecting
  CD discs, 66, 91
  DVD discs, 91
  PC Cards, 67
electric motors, keeping away from, 254
Electrostatic Discharge (ESD), 39
e-mail. *See also* Internet connection
  accessing from friend's computer,
    217–218
  accessing on the road, 215–216
  alternatives to Outlook Express, 208
  antivirus software, 205–208, 213
  author's address, 3
  deleting Web-based e-mail, 216
  disabling automatic checking, 221–222
  disconnecting after picking up, 221
  forwarding for pickup on the road,
    218–219
  leaving a copy on the server, 222–223
  mail rule for Outlook Express, 219
  password, removing, 220–221
  on the road, tips for, 215–224
  sending messages in one batch, 222
  skipping messages over a given size, 224
  viruses, avoiding, 208
  Web-based access, 171–172, 216–218, 223
enabling. *See also* disabling; turning on
    and off
  Hibernation mode, 59
  System Restore feature, 279–281
  Windows firewall, 202–203
encrypting files or folders, 264–265
energy management. *See* power
    management
engraving your laptop, 258
erasing. *See* removing
ergonomics, 40

Esc or Escape key, 74
ESD (Electrostatic Discharge), 39
Ethernet
  buying a laptop and, 28
  cables, 150
  Internet connection, 172–175
  PC Cards for, 28
  RJ-45 port, 70, 71, 150, 151
Eudora e-mail software, 208, 224
evolution of laptops
  desire for portability and, 7
  early PC laptops, 13–14
  future, 17
  luggables, 9–11
  lunch buckets, 12–13
  modern notebooks, 16–17
  NEC UltraLite laptop, 15–16
  Osborne 1 portable, 8–10
  Radio Shack Model 100, 11–12
  search for weightlessness and, 15
exchangeable drives, 27, 28
expansion options
  buying a laptop and, 25, 27–28
  exchangeable drives, 27, 28
  PC Cards, 27
  portability and, 25
  ports, 28
expansion slots, 25
extended warranties
  buying a laptop and, 30
  filling out, 36
  sending in, 37–38
  start date for, 38
extension cables for USB, 118
external devices. *See also* printers; *specific
    devices*
  adding a USB device, 118, 120–122
  battery charging unit, 142
  drives, 294
  getting rid of the dialog box, 122
  keyboard, 115, 126–127, 308
  modems, 185–187, 294
  monitors, 127–128

mouse, 82–83, 115, 128–129, 253, 308–309, 312

numeric keypad, 127

removing a USB device, 118, 123–124

types of USB storage, 114

video projector, 127

• F •

FAT32 file system, 263

Fax Console, 199, 200

Fax Monitor window, 198, 200

faxing
  canceling a pending fax, 198, 199
  cover templates for, 198
  Fax Console, 199, 200
  modem capability for, 195
  modem setup for, 195–196
  overview, 100, 101, 195
  receiving a fax, 200
  sending a fax, 196–198
  using fax machines as printers, 132, 253

File menu
  Add Password command, 266
  Eject command, 66, 91
  New Briefcase command, 231
  New Compressed (zipped) Folder command, 266
  Print command, 196
  Save As command, 214

filename extensions
  saving Web pages and, 214
  viruses and, 208

firewalls
  alternatives to Windows, 204
  defined, 174, 201
  monitoring, 204–205
  need for, 202
  overview, 201–202
  remote access and, 237
  router Internet connection and, 173
  spyware and, 209

Windows XP firewall, 202–204
  Zone Alarm firewall, 204–205

FireWire port, 69, 120, 125

flash drives
  adding a USB device, 120–122
  memory cards versus, 314
  packing, 313
  removing a USB device, 123–124

floppy drives, 25, 27, 67, 144

Fn (function) key, 76–77

folders. *See also specific folders*
  accessing shared folders, 156–157
  defined, 89
  for digital camera images, 122
  sharing, 157–159
  unsharing, 159

F1 through F12 keys, 74

food and drink, dangers from, 40, 253

forgetting passwords, cautions about, 50, 109, 262

forwarding your e-mail, 218–219

free services
  Internet access, 170
  Web-based e-mail access, 217

fuel cells, 17, 135

function (Fn) key, 76–77

Function keys, 74

future of laptops, 17

• G •

games
  hardware requirements for, 23
  USB port for controllers, 115

Gookin, Dan
  Buying a Computer For Dummies, 21
  e-mail address, 3
  Laptops For Dummies, 1–3
  PCs For Dummies, 89, 171, 253
  Troubleshooting Your PC For Dummies, 30, 285
  Web sites, 3
  weekly newsletter, 3

graphic applications, monitors and, 23
graphics files
  DCIM folder for digital camera images,
    122
  faxes as, 200
  hard drive space and, 25
  user account image, 53, 109
Guest account, disabling, 110, 263

• _H_ •

handheld devices for presentations, 269
happy stick, 80–81
hard drive storage
  accessing shared folders, 156–157
  battery life and, 144, 145, 146, 299
  buying a laptop and, 24, 25
  defined, 24
  exchangeable drives, 27, 28
  external USB storage, 114, 118,
    120–124, 294
  freeing up space, 106
  graphics files and, 25
  Hibernation mode and, 59
  PC Cards for, 125
  plugging external drives into UPS, 41
  printing to disk and Windows XP, 132
  sharing drives, avoiding, 159
  software requirements and, 23, 24
  status indicator, 72
  upgrading, 293–294
hardware. _See also specific kinds_
  buying a laptop and, 24–29
  compatibility in modern notebooks, 16
  defined, 65
  devices that consume battery power, 144
  future of laptops, 17
  modem, 181–182
  networking, 150–151
  not used, disabling, 99, 255
  ports, overview, 68–71
  for power management, 29
  software requirements and, 23, 24

tour of laptop, 65–71
unpacking the laptop, 35–38
upgrading, 293–294
USB port for, 114–116
USB-powered, 119
wireless networking, 161
headphone port, 69
headphones, 314
heat. _See_ temperature
Hibernation mode
  closing the lid and, 62–63
  defined, 57
  enabling, 59
  entering, 58, 62–63
  files saved by, 255
  hard drive space and, 59
  "lost" in (won't wake up), 287–288
  power button setting for, 60–62
  sleep button setting for, 62
  Stand By (sleep) mode versus, 58–59
  starting up from, 58
hijacking, avoiding, 211
HijackThis anti-hijacking software, 211
hot battery, dangers of, 136
hot swapping
  batteries, 142
  USB devices, 118
hotel room computing, 253–254
.htm or .html files, saving Web pages as,
    214, 215
hubs for networking, 151
hubs for USB ports, 119–120

• _I_ •

IBM TrackPoint, 80–81
icons. _See also_ Control Panel; System Tray
    or Notification Area
  defined, 51
  in margins of this book, 3
  My Computer, 90–91
  My Network Places, 91
  Network Connections, 91–92

for network connections, 92
for network printers, 100, 157
New Briefcase, 231
Safely Remove Hardware, 123, 124
for shared folders, 159
in System Tray, 102
ID card, 309
IEEE 1394 port, 69, 120, 125
iGo battery store online, 142
images. *See* graphics files
infrared port
buying a laptop and, 28
Control Panel icon for, 101
for desktop-laptop connection, 228
disabling, 266–267
overview, 69
inserting PC Cards, 124–125
installing hardware
assembling your new laptop, 39
Electrostatic Discharge (ESD) and, 39
external modem, 185–187
overview, 293–294
installing software. *See also* updating;
    upgrading
from CD or DVD, 104
creating a restore point before, 281–282
disabling antivirus software before,
    207–208
for external mouse, 83
licensing agreements and, 23
reinstalling Windows, avoiding, 279
Windows components, 106
Internet connection. *See also* networking
anti-spyware software for, 208–211
antivirus software for, 205–208, 213
cable modem, 173
dial-up connection, 171, 176–180
disconnecting, 172, 179–180
DSL, 173
Ethernet connection, 172–175
firewall for, 173, 174, 201–205
free access, 170
further information, 171

hijacking, avoiding, 211
Internet Explorer security flaws, 205
ISP for, 170, 171–172
on planes, 249
ports, 202
requirements, 170–171
router connection, 173–174
sharing, 174–175
Web-based e-mail access, 171–172, 223
wireless, 173, 175
Internet Explorer security flaws, 205
Internet Options dialog box, 209–210
Internet resources
anti-hijacking software, 211
anti-spyware software, 210
antivirus software, 206
author's Web sites, 3
author's weekly newsletter, 3
browser alternatives, 205
for buying a laptop, 31, 32
e-mail software, 208
Klear Screen, 85
laptop cases, 244
phone home services, 268
RealVNC remote access software, 235
for spare batteries, 142
STOP program, 259
for troubleshooting, 278
Web-based e-mail access, 171–172,
    216–218
Windows knowledgebase, 285
Zone Alarm firewall, 204
"Into the Comet" (Clarke, Arthur C.), 9
IR port. *See* infrared port
ISP (Internet Service Provider)
dial-up connection configuration, 176–177
firewall and, 202
leaving e-mail copy on server, 222–223
required for Internet connection, 170
selecting, 171–172
Web-based e-mail access, 216

• J •

jacks. *See* ports
joysticks, 294

• K •

Kaspersky antivirus software, 206
keyboard
  cleaning, 84
  color coding, 74
  custom keys and buttons, 78
  external, 115, 126–127, 308
  Fn key, 76–77
  general layout, 73–75
  numeric keypad, 75–76
  screen stained by, 85
  shortcuts for PowerPoint, 272–273
  size of, 73
  troubleshooting, 286–287
keyboard port, 69, 71
Klear Screen (Meridrew Enterprises), 85

• L •

labeling your laptop, 258–259
lamp, USB, 115, 307–308
LAN (Local Area Network). *See* networking
laptop carrying case
  as carry-on luggage, 247
  features to look for, 243–244
  manufacturer's case, avoiding, 242–243
  need for, 241–242
  recommended brands, 244
  theft, avoiding, 259
  things to pack, 246, 311–315
laptops, defined, 2
Laptops For Dummies (Gookin, Dan)
  assumptions about the reader, 1, 2
  icons in book margins, 3
  overview, 1–2
  using, 3

LCD display. *See also* monitors
  battery life and, 27, 144, 145, 255, 298–299
  buying a laptop and, 23, 26, 27
  cleaning, 84–85, 313
  DVD movies and, 27
  games and, 23
  graphic applications and, 23
  large displays, 126
  settings, 96–97
  size of laptop and, 27, 126
  weight and, 27
lead acid batteries, 134
lease for wireless networks, 167
legacy adapters, USB port for, 115
lights
  on the laptop, 72–73
  USB lamp, 115, 307–308
Limited account, 110
line filtering for laptop, 41–42
line in port, 69
line out port, 69
Linux operating system, 2
Lithium-Ion batteries. *See also* batteries;
    battery life; power management
  cycling, 143, 298
  NiCad batteries versus, 26, 134
  NiMH batteries versus, 134
  overview, 134
  trivia, 298
Local Area Network (LAN). *See* networking
local dealers, 31
location setup for modems, 188–190
locking Windows XP, 263–264
logging on to routers, 175
logging on to Windows XP. *See also* user
    accounts
  as administrator, 110–111
  after locking Windows, 264
  defined, 107
  password for, 50, 51, 108–109
  removing the need to log on, 111
Low Battery Alarm, 139
low battery warnings, 139–141, 255

LPT (printer) port, 70, 130, 227
luggables, 9–11
lunch buckets, 12–13

• *M* •

MAC Address, 166
Macintosh computers (Apple), 2
magnets, keeping away from, 254
main computer, laptop as, 18
malware, 209
manuals with the laptop, 37
marking your laptop, 258–259
McAfee
  firewall, 204
  VirusScan, 206
memory card readers
  adding a USB device, 120–122
  buying a laptop and, 25
  DCIM folder for images, 122
  PC Cards for, 27
  for removable storage, 314
  removing a USB device, 123–124
memory or RAM
  buying a laptop and, 24–25
  disk swapping and, 299–301
  installing in new laptop, 39
  software requirements and, 23, 24
  upgrading, 293
memory, virtual, 299–301
Meridrew Enterprises' Klear Screen, 85
.mht files, saving Web pages as, 214
mic port, 69
microprocessor
  buying a laptop and, 24, 25
  defined, 24
  power-miser, 29
  software requirements and, 23, 24
  speed and battery life, 146
Microsoft. *See also* Outlook Express;
    Windows XP
  Office Pack and Go Wizard, 271
  PowerPoint, 269, 271–273
  Windows knowledgebase, 285

mini-vac, 307
mobile phone, USB port for recharging, 116
Model 100 computer (Radio Shack), 11–12
Modem Properties dialog box
  general modem timeout setting, 194
  modem command settings, 184
  volume setting, 182–183
modems. *See also* dial-up Internet
    connection
  adding a new location, 190
  area code rules, 191–193
  battery life and, 144
  buying a laptop and, 28
  cable modem Internet connection, 173
  call waiting and, 189
  calling cards with, 193
  command settings, 184
  connecting to phone jack, 178
  dialing rules, 188–193
  digital phone systems and, 179, 254
  disabling, 184–185
  external, 185–187, 294
  faxing and, 100
  faxing with, 195–200
  hardware, 181–182
  internal versus external, 185–186
  location setup, 188–190
  long-distance charges and, 182
  meaning of the term, 182
  on networks, 156
  PC Cards for, 28
  port or jack, 69, 71, 181
  portable computing and, 10
  pulse dialing and, 189–190
  timeouts, 180, 194–195
  types of, 181
  volume setting, 182–183
monitoring
  batteries, 136–139
  firewalls, 204–205
monitors. *See also* LCD display
  connecting to your laptop, 127
  large, LCD displays versus, 126
  using two at once, 128

moon button. *See* sleep button

moon icon, 47, 62. *See also* sleep button

mounting external USB storage, 118, 120–122

mouse, external
 buying, 82–83, 128–129, 308
 for café computing, 253
 packing, 312
 touch pad with, 309
 as USB device, 115

mouse pad. *See* touch pad

mouse pointer, making more visible, 287

mouse port, 70, 71

Mouse Properties dialog box, 81–82, 287

Mozilla Firefox Web browser, 205

MP3 players, 114

MS Config, 284–285

multitasking, battery life and, 301–302

My Computer window, 90–91, 99

My Documents folder, 88–89

My IE Web browser, 205

My Music folder, 89

My Network Places window
 finding other computers, 154–156
 overview, 91
 View Network Connections link, 92

My Pictures folder, 89

• *N* •

names and naming. *See also* passwords
 Briefcase icon, 231
 desktop-laptop connection, 229
 for Internet connection, 176–177
 network computers, 152–153
 network printers, 157
 restore points, 281
 viruses and filename extensions, 208

NEC UltraLite laptop, 15–16

network adapters, 114, 144

Network Connections window
 adding a wireless network, 165
 dial-up Internet connection using, 178

direct connection (desktop-laptop), 228

disconnecting from a wireless network, 167

firewall setup, 202–203

network connection setup, 151–153

overview, 91–92

timeout for dial-up Internet connection, 180, 194–195

viewing available wireless networks, 161

Network Setup Wizard, 158

networking. *See also* Internet connection; wireless networking
 accessing printers, 157
 accessing shared folders, 156–157
 buying a laptop and, 28
 computer names, 152–153
 connecting and disconnecting, 153–154
 connection setup in Windows, 151–153
 creating a restore point before configuring, 281–282
 for desktop-laptop connection, 226
 etiquette, 157
 finding other computers, 154–156
 hardware, 150–151
 installing adapter in new laptop, 39
 LAN parties, 155
 network printers, 100, 101, 156, 157
 office setting and, 149
 peer-to-peer, 151
 shared resources, 155–156
 sharing a folder, 157–159
 unsharing a folder, 159
 viewing shared resources, 155–156

NetZero Internet service, 171

New Area Code Rule dialog box, 191–193

New Briefcase command (File menu), 231

New Briefcase icon, 231

New Compressed (zipped) Folder command (File menu), 266

New Connection Wizard
 for direct connection (desktop-laptop), 228–230
 for Internet connection, 173, 176–177

Nickel-Cadmium (NiCad) batteries, 26, 134, 135
Nickel-Metal Hydride (NiMH) batteries
  cycling, 143, 298
  Lithium-Ion batteries versus, 134
  overview, 135
Norton
  Cleansweep utility, 106
  firewall, 204
notebooks, 16
Notification Area. *See* System Tray or Notification Area
NTFS file system, 262–263, 264
Num Lock key
  keyboard troubles and, 286–287
  numeric keypad and, 76
  status indicator, 72
numeric keypad, 74, 75–76, 127

• *O* •

Office Pack and Go Wizard (Microsoft), 271
Office suites, 23
on-the-road computing. *See* portability; travel
opening the laptop lid, 44–46
Opera Web browser, 205
operating systems, 2, 23. *See also* Windows XP
Organization name for Windows XP, 50
Osborne, Adam (inventor), 8
Osborne 1 portable computer, 8–10
Outlook Express (Microsoft). *See also* e-mail
  disabling automatic checking, 221–222
  disconnecting after picking up e-mail, 221
  forwarding mail rule, 219
  leaving e-mail copy on server, 222–223
  removing your e-mail password, 220–221
  sending messages in one batch, 222
  skipping messages over a given size, 224
  viruses and, 208
overheating, avoiding, 255–256

• *P* •

Pack and Go Wizard (Microsoft Office), 271
packing slip, 36
packing your laptop case, 246, 311–315
parallel (printer) port, 70, 130, 227
pass-through USB devices, 118
passwords
  administrator, 50
  BIOS, 261–262
  changing, 108–109
  for compressed files or folders, 266
  creating strong passwords, 50, 109, 264
  data protection and, 261
  e-mail, removing, 220–221
  files or folders and, 266
  forgetting, cautions about, 50, 109, 262
  Internet connection, 176
  for screen saver, 264
  for Setup program, 49
  for shared folders, 156
  for user account, 50, 51, 108–109, 263
  for wireless networks, 162
patches. *See* updating
pay wireless access, 167
PC Cards
  buying a laptop and, 27
  for communications options, 28
  defined, 27
  ejecting, 67
  inserting, 67, 124–125
  overview, 67–68
  removing, 125–126
  USB options versus, 124
  for USB ports, 116, 120
  using, 125
  for wireless networking, 28, 124, 125
PCMCIA (Personal Computer Memory Card International Association) cards. *See* PC Cards
PCs For Dummies (Gookin, Dan), 89, 171, 253
PDF files, 132

peer-to-peer networking, 151. *See also* networking

Phone and Modem Options dialog box
    area code rules for modems, 191–193
    Dialing Rules tab, 188–190
    Modems tab, 182–183, 184, 185
phone home services, 268
phone port, 69, 178
pictures. *See* graphics files
pin-on area of Start panel, 53
plugging in
    in cafés, 252–253
    in hotel rooms, 254
    laptop power cord, 40–41
    lightning storms and, 42
    modem to phone jack, 178
    network cable, 153–154
    peripherals to docking station or port
        replicator, 40
    on planes, 249
    surge protection and line filtering, 41–42
    UPS and, 41–42
pointer, making more visible, 287
port replicators
    buying a laptop and, 29
    defined, 29, 70–71
    docking stations versus, 71
    for non-USB keyboards, 127
    for non-USB printers, 130
    overview, 306
    storing, 40
    for USB ports, 116
portability. *See also* travel
    batteries and, 133–134
    buying a laptop and, 25
    communications and, 10
    evolution of laptops and, 7–18
    as reason for owning a laptop, 19, 113
    trade-offs for gizmos, 113
ports. *See also specific kinds*
    defined, 68
    for direct connection (desktop-laptop),
        227, 229

Internet, 202
    overview, 68–70
power brick
    packing, 312
    plugging in, 41
    removing battery if used primarily,
        143–144
    wall socket in cafés, 252–253
    wall socket in hotel rooms, 254
    wall socket on planes, 249
    weight calculation and, 14
power button
    finding, 46
    on-off switch versus, 44
    setting the function of, 60–62
    sleep button and, 46
    symbols for, 47
    types of, 46
power cord
    packing, 312
    plugging in, 40–41
power jack, 70, 71
power management. *See also* batteries;
        Hibernation mode; Stand By (sleep)
        mode
    buying a laptop and, 29
    changing batteries, 142
    cycling the battery, 143, 298
    devices that consume power, 144
    fuel cells and, 135
    low battery warnings, 139–141, 255
    microprocessor and, 29
    monitoring the battery, 136–139
    saving custom settings, 146
    smart batteries and, 136, 139
    spare battery and, 142
    Stand By (sleep) mode and, 57
    tips, 144–146
    troubleshooting, 287–288
Power Options Properties dialog box
    Advanced tab, 60–63
    closing the lid, options for, 62–63
    low battery alarms, 139–141

overview, 97–98

power button function settings, 60–62

Power Meter tab, 137

Power Schemes tab, 145–146

sleep button function settings, 62

Stand By mode settings, 58

power sockets. *See* wall sockets

powering on or up. *See* turning on your laptop

PowerPoint (Microsoft), 269, 271–273

presentations

CD discs for, 269

creating, 269–270

Display Properties dialog box settings, 96

handheld devices for, 269

PowerPoint keyboard shortcuts, 272–273

setting up, 269–270

video projector connection, 127, 271–272

Print command (File menu), 196

Print dialog box, 131–132, 196

printer port, 70, 130, 227

printers

adding, 100

connecting to your laptop, 129–130

default, 100

doing without, 132

drivers for, 130

network, 100, 101, 156, 157

portable, 129

printing in Windows, 131–132

setting up, 129–130

sharing, 101

travel and, 129, 132, 253

USB port for, 114

Printers and Faxes window

adding a printer, 130

fax modem setup, 195–196

overview, 99–101

printing. *See also* faxing

to disk, 132

when you don't have a printer, 132, 253

in Windows, 131–132

PRN (printer) port, 70, 130, 227

processor. *See* microprocessor

Program Files folder, 89, 103, 104

programs. *See* software

protection. *See* security

pulse dialing, modems and, 189–190

purchasing a laptop. *See* buying a laptop

• *R* •

Radio Shack Model 100 computer, 11–12

RAM. *See* memory or RAM

reading e-mail

accessing from friend's computer, 217–218

accessing on the road, 215–216

disabling automatic checking, 221–222

disconnecting after picking up, 221

forwarding for pickup on the road, 218–219

leaving a copy on the server, 222–223

skipping messages over a given size, 224

on the Web, 216

Web-based access, 171–172, 216–218, 223

RealVNC remote access software, 235–236

rebooting. *See* restarting

receiving a fax, 200

Recently Used Programs menu (Start panel), 53

recharging batteries, 38–39, 141–142

registering the laptop and software, 259

Registry Editor, 103

reinstalling Windows, avoiding, 279

Remember icon, 3

remote access

firewalls and, 237

RealVNC for, 235–237

security issues for, 234, 237

Windows Remote Desktop and, 234–235

Remote Desktop feature, avoiding, 234–235

removable media, packing, 313–314

removing. *See also* ejecting

automatic updates, 292

battery when using AC power, 143–144

removing *(continued)*
  CD/DVD drives to save power, 255
  data files for software, 106
  discs before traveling, 246
  e-mail password, 220–221
  external modem, 187
  external USB storage, 123–124
  hardware, creating a restore point before,
    281–282
  laptop from network, 154
  PC Cards, 125–126
  printers (unplugging the USB cable), 130
  shared folders (unsharing), 159
  software (uninstalling), 105–106, 107
  System Tray icons, 102
  USB devices, 118
  user accounts, 110
  Web-based e-mail, deleting, 216
  Windows components, 106
  wireless network connection, 167
repairs, 30
resetting your laptop. *See* restarting
resolution of LCD display, 96, 97
restarting, 48, 55–56, 166, 278
restore points. *See* System Restore feature
RJ-45 port, 70, 71, 150, 151. *See also*
    Ethernet
road trips. *See* portability; travel
root USB ports, 120
routers, 151, 173–174
RS-232C (serial) port, 70, 186, 187, 227

• *S* •

Safe Mode
  advantages for troubleshooting, 284
  entering, 284–285
  laptop always starts in, 286
  returning from, 286
  testing in, 285–286
Safely Remove Hardware dialog box,
    123–124, 125–126
Save As command (File menu), 214

Save As dialog box
  My Documents folder and, 89
  saving Web pages, 214–215
saving files
  before entering Stand By mode, 56, 57
  before shutting down Windows, 54
  custom Power Scheme, 146
  Hibernation mode and, 255
  Web pages, 214–215
scanners, 114
scanning
  for viruses, 206–207
  for wireless networks, 164
school, laptops at, 20
screen. *See* LCD display
screen saver
  password for, 264
  power settings and, 146
second computer, laptop as, 19
Secure Digital card reader. *See* memory
    card readers
security. *See also* passwords
  anti-spyware software, 208–211
  antivirus software, 205–208, 213
  automatic updates and, 293
  backing up your data, 267
  café computing and, 253
  disabling the Guest account, 110, 263
  disabling the infrared port, 266–267
  encrypting files or folders, 264–265
  firewall, 173, 174, 201–205
  having the laptop phone home, 268
  hijacking, avoiding, 211
  hotel rooms and, 254
  Internet Explorer and, 205
  locking Windows, 263–264
  NTFS file system and, 262–263, 264
  protecting your data, 261–267
  remote access and, 234, 237
  sharing folders and, 159
  theft, avoiding, 253, 254, 257–261
  thumbprint readers, 268

USB port devices, 116
wireless networking, 162, 163, 164–166, 253
Security Tracking of Office Property (STOP) program, 259
Send Fax Wizard, 196–198
sending e-mail messages
  forwarding for pickup on the road, 218–219
  in one batch, 222
serial number, 259
serial port, 70, 186, 187, 227
service and support
  buying a laptop and, 22, 29–31
  defined, 30
  extended warranties for, 30
  hardware versus software and, 30
  sending in the warranty, 37–38
Service Pack 2 (Windows XP), 202, 203
Service Set Identifier (SSID), 162, 164–165
setting up your laptop
  assembly, 39
  before turning it on, 44
  charging the battery, 38–39
  finding a place to keep it, 39–40
  instructions for, heeding, 38
  plugging it in, 40–41
  UPS and, 41–42
Setup program, 49
shared resources. *See also* networking
  accessing printers, 157
  accessing shared folders, 156–157
  Internet connection, 174–175
  sharing a folder, 157–159
  unsharing a folder, 159
  viewing, 155–156
shift keys, 73–74
shorting batteries, avoiding, 142
shutting down Windows. *See also* turning off your laptop
  power button setting for, 60–62
  properly, from Start panel, 54–55
  sleep button setting for, 62

signature files for viruses, 207
size
  buying a laptop and, 26
  evolution of laptops and, 7–18
  LCD display and, 27
sleep button. *See also* Stand By (sleep) mode
  overview, 46–47
  setting the function of, 62
slide shows. *See* presentations
smart batteries, 136, 139
software. *See also* installing software; *specific kinds*
  anti-hijacking, 211
  anti-spyware, 208–211
  antivirus, 205–208, 213
  bundled with laptops, 23, 107
  defined, 65
  finding before buying a laptop, 22–23
  hardware requirements for, 23, 24
  for Internet connection, 170
  licensing agreements, 23
  for PC Cards, 125
  phone home programs, 268
  for presentations, 269–270
  printer drivers, 130
  Program Files folder for, 89, 103–104
  RealVNC remote access software, 235–236
  registering, 259
  sharing programs, avoiding, 159
  special deals and advertisements, 51
  support and, 30
  uninstalling, 105–106, 107
  upgrading, 289–290
  wireless scanners, 164
sound hardware, 115
space-saving, laptop for, 18–19
speakers
  keeping away from, 254
  muting to save power, 255
  USB port for, 115
Spybot Search & Destroy anti-spyware software, 210

spyware. *See* anti-spyware software
SpywareBlaster anti-spyware software, 210
SSID (Service Set Identifier), 162, 164–165
Stand By (sleep) mode
  closing the lid and, 57, 62–63
  computer enters by itself, 58
  hardware sleep button for, 46–47
  Hibernation mode versus, 58–59
  "lost" in (won't wake up), 57, 287–288
  power button setting for, 60–62
  removing USB devices and, 118
  shared folders and, 159
  shutting down versus, 56
  sleep button setting for, 62
  status indicator, 72
  using, 56–57
  waking up from, 57
  Windows Stand By button for, 56
standards for wireless networking, 28, 160
Start button and panel
  account image, 53
  All Programs menu, 53
  Control Panel fly-out menu, 94–96
  Control Panel link, 54, 93
  defined, 51
  My Documents folder on, 88–89
  pin-on area, 53
  Recently Used Programs menu, 53
  Turn Off Computer button, 54
  using, 52–54
starting your laptop. *See* turning on your
  laptop
Startup program, 49
statistics on laptop theft, 258
Status dialog box (Internet connection),
  179–180
stolen laptop. *See* theft, avoiding
STOP (Security Tracking of Office
  Property) program, 259
stopping
  e-mail forwarding after returning home,
   218
  pending faxes, 198, 199

storing
  battery when not in use, 143, 302–303
  docking station, 40
  laptop, 39–40
  port replicator, 40
sub-notebooks, 16
sunlight, avoiding direct, 256
support. *See* service and support
surge protection for laptop, 41–42
suspend mode. *See* Stand By (sleep) mode
S-video out port, 70, 71, 127
swappable drives, 27, 28
switch, networking, 151
switching on. *See* turning on your laptop
symbols
  for computer lights, 72–73
  for ports, 69–70
  power button, 47
synchronizing files (synch). *See also*
   desktop-laptop connection
  before traveling, 245
  copying items to the Briefcase, 232
  creating Briefcase for, 231
  defined, 19
  moving the Briefcase to the laptop, 233
  synchronizing the files, 233–234
  using Briefcase files, 233
System Configuration Utility, 284–285
System Properties dialog box
  Advanced tab, 300
  Computer Name tab, 153
  Device Manager button, 98
  Hardware tab, 266–267
  overview, 98–99
  System Restore tab, 280–281
System Restore feature
  enabling, 279–281
  restoring your system, 282–283
  setting a restore point, 281–282
  when to run, 281
System Tray or Notification Area
  antivirus software icon, 207
  balloon tips, disabling, 103

battery icon, 137
defined, 52, 102
removing icons from, 102
Safely Remove Hardware icon, 123, 124, 125
using, 102

● *T* ●

Tablet PCs, 18
taskbar, 52
Taskbar and Start Menu Properties dialog box
Control Panel fly-out menu setting, 95–96
My Documents folder settings, 88–89
Technical Stuff icon, 3
temperature
avoiding overheating, 255–256
battery life and, 302
cooling pad, 115, 256, 306–307
hot battery, dangers of, 136
storing laptops and, 39–40
terminals, battery, 302
testing your laptop in Safe Mode, 285–286
text files, saving Web pages as, 214
theft, avoiding
anti-theft alarms, 309, 313
being mindful of the environment, 260
café computing and, 253
hotel rooms and, 254
marking your laptop, 258–259
nondescript laptop carrying case for, 259
registering and, 259
statistics on laptop theft, 258
USS (Universal Security Slot) for, 71, 260–261
third-party cookies, disabling, 209–210
1394 port, 69, 120, 125
thumb-ball mouse, 78, 79
thumbprint readers, 268
TIFF files, faxes as, 200
timeouts, 180, 194–195

Tip icon, 3
tools, packing, 314
touch pad
defined, 78
disabling, 82, 83, 129
external mouse and, 129
illustrated, 80
settings, 81–82
using, 79
wheel button and, 80
trackball, 312
TrackPoint (IBM), 80–81
transferring files. *See* desktop-laptop connection
travel. *See also* portability
airport inspections and, 247–248, 260
avoiding overheating, 255–256
café computing, 251–253
carrying on the laptop case, 247
checklist of things to do before, 245–246
checklist of things to pack, 246, 311–315
e-mail tips, 215–224
hotel room computing, 253–254
laptop as road computer, 19
laptop case for, 241–245
low battery warnings and, 255
printing and, 129, 132, 253
shared folders and, 159
storing your laptop on the plane, 248
theft, avoiding, 253, 254, 257–261
using your laptop on the plane, 248–249
wall sockets, 249, 252–253, 254
Web browsing tips, 214–215
troubleshooting
battery won't charge, 288
differences in computers and, 277
further information, 285
Internet resources for, 278
keyboard problems, 286–287
laptop always starts in Safe Mode, 286
laptop won't wake up, 57, 287–288
making the pointer more visible, 287

troubleshooting *(continued)*
  power management problems, 287–288
  recent changes and, 278
  reinstalling Windows, avoiding, 279
  restarting Windows, 278
  Safe Mode for, 283–286
  System Restore feature for, 279–283
  turning off locked up system, 60
Troubleshooting Your PC For Dummies
    (Gookin, Dan), 30, 285
Turn Off Computer button, 54
Turn Off Computer dialog box, 55–56
turning off items. *See* turning on and off
turning off your laptop. *See also*
    Hibernation mode; Stand By (sleep)
    mode
  multitude of options for, 54
  power button setting for, 60–62
  restarting, 48, 55–56, 166, 278
  shutting down properly, 54–55
  Start panel button for, 54
  when the system is locked up, 60
turning on and off. *See also* disabling;
    enabling; turning off your laptop;
    turning on your laptop
  antivirus software, 207–208
  numeric keypad, 76
turning on your laptop
  after hibernating, 58
  finding the power button, 46
  laptop always starts in Safe Mode, 286
  moon button and, 46–47
  opening the lid, 44–46
  other terms for, 48
  power button for, 43, 46–48
  restarting, 48, 55–56, 166, 278
  returning from Safe Mode, 286
  in Safe Mode, 284–285
  setting up before, 44
  status indicator, 72
"typewriter" keys, 73

• U •

UltraLite laptop (NEC), 15–16
uninstalling software
  automatic updates, 292
  bundled with laptops, 107
  overview, 105–106
  updating and, 290
Uninterruptible Power Supply (UPS),
    41–42, 144
Universal Security Slot (USS), 71, 260–261
universities, laptops at, 20
unmounting external USB storage, 118,
    123–124
unpacking the laptop
  how long to keep the box, 37
  making piles for box contents, 36–37
  sending in the warranty, 37–38
  tips, 35–36
unplugging
  external keyboard, 126–127
  network cable, 154
  printer USB cable, 130
unsharing a folder, 159
updating
  creating a restore point before, 281–282,
    290
  defined, 290
  upgrades versus updates, 290
  Windows XP, 291–292, 293
upgrading
  creating a restore point before, 281–282,
    290
  defined, 290
  hardware, 293–294
  software, 289–290
  updates versus upgrades, 290
  Windows XP, avoiding, 292
UPS (Uninterruptible Power Supply),
    41–42, 144

USB ports
  adding, 116, 119–120
  cables, 116, 117–118
  connecting devices, 118
  for external mouse, 82
  for floppy drive, 67
  hot swapping devices, 118
  overview, 70
  pass-through devices, 118
  PC Cards versus USB options, 124
  root ports, 120
  Stand By mode and, 118
  USB 2.0 standard, 117
  USB-powered devices, 119
  uses for, 114–116
user accounts
  administrator, 110–111
  creating, 50, 109–110
  Guest, disabling, 110, 263
  image for, 53, 109
  Limited, 110
  passwords for, 50, 51, 108–109, 263
  removing, 110
  updating to Administrator status, 111
  using multiple accounts, 51
User Accounts dialog box
  adding new accounts, 109–110
  changing image for account, 109
  changing your password, 108–109
  Guest account, disabling, 110, 263
  opening, 107
  removing accounts, 110
username for Internet connection, 176, 177
USS (Universal Security Slot), 71, 260–261

• *V* •

vacations. *See* portability; travel
vents, 71
video camera, USB port for, 115
video port, 70

video projector, connecting, 127, 271–272
viewing
  computers on network, 154–156
  displaying My Documents folder, 88–89
  shared resources, 155–156
  wireless networks available, 161–162
virtual memory settings, 299–301
virtual printers, 100
viruses, protecting against, 205–208
VirusScan (McAfee), 206
VNC (virtual network computing), 235–237
volume setting for modem, 182–183

• *W* •

waking up
  hard drive after suspending, 146
  from Hibernation mode, 58
  from Stand By (sleep) mode, 57
wall sockets
  finding for café computing, 252–253
  in hotel rooms, 254
  on planes, 249
wallpaper, 51, 96
warm boot, 48. *See also* turning on your
    laptop
Warning! icon, 3
warnings for low batteries, 139–141, 255
warranties
  extended, buying, 30
  filling out, 36
  sending in, 37–38
  start date for, 38
Web browsing. *See also* Internet
    connection
  firewall for, 201–205
  hijacking, avoiding, 211
  Internet Explorer alternatives for, 205
  on the road, 214–215
  saving Web pages, 214–215
  spyware and, 208–211

Web pages, saving, 214–215
Web sites. *See* Internet resources
Web-based e-mail access, 171–172,
    216–218, 223
weight
  buying a laptop and, 26, 27
  calculation by computer companies, 14
  Compaq SLT computer, 14
  LCD display and, 27
  lunch buckets, 13
weight *(continued)*
  NEC UltraLite laptop, 15
  notebooks, 16
  Osborne 1 portable computer, 8
  power brick and, 14
  Radio Shack Model 100 computer, 12
Welcome to System Restore window,
    281–283
wheel button, 80
Win key, 73–74
Windows XP. *See also specific components*
  adding and removing components, 106
  automatic updates, 291–292, 293
  desktop, 51–52
  firewall, 202–204
  Internet software, 170
  knowledgebase, 285
  laptops versus desktops and, 49
  locking, 263–264
  logging on, 107–111
  My Computer window, 90–91
  My Documents folder, 88–89
  My Network Places window, 91
  network connection setup, 151–153
  Network Connections window, 91–92
  as operating system in this book, 2, 23
  printing in, 131–132
  printing to disk and, 132
  reinstalling, avoiding, 279
  Remote Desktop, avoiding, 234–235

  restarting, 48, 55–56, 166, 278
  Service Pack 2, 202, 203
  shutting down properly, 54–55
  starting for the first time, 49–50
  updating, 291–292, 293
  upgrading, avoiding, 292
  user accounts, 50, 107–110
Wireless Network Connection dialog box,
    161–163
Wireless Network Connection Properties
    dialog box, 163, 203
wireless networking. *See also* networking
  accessing pay service networks, 167
  buying a laptop and, 28
  connecting to a network, 161–163,
    164–165
  connection setup in Windows, 151–153
  disadvantages of, 160
  disconnecting, 167
  e-mail access on the road and, 218
  hardware, 161
  Internet connection, 173, 175
  MAC Address, 166
  PC Cards for, 28, 124, 125
  popularity of, 159–160
  renewing your lease, 167
  scanning for networks, 164
  security, 162, 163, 164–166, 253
  SSID (Service Set Identifier), 162, 164–165
  standards, 28, 160
  status indicator, 72
  switching connections, 163
  topics not covered, 150
workgroups, naming, 152–153

• Z •

Zip disks, 25
Zone Alarm firewall (Zone Labs), 204–205

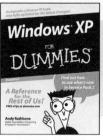

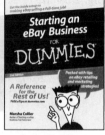

SPORTS, FITNESS, PARENTING, RELIGION & SPIRITUALITY

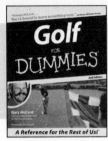

0-7645-5146-9

0-7645-5418-2

Also available:
- Adoption For Dummies
  0-7645-5488-3
- Basketball For Dummies
  0-7645-5248-1
- The Bible For Dummies
  0-7645-5296-1
- Buddhism For Dummies
  0-7645-5359-3
- Catholicism For Dummies
  0-7645-5391-7
- Hockey For Dummies
  0-7645-5228-7

- Judaism For Dummies
  0-7645-5299-6
- Martial Arts For Dummies
  0-7645-5358-5
- Pilates For Dummies
  0-7645-5397-6
- Religion For Dummies
  0-7645-5264-3
- Teaching Kids to Read For Dummies
  0-7645-4043-2
- Weight Training For Dummies
  0-7645-5168-X
- Yoga For Dummies
  0-7645-5117-5

TRAVEL

0-7645-5438-7

0-7645-5453-0

Also available:
- Alaska For Dummies
  0-7645-1761-9
- Arizona For Dummies
  0-7645-6938-4
- Cancún and the Yucatán For Dummies
  0-7645-2437-2
- Cruise Vacations For Dummies
  0-7645-6941-4
- Europe For Dummies
  0-7645-5456-5
- Ireland For Dummies
  0-7645-5455-7

- Las Vegas For Dummies
  0-7645-5448-4
- London For Dummies
  0-7645-4277-X
- New York City For Dummies
  0-7645-6945-7
- Paris For Dummies
  0-7645-5494-8
- RV Vacations For Dummies
  0-7645-5443-3
- Walt Disney World & Orlando For Dummies
  0-7645-6943-0

GRAPHICS, DESIGN & WEB DEVELOPMENT

0-7645-4345-8

0-7645-5589-8

Also available:
- Adobe Acrobat 6 PDF For Dummies
  0-7645-3760-1
- Building a Web Site For Dummies
  0-7645-7144-3
- Dreamweaver MX 2004 For Dummies
  0-7645-4342-3
- FrontPage 2003 For Dummies
  0-7645-3882-9
- HTML 4 For Dummies
  0-7645-1995-6
- Illustrator CS For Dummies
  0-7645-4084-X

- Macromedia Flash MX 2004 For Dummies
  0-7645-4358-X
- Photoshop 7 All-in-One Desk
  Reference For Dummies
  0-7645-1667-1
- Photoshop CS Timesaving Techniques
  For Dummies
  0-7645-6782-9
- PHP 5 For Dummies
  0-7645-4166-8
- PowerPoint 2003 For Dummies
  0-7645-3908-6
- QuarkXPress 6 For Dummies
  0-7645-2593-X

NETWORKING, SECURITY, PROGRAMMING & DATABASES

0-7645-6852-3

0-7645-5784-X

Also available:
- A+ Certification For Dummies
  0-7645-4187-0
- Access 2003 All-in-One Desk
  Reference For Dummies
  0-7645-3988-4
- Beginning Programming For Dummies
  0-7645-4997-9
- C For Dummies
  0-7645-7068-4
- Firewalls For Dummies
  0-7645-4048-3
- Home Networking For Dummies
  0-7645-42796

- Network Security For Dummies
  0-7645-1679-5
- Networking For Dummies
  0-7645-1677-9
- TCP/IP For Dummies
  0-7645-1760-0
- VBA For Dummies
  0-7645-3989-2
- Wireless All In-One Desk Reference
  For Dummies
  0-7645-7496-5
- Wireless Home Networking For Dummies
  0-7645-3910-8